RAINBOW PIE

JOE BAGEANT frequently appears on US national public radio and the BBC, and writes for newspapers and magazines internationally. A commentator on the politics of class in America, he has been featured in documentary films in Germany, Greece, Switzerland, Italy, Sweden, and Britain. His book *Deer Hunting with Jesus: Guns, Votes, Debt and Delusion in Redneck America* has been adapted for the theatre and is being developed as a dramatic television series in America. Bageant spends much of each year in Belize, Central America, and in Jalisco, Mexico, where he writes, and in which he sponsors small health-and-shelter development projects. He also writes an online column (www.joebageant. com) that has made him a cult hero among gonzo-journalism junkies and progressives.

For my children: Timothy, Patrick, and Elizabeth

RAINBOW PIE

A MEMOIR OF REDNECK AMERICA

JOE BAGEANT

Portobello
BOOKS

Published by Portobello Books Ltd 2010

Portobello Books Ltd
12 Addison Avenue
London
W11 4QR

First published in Australia 2010 by Scribe Publications Pty Ltd,
Carlton North, Victoria

A CIP catalogue record is available from the British Library

9 8 7 6 5 4 3 2 1

ISBN 978 1 84627 257 8

www.portobellobooks.com

Typeset in 12/17 pt Iowan Old Style.

Offset by Avon DataSet Ltd, Bidford on Avon, Warwickshire

Printed in the UK by CPI William Clowes Beccles NR34 7TL

Lose all your troubles, kick up some sand
And follow me, buddy, to the Promised Land.
I'm here to tell you, and I wouldn't lie,
You'll wear ten-dollar shoes and eat rainbow pie.
— 'The Sugar Dumpling Line', American hobo song

A note from the author

While the events in this book are true, the names and identifying characteristics of some of the people in it have been changed to protect their privacy.

Contents

INTRODUCTION

Lost in the American Undertow

Did you ever stand and shiver, because you was lookin' in a river ...?
— American folksinger Ramblin' Jack Elliott

The United States has always maintained a white underclass—citizens whose role in the greater scheme of things has been to cushion national economic shocks through the disposability of their labour, with occasional time off to serve as bullet magnets in defence of the Empire. Until the post–World War II era, the existence of such an underclass was widely acknowledged. During the US Civil War, for instance, many northern abolitionists also called for the liberation of 'four million miserable white southerners held in bondage by the wealthy planter class'. Planter elites, who often held several large plantations which, together, constituted much or most of a county's economy, saw to it that poor whites got no schools, money, or political power. Poll taxes and literacy requirements kept white subsistence farmers and poor labourers from entering voting booths. Often accounting for up to 70 per cent of many deep-southern counties,

1

they could not vote, and thus could never challenge the status quo.

Today, almost nobody in the social sciences seems willing to touch the subject of America's large white underclass; or, being firmly placed in the true middle class themselves, can even agree that such a thing exists. Apparently, you can't smell the rabble from the putting green.

Public discussion of this class remains off limits, deemed hyperbole and the stuff of dangerous radical leftists. And besides, as everyone agrees, white people cannot be an underclass. We're the majority, dammit. You must be at least one shade darker than a paper bag to officially qualify as a member of any underclass. The middle and upper classes generally agree, openly or tacitly, that white Americans have always had an advantage (which has certainly been the middle- and upper-class experience). Thus, in politically correct circles, either liberal or conservative, the term 'white underclass' is an oxymoron. Sure, there are working-poor whites, but not that many, and definitely not enough to be called a white underclass, much less an American peasantry.

Economic, political, and social culture in America is staggering under the sheer weight of its white underclass, which now numbers some sixty million. Generally unable to read at a functional level, they are easily manipulated by corporate-political interests to vote against advances in health and education, and even more easily mustered in support of any proposed military conflict, aggressive or otherwise. One-third of their children are born out of wedlock, and are unemployable by any contemporary industrialised-world standard. Even if we were to bring back their jobs from China and elsewhere—a damned unlikely scenario—they would be competing at a wage scale that would not meet even their basic needs. Low skilled, and with little understanding of the world beyond either what is presented to them by kitschy and simplistic television, movie, and other media entertainments, or their experience as armed grunts in foreign combat, the future of the white underclass not only looks grim, but permanent.

Meanwhile, the underclass, 'America's flexible labour force' (one must be pretty flexible to get screwed in some of the positions we are asked to), or whatever you choose to call the unwashed throngs mucking around down here at the bottom of the national labour tier, are nevertheless politically potent, if sufficiently taunted and fed enough bullshit. Just look at the way we showed up in force during the 2000 elections, hyped up on inchoate anger and ready to be deployed as liberal-ripping pit bulls by America's ultra-conservative political machinery. Snug middle-class liberals were stunned. Could that many people actually be supporting Anne Coulter's call for the jailing of liberals, or Rush Limbaugh's demand for the massive, forced psychiatric detention of Democrats? Or, more recently, could they honestly believe President Obama's proposed public healthcare plan would employ 'death panels' to decide who lives and who dies? Conservatives cackled with glee, and dubbed them the only real Americans.

But back in 2000, before the American economic implosion, middle-class people of both stripes could still have confidence in their 401(k)s and retirement stock portfolios, with no small thanks to the cheap labour costs

3

provided by the rabble out there. And they could take comfort in the knowledge that millions of other middle-class folks just like themselves were keeping the gears of American finance well oiled and humming. Our economy had become fat through financialisation. Who needed manufacturing? We were now a post-industrial nation of investors, a 'transactional economy'. Dirty work was for … well … Asians. In this much-ballyhooed 'sweat-free economy', the white underclass swelled with every injection mould and drill press shipped across the Pacific.

Ten years later, with the US economy as skinny as the running gears of a praying mantis, the middle class—what's left of it now—is having doubts about its traditional class security. Every day it gets a bit harder not to notice some fifty or sixty million people scratching around for any kind of a job, or working more hours than ever in a sweating, white-knuckled effort to hang onto the jobs they do have. With credit cards melting down and middle-class jobs evaporating, there is the distinct possibility of them slipping into the classes below them. And who are they anyway—those people wiping out the ramen noodle shelf at the supermarket, and looking rather surly as they are moved out of their repossessed houses?

True, with the right selection of lefty internet bookmarks, you can find discussions of the white underclass, and occasionally even a brief article in the *New York Times* about some scholarly book that asks, 'Does a white underclass exist in America?' But most of the shrinking middle class pulls its blinds shut, hoping that if they don't see bad fortune, perhaps bad fortune can't see them and will not find their doors. Behind those doors, however, some privately wonder how the ranks of desperate and near-desperate American whites ever became so numerous. Where did all those crass people with their bad grammar and worse luck suddenly come from?

Seldom are such developments sudden, of course. It's only the realisation of them that happens overnight. The foundation of today's white underclass was laid down in the years following World War II. I was there, I grew up during its construction, and spent half my life trapped in it.

When World War II began, 44 per cent of Americans were rural, and over half of them farmed for a living. By 1970, only 5 per cent were on farms. Altogether, more than twenty-two million migrated to urban areas during the post-war period. If that migration were to happen in reverse today, it would be the equivalent of the present populations of New York City, Chicago, Miami, Philadelphia, Boston, and Saint Louis moving out into the countryside at a time when the US population was half of its present size.

In the great swim upstream toward what was being heralded as a new American prosperity, most of these twenty-two million never made it to the first fish ladder. Stuck socially, economically, and educationally at or near the bottom of the dam, they raised children and grandchildren who added another forty million to the swarm.

These uneducated rural whites became the foundation of our permanent white underclass. Their children and grandchildren have added to the numbers of this underclass, probably in the neighbourhood of 50 or 60 million people now. They outnumber all other poor and working-poor groups—black, Hispanics, immigrants.

Even as the white underclass was accumulating, it was being hidden, buried under a narrative proclaiming otherwise. The popular imagination was swamped with images that remain today as the national memory of that era. Nearly all of these images were products of advertising. In the standard depiction, our warriors returned to the land kept free by their valour, exhilarated by victory, and ready to raise families. They purchased little white cottages and Buick Roadmaster sedans, and then drove off into the unlimited horizons of the 'land of happy motoring'. A government brochure of the time assured everyone that 'An onrushing new age of opportunity, prosperity, convenience and comfort has arrived for all Americans.' I quoted this to an old World War II veteran named Ernie over an egg sandwich at the Twilight Zone Grill near my home in town. Ernie answered, 'I wish somebody had told me; I would have waved at the prosperity as it went by.'

According to this officially sanctioned story of the great post-war migration, these people abandoned farm life in such droves because the money, excitement, and allure of America's cities and large towns was just too great to resist. Why would anyone stay down on the farm when he or she could be 'wearing ten-dollar shoes and eating rainbow pie'? One catches a whiff of urban-biased perception here; but then, the official version of all life and culture in America is written by city people. Our dominant history, analysis, and images of America are generated in the urban centres. Social-research institutions, major universities, and the media—such as ABC, HBO, PBS, and the Harvard University sociology department—are not located in Keokuk, Iowa; Fisher, Illinois; Winchester, Virginia; or Lubbock, Texas.

I grew up hard by the Blue Ridge Mountains of Virginia and West Virginia, and am a product of that out-migration; and, as I said, grew up watching it happen around me. I'm here to tell you, dear hearts, that while all those university professors may have their sociological data and industrial statistics verified and well indexed, they're way off-base; they've entirely overshot the on-the-ground experience. In fact, they don't even deal with it. You won't be surprised to hear that the media representation of the post-war era—and, let's face it, more people watch The History Channel than read social history texts—it is as full of crap as an overfed Christmas goose.

My contemporaries of that rural out-migration, now in their late fifties and mid sixties, are still marked by the journey. Their children and grandchildren have inherited the same pathway. The class competition along that road is more brutal than ever. But the sell job goes on that we are a classless society with roughly equal opportunity for all. Given the terrible polarisation of wealth and power in this country (the top 1 per cent hold more wealth than the bottom 45 per cent combined, and their take is still rising), we can no longer even claim equal opportunity for a majority. Opportunity for the majority to do what? Pluck chickens, and telemarket to the ever-dwindling middle class?

AS FOR THE MEMOIR ASPECT OF THIS BOOK, IT took a while to get up the nerve, both personally and professionally. It was approached with trepidation. I'd be willing to bet that my generation—the baby boomers—has produced more damned memoirs than all others combined. Angry memoirs weeping over some metaphorical pony the author did not get for Christmas in 1958 have left a sour wad in the gullet of serious readers. I always thought I had better sense than to add to that heap. I was wrong.

Beyond that, I am advised by some editors that the word 'memoir', like the word 'essay', can be the kiss of death in today's suffering book market. But this book is being published first in Australia, where I have with my very eyes seen real customers in bookstores, there to purchase a book, not a talking greeting-card or a Shakespeare coffee mug to prove they have been inside a bookstore. So I nurse a shred of optimism.

Nearly a year after the publication of my first book, *Deer Hunting With Jesus: dispatches from America's class war*, I decided that, at the age of 63, I just might be a grizzled enough old rooster who had scratched up enough American gravel to justify recording some of it. I was among the last to witness horse-drawn mould-board ploughs at work. I went to a one-room school with a woodstove and an outhouse. Yet, by dint of fate, here I am sitting at a Toshiba laptop hurling electrons across the planet that will magically reassemble themselves into a published work, a narrative and observations on the American class system.

The narrative begins with the voices of a 1950s post-war boyhood in the Appalachian Mountains, and ends in America's industrial towns. I've not had a day in my life when I did not hear those Appalachian voices in the back of my mind, as if to follow me from the family farm along Shanghai Road in West Virginia, out of the hills and hollers, no matter where I go in this world:

> The Devil, he wears a hypocrite shoe, better watch out he'll slip it on you ... Ezekiel seen that fireball burning way in the middle of the air ... the big little wheel turns by man, lord, but the big wheel turns by the grace of God ... and our rabbit dog Nellie got gored in the corn crib by a 10-point buck ... it's bad luck to bury a man barefooted ... this old road runs along Sleepy Crick, clean past Shanghai and up to Cumberland boy, this old road runs on forever.

Shanghai Road was a red-dirt scratch across the green mountains to a post office/general store crossroads community called Shanghai. Our lives on that road exemplified four-fifths of the American historical experience—which is to say, rural and agrarian. They are not just my roots but, with variations on the theme, the rootstock of a large portion of working-class Americans, especially those we must now call an underclass. Excepting immigrants whose ancestors came through Ellis Island, most of us don't have to dig too deeply into our genealogical woodpile to find a rural American progenitor tearing up dirt to plant corn, or racing a thunderstorm to get in a hay crop.

But, isolated as that life was at times, there was community. Neighbours along Shanghai Road banded together to make lard and apple butter, put up feed corn, bale hay, thresh wheat, pick apples, and plough snow off roads. One neighbour cut hair; another mended shoes. From birth to the grave, you needed neighbours and they needed you. I was very lucky to have seen that culture, which showed me that a real community of shared labour toward the shared good is possible—or was at one time in my country.

The nature and substance of their efforts and endurance causes me to reflect on the ecology of human labour then, and what we now call 'our jobs'. Especially how our degraded concepts of community and work have contributed to the development of physical and cultural loneliness in America. Not to mention the destruction of a sense of the common good, the economy, and the natural world.

This book covers about eleven years, with short jumps into the past and the present for reasons of context. But, like its writer, it always returns to the Shanghai Road farm to find meaning in America, its people, and its land.

So here it is in your hands. Now all I can do is ask your forbearance and the forgiveness of the larches and Douglas firs, the loblolly and white pines that were cut and pulped to make this book. I hope to have testified to what was, and still is, worthwhile in the human rush and flow, the still pools and eddies of things witnessed.

Even so, it's hard not to shiver when you're looking at that river.

CHAPTER ONE

A Panther in a Sycamore Tree

I'm going there to meet my loved ones,
To dwell with them and never roam
I'm only going over Jordan,
I'm only going over home.
— 'Wayfaring Stranger', traditional Appalachian ballad

It happens perhaps once or twice every August: a deep West Virginia sundown drapes the farmhouses and ponds in red light, as if the heat absorbed during the dog days will erupt from the earth to set the fields afire. Distant cars raise dust clouds that settle on the backs of copperhead snakes lying in wait for the night's coolness and the hunt, and that red light flashes briefly in the eyes of old farmers setting out salt blocks for white-faced cattle.

It is during exactly such a dusk in 1951 that Uncle Nelson and I see the panther, in the meadow sycamore tree—a panther so black it is almost blue. Neither Nelson nor I had ever seen a panther, nor expected to in our lives. But there it is. Big as life. Nelson's face shows almost holy amazement. He takes his pipe away from his quivering lip. Not that fear is a part of it; only awe of this beast. The panther drops weightlessly to the ground and glides into the loblolly pines in all its lithe power. We let out our breath. We gesture at each other for a moment—Uncle Nelson being deaf—then trot for home. By the time we reach my grandparent's house, twilight has settled.

'Maw,' I blurt. 'We seen a panther down by the big sycamore. Black as night. Long and black as night.'

My grandmother turns away from the hand pump by the galvanised sink where she had been drawing dishwater. 'Never been a panther in these parts I know of,' she says. But the set of Nelson's wide, dark semi-mongoloid face tells her this is a true thing. 'Hear that, Pap?' she asks. 'The boys seen a panther. A panther is a sign of war and troubles of war for one of your own kin.'

My grandfather frowns, says nothing, then raises his lanky frame from his chair, picks up the kitchen slops-bucket, and heads for the hog pen.

What about the sign of war? I wanted to know. Well, if it was an omen, I figured Maw would surely know about it. She knew everything. She knew how to plant by the moon signs. And she knew the mark of the witch and that Miss Beddow down the road was for sure a witch (thus we kids hid under the porch when she passed along the road). She knew doctoring, too, and had saved Clarkie Unger's life that time he got his head run over by his daddy's tractor. Clarkie's father, Clarence, had wrapped his son's head in kerosene-soaked rags and Bag Balm cow-udder salve, and had prayed over Clarkie all night to no avail. Maw declared that she had never seen 'such a mess of heathen doctoring', burned the rags, and set about healing the boy.

Clarkie pulled through. A little lopsided in the face, but he pulled through. But for all her powers, she couldn't make Pap talk if he didn't want to.

'I swear, if talk was corn, that old man couldn't buy grain,' Maw grumbled at Pap's non-response to the sign of the panther. And that was all I ever got in the way of answers about the panther and the sign of war.

I would one day learn that panthers were among the first beasts killed off by the settlers in our region, along with red wolves and the eastern woodland bison. Also that black is just one of the colour possibilities of panthers anywhere on the planet. But on that day in the dead centre of the twentieth century, and in our world on Shanghai Road in Morgan County, West Virginia, along the drains of Sleepy Creek, phantom panthers inhabited their place alongside witches, wolf trees, milk-drinking snakes, and such other creatures as prowled the subconscious and gave a folk explanation for the greater unknown. For the English, Scots–Irish, and German souls strung out along the front hollers of the Blue Ridge Mountains, life was still animated on interior levels by the idea of such spirits. Things both tangible and impalpable lived alongside one another with equal importance — and the panther, an Appalachian folk sign of the devil's anvil, war, was an augury to be fulfilled. Indeed, the Korean War started that same year.

Still, as much as some part of me still wants to find veracity in a sign of war divined by my long-dead grandmother, I cannot. The Bageant family has been birthing willing and flinty soldiers for every American war since General Edward Braddock's fatal 1755 frontier march on the French and Indians. Yet we were never touched by the conflict that scorched Korea from 1950 to 1953. No one we knew even served during those years, except for Pink Brannon, who was an army cook at the Newton D. Baker Veteran's Hospital in nearby Martinsburg. To us kids, that didn't count, since he didn't kill any Japs or Germans in Korea. (We children had no idea who America was fighting in 'Kria', but World War II was still a fresh reality.)

So I am left with no meaning for the sign—just the awesome impression of it. The memory of it anchors an entire world I once knew.

MAW AND PAP WERE MARRIED IN 1917. He was twenty-three; she was seventeen. Pap had walked nine miles each way for over a month to court her, a fact which may have helped overcome her father's objections to their age difference, if he had any. The year they were married, Woodrow Wilson was inaugurated for a second term and Sigmund Freud published *The Psychology of the Unconscious*. But Woodrow Wilson had damned-little to do with life along Shanghai Road, and Maw and Pap went to their graves never hearing of Sigmund Freud. Their world was mostly just birth-to-death work, and pride in the fact that it was such. 'My man is sure enough a worker,' Maw observed. 'By Jesus, he even got married in his work clothes. The preacher barely finished saying his do-yous before Pap was hitching up his jack leg Purcheron [a type of draught horse]. An hour later we topped this ridge, Pap hauled in the reins, turned, and said: "Now, Virginia, I love you. And that's the last I want said about it."'

14

'I never took it in a bad way,' she said. 'Pap can be a hard, stubborn man, but he's always as good as his word and a good provider. He promised I'd never be hungry, cold, or beat-on, and that he would build me a "home in glory". We had an orchard, peaches, pears, and Pippin apples mostly. We did good. The hillsides come full of corn, and we fed five or six Poland China hogs.'

As a child, I can remember how the stove woodpile would grow almost half as big as the house every autumn. Pap was a good provider, alright. Nor was he as hard as he sometimes acted. In symbolisation of their union, Pap planted two rose bushes that he fussed over and nurtured until his final days.

Neither of them were attractive people by any measure. Pap was gangly and heavy browed, not unlike Jean-Francois Millet's 'Man With a Hoe', but in bib overalls. Maw was squat, fat, with grey eyes that slanted downward at the outside corners like those of a Greek tragedy mask.

But, as Maw said, 'Looks don't mean shit.' They meant even less in the world of farming. When Virginia Iris Gano and Harry Preston Bageant crested that ridge in their buggy and began their life together, they stood an excellent chance of making it. For starters, in that world the maths of life was easier, even if the work was harder. If you could show the bank or the seller of the land that you were healthy and sober, and knew how to farm, you pretty much had the loan (at least when it came to the non-arid eastern American uplands; the American West was a different matter). At 5 per cent simple interest, Pap bought a 108-acre farm—house, barn, and all—for $400. (It was a cash-poor county, and still is. As recently as 1950 you could buy a 200-acre farm there for about $1,000.) On those terms, a subsistence farmer could pay off the farm in twenty years, even one with such poor soils as in these Southern uplands. But a subsistence farmer did not farm to sell crops, though he did that, too, when possible. Instead, he balanced an entire life with land and human productivity, family needs, money needs, along with his own and his family's skills in a labour economy, not a wealth economy. The idea was to require as little cash as possible, because there wasn't any to be had.

Nor was much needed. The farm was not a business. It was a farm. Pap and millions of farmers like him were never in the 'agribusiness'. They never participated in the modern 'economy of scale' which comes down to exhausting as many resources as possible to make as much money as possible in the shortest time possible. If you'd talked to him about 'producing commodities under contract to strict specifications', he wouldn't have recognised that as farming. 'Goddamned jibber-jabber' is what he would have called it. And if a realtor had pressed him about the 'speculative value' of his farmland as 'agronomic leverage', I suspect the old 12-gauge shotgun might have come down off the rack. Land value was based upon what it could produce, plain and simple. These farms were not large, credit-based 'operations' requiring annual loans for machinery, chemicals, and seed.

Sure, farmers along Shanghai Road and the Unger Store community bought things at the junction store on credit, to be paid for in the autumn. Not much, though. The store's present owners, descendants of the store's founders, say that an annual bill at the store would run to about ten dollars. One of them, Richard Merica, told me, 'People bought things like salt and pepper. Only what they couldn't make for themselves, like shotgun shells or files.' Once I commented to an old Unger Store native still living there that, 'I suspect there wasn't more than $1,000 in the Unger Store community in the pre-war days.'

'You're guessing way too high,' he said. 'Try maybe $400 or $500. But most of it stayed here, and went round and round.'

So if Pap and the other subsistence farmers there spent eight bucks a year at the local crossroads store, it was eight bucks in a reciprocal exchange that made both their subsistence farming and the Unger Store possible as a business and as a community.

Moneyless as it was, Maw and Pap's lives were far more stable than one might think today. In fact, the lives of most small farmers outside the nasty cotton sharecropping system of deep-southern America were stable. Dramatic as the roller-coaster economics of the cities and the ups and downs caused by crop commodity speculators in Chicago were, American farm life remained straightforward for the majority. Most were not big Midwestern broad-acre farmers who could be destroyed by a two-cent change in the price of wheat. Wheat in Maw and Pap's time hovered at around fifty to fifty-five cents a bushel; corn, at forty-five; and oats at about fifty-six. Multiply the acreage by average bushels per acre for your piece of land, and you had a start at figuring out a realistic basis for your family's future. It was realistic enough that, after making allowances for bad years, plus an assessment of the man seeking the loan, the banks lent Pap the price of a farm.

That assessment was not shallow.

Pap was expected to bring to the equation several dozen already-honed skills, such as the repair, sharpening, and use of tools (if you think that is simple, try laying down wheat with a scythe sometime); the ability to husband several types of animal stock; and experience and instinct about soils and terrain, likely weather, and broadcasting seed by hand. Eastern mountain subsistence farms needed little or no planting equipment because plots were too small and steep. What harvesting equipment such as reapers and threshers might be needed was usually owned by one man who made part of his living reaping and threshing for the rest of the community. Other skills included planting in cultivated ridges, managing a woodlot, and estimating hours of available sunlight for both plant growth and working. The subsistence farm wife's life required as much experience and skill on a different front of family provision.

That said, Pap wasn't a particularly good farmer. He wasn't a bad farmer, either. He was just an average farmer among millions of average farmers. The year my grandparents married, about 35 million Americans were successfully engaged in farming, mostly at a subsistence level. It's doubtful that they were all especially gifted, or dedicated or resourceful. Nevertheless, their kind of human-scale family farming proved successful for twelve generations because it was something more—a collective consciousness rooted in the land that pervaded four-fifths of North American history.

They farmed with the aid of some 14 million draught horses and God only knows how many mules. Pap wasn't much for mules; all the farming he had to do could easily be done with one horse. Without going into a treatise on horse farming, let me say that, around 1955 at the age of ten, I saw the last of Pap's work horses in use, a coal-black draught animal named 'Nig' (short for nigger, of course). By then, Nig, who was Nig number three, if I remember correctly, was over twenty years old, and put out to pasture—a loose use of the term, given that he spent his time in the shade of the backyard grape arbour waiting to be hand-fed treats. But Nig still pulled a single tree-plough in a four-acre truck garden down in the bottom land—mostly melons, tomatoes, and sweet corn—while I sometimes rode atop barefoot holding onto the wooden hames at the collar. Pap walked behind, guiding the plough. 'Gee Nig! Haw Nig! Step right ... Turn and baaack. Cluck-cluck.' The rabbit dogs, Nellie and Buck, trotted alongside in the spring sun.

Though Pap owned a tractor by then—a beaten-up old Farmall with huge, cleated steel wheels, a man-killer prone to flipping over backward and grinding the driver bloodily under the cleats—he could still do all his cultivation walking behind Nig in the spring. In summer he'd scratch out the weeds with a horseless garden plough, or 'push plough', and pick off bugs by hand, dropping them into a Maxwell House coffee can half-filled with kerosene. Pap hand-harvested most things, even large cornfields, using a corn cutter fashioned from an old Confederate sword. But it is that old horse and that old man with the long leather lines thrown up over his shoulders, the plough in his iron grip, and cutting such straight lines in the red clay and shale, that I remember most fondly. He made it look easy.

Fifty years in the furrows will do that.

The last I saw of old Nig was a few years later on a sunfish-catching expedition to the farm pond. Red-winged black birds ch-ch-chrilled in the cattails. Nig was a skeleton trapped in wild grapevines deep in a sumac thicket. He stood upright, his bones encased in a brittle, sun-baked hide, with his nose touching the ground, as if he were grazing somewhere beyond the grave. And for the first time I understood something. I didn't quite know what, but I knew it had to do with the passing of all things, and that eternity does not care about that passing.

BY 1930, MAW WAS, IN HER WORDS, 'PLUM DONE WITH having babies'. This was the same year that the last of Maw's children, my aunt Ony Mae, was born, letting out her first squalls of mortal indignation upstairs in the bedroom with the balcony, where her siblings before her had done the same—Big Joe (my daddy), Ruth, Harry Jr, whom everyone called Toad, and Nelson, the oldest.

'Nelson come along in 1919, smack in the middle of canning season,' Maw said. In 1919, there was a war on, with doughboys in the trenches of Europe, but canning is its own war between quickly ripening acres of vegetables and the slow process of hand canning. 'Pap took on my canning and put up fifty quarts of green beans the night Nels come into the world. The bean baskets had already been on the porch almost two days and was getting limp. "Cain't let 'em go to waste," he said. Pap wasn't about to come upstairs among women and birthing and such!'

Pap's explanation was simple and brusque: 'Canning was the next thing that needed doing, dammit.'

Uncle Nelson, the product of all that moaning and hen-cackle upstairs, was born mentally deficient and 99 per cent deaf. Consequently, he never left the farm, never married, nor learned to read and write. For a couple of weeks he did attend the free state school for the deaf in nearby Romney. But Pap and Maw pulled him out. There was no telling what wickedness lay in Romney, a town of perhaps a thousand, back then. At the same time they knew that, barring him losing a hand on the tractor's side-mounted buzz saw, the farm was a safe-enough place for Nelson. 'So we just kept him home. He come up to size right here on the place, workin' like everybody else as soon as he got his growth.'

'Working' is an understatement. My daddy recalled, 'Nelson and I were, oh, about twelve or thirteen years old when we camped up on the Potomac River for a couple of months fellin' and hewin' green oak cross-ties. You know how heavy a green oak tie is? [240 pounds] Pap had to keep up the farm, so there we'd be up there on the river, and he'd come by once a week. A guy named Guy Spriggs hauled 'em over to the B&O rail yard at Martinsburg. But we never thought it was tough doings. We fished and hunted for food, and cooked on a fire. Once, Nelson killed a damned 10-point buck with an axe! The dogs had it cornered in a blackberry thicket. I sunk the meat in a lard bucket in the river, and Nelson and me ate on it for almost a week.'

Every time I see the ties in a railroad track, I think of those two boys doing such strongman's work by the rushing river. And I think about how one of those boys, Daddy, had a congenital heart defect that would cause him to pass out in those woods, and later while he was standing in military formations during the war. And how, later, knowing that, he could still say it wasn't 'tough doings'.

WE REFERRED TO THE FAMILY FARMSTEAD AS 'Over Home'. As in, 'Are you going Over Home this weekend?', or 'The deer are just thick as fleas on a wild hog Over Home this year. Good hunting.' No matter what direction you drove from to get there, you were still headed Over Home.

For a kid, life Over Home was somewhere between a Tarzan movie, *The Adventures of Huckleberry Finn*, and unrestrained redneck aboriginalism. Admirers of Americans Indians in all things, we made Osage orangewood bows and cedar arrows tipped with ancient triangulate-notched arrowheads lost centuries ago by Manahaoc, Tutelo, and Shawnee Indian hunters. So many of them turned up in freshly ploughed fields, and were so easily spotted after a rain, that farmers would accumulate a crate or rusty bucket full of them in their barns. We took imaginary scalps and set bent-sapling snares for small animals, just as our fathers had. There are still trees in the woods which my father and uncles bent down and staked seventy years ago when they were saplings. Those saplings sent up tall, straight 'suckers', which grew into multiple trees off the original bent one, which turned into a strange, thick, horizontally curved mother trunk for them all—living monuments of childhoods past and to come. And if we still managed to get bored, we could always go shoot someone's bull in the balls with the BB gun ('I don't know what's got into that bull lately, he's tore through two sections of fence in two weeks!' said neighbouring farmer Jackson Luttrell, who probably had a pretty good idea what was up.) Along with the dogs, we were turned loose in the woods and fields until dark. 'Let 'em follow the cows home.'

When the cows did come home, we sometimes did not. So it was the job of deaf, grinning Uncle Nelson, with his semi-mongoloid visage and muscular stride, to retrieve us before night fell. In a house jammed with uncles, Nelson was the special one for the kids. He babysat in those times when the rest of the family went to a funeral or camped in the orchards of adjoining Frederick County, Virginia, to work on the millionaire Byrd family's apple plantation to earn cash. That left Nelson to revert to the childhood from which he'd never really emerged. He'd jack up the woodstove so the mice would scurry out and we could plug them with the BB gun he kept stashed under his bed. And there were fast downhill rides in the wheelbarrow, giddy feed-corn battles in the granary, and long slides through the haymow.

There was also a dark side to Nelson's relationship with children. At times when babysitting, he would sexually fondle some of the younger kids. Being the oldest of the grandchild-and-cousin network, I knew nothing of it at first. Once I found out, I was shocked, sickened inside. I also felt compelled to tell my parents and grandparents. I could never have expected or been prepared for their unified wall of denial. 'How can you say something like that about your uncle Nelson? Why do you tell such a lie, boy?' All the adults seemed outraged by me; not a one was on my side. Then came the permanent silence about the matter, which was never again, even to this day, mentioned by anyone in the family, including the kids that I know of. But the fondling ceased immediately after that, so somebody must have talked to Nelson afterward. (He could read lips a bit, and hear a bit if you yelled directly in his ear.) Then life went on like it had never happened. When I look back on it, I can see that it was the only kind of sexual intimacy that Nelson ever knew in his life, which was that of a child—the mentally handicapped child that was himself.

For the adults, life was about work. Hard work. And, for their back-breaking efforts, most of the clan expected to live on that place any time and at will—or at least hunt and 'run a patch' (keep a garden) there. My grandfather's will specifically granted all future Bageants perpetual gardening and hunting rights on the place. The late attorney David Savastian, a young lawyer travelling along the back roads looking for small legal work at the time he wrote Pap's will, told me later, 'Your grandfather didn't know it was impossible to grant such a right after you're dead, and I didn't have the heart to tell him.' Pap couldn't imagine a life without the security of a garden. He came from an ancient lineage of such people. (*They have bones of clay and blood of the earth's rains, and make to rise up the goodness of creation.*) Planting was necessary to life as he knew it, and as those before him knew it. All his children would plant gardens most of their lives, no matter where they lived. Nor could he imagine life without chickens and at least one hog, nor a house that didn't contain at least two generations — usually newly married sons or daughters, plus an old man or woman or both living out their last years somewhere in the back rooms. So rooted in the home place was the family that in the years after the war, when my father, aunts, and uncles all ended up taking jobs and apartments in the towns and cities, it was unforgiveable for them not to spend every weekend and holiday there. My father, Aunt Ony, and Uncle Toad managed to drop by there a couple of evenings during the week to boot, until the day they died.

Childhood there, nevertheless, held its dangers. Warnings and admonitions were constant. In late autumn on butchering day, you could count on hearing, 'Now you kids stay away from that hog-scalding trough, or you'll end up like that little Brannon girl who fell in and was boiled alive. Yessir, cooked all the way through, and the skin come right off her by the time they fished her out.' Which, as I learned later, happened in 1911. Talk about community memory! Or maybe it would be about some boy who had gotten his hand cut off messing with the buzz saw on the tractor's power take-off.

A far more likely danger, though, was snakes. Everyone at some point in their lives pretty near got bitten while hoeing gardens, cutting firewood, pulling down hay bales, or bringing up a stringer of fish at night along the Potomac River, when water moccasins swallowed the smaller fish on the stringer and you pulled up a bundle of engorged serpents. You never quite got used to it.

People died as well as lived at the old home place. And when they did, they were 'laid out' in the living room.

Maw's pappy, Old Jim—an offensive, cranky old coot — spent most of his last years nailed to the one spot, his big leather chair by the living-room window, where he spat tobacco juice into a cut-down molasses can and cussed FDR. When he died, he only moved about six feet from that chair, to the centre of the room—to his funerary bier, which consisted of two sawhorses draped in black cloth. Old Jim was quiet at last in that satin-lined box. Roosevelt had one less detractor, and Maw could throw his much-reviled spit can on the trash heap. But Old Jim managed to remain offensive to the end. The deceased had picked out his 'burying suit' years before, and stored it mightily against moths and worms. Consequently, the coffin smelled overpoweringly of mothballs and what must have been a quart of eye-watering camphor.

In those days, the embalmer or mortician often came to your house the next morning to lay out the body. Kerosene lamps burned low all that night; and if you happened to be a small kid, that first realisation of mortality struck, killing that innocent place it kills in children. Maw leaned through the lantern glow and said, 'Just be real still, and you'll hear the angels sing.' None did, of course. There was no sound, except for the breathing of Old Jim's equally cranky black dog, Prince, peering from under the bier, his green eyes flashing as if to say, 'You folks just *think* I'm outta yer hair! I done been reincarnated in this here old dog, be damned ya!'

Old Jim's laying-out was a calm affair, as might be expected from any situation in which the primary attendant is a dead man. Calm except for when the mortician, wearing stockyard gumboots and a three-piece suit, got his truck stuck in the mud trying to back it up to the porch steps to unload Jim's coffin. He finally lost his composure when he tried sliding the coffin along an eight-foot plank that didn't quite reach the steps.

Old Jim retained his cool composure (and decomposure) through it all. There he lay, at first in the cellar, amid a quarter ton of potatoes, canned sweet pickles, and a side of salted pork in the cellar, where his earthly hide had been washed, and laid on a door placed across the aforementioned sawhorses to chill. By the time the mortician was ready to box Jim up, the neighbours had arrived—the women with food, the men with fedora hats in their hands, and floundering expressions. Though most of the family members were Christian teetotallers, a modest pint of corn essence was being passed around in the unsavoury environment of the two-holer outhouse. You would never go sit in the car to do your drinking. That would have been an instant tip-off to the womenfolk.

Later, a sideways cousin of mine named Burt, one of those congenital bullies you just knew was going to grow up to kill somebody, told me that the mortician had dumped Jim's blood in what we called 'the nansy patch', a plot of wavering red poppies down by the garden—which, for some unknown reason, my grandmother had dubbed nansies. Now a mortician is sort of a beautician to the dead, and not necessarily an embalmer, and the one who came probably hadn't done any blood pumping on Old Jim. The portable blood pump was large and noisy, and any resort to it would have been noted or remembered. But I didn't know that and, given what Burt had told me, I was forever after struck numb at the sight of those ominous blossoms lunging vulgarly forward in the sun, rooted in blood and red clay. In summer, the sun glared down and the garden dirt was hot. Katydids buzzed their atomic hymn to the void while the nansies nodded in silent agreement. I played in the barn and under the high, cool front porch, but stayed damned-clear of that nansy patch.

Except whenever Cousin Burt came around—which, thank God, was not often. Burt lived up on Sleepy Creek Mountain, and was one of those oafish children born late in his parents' lives. His father, who was some kind of kin to Maw, was a tall, cadaverous man with a cruel streak that often shows up in these hills. So Burt 'got his meanness honest', as they say. Once Burt burned some baby birds alive with lighter fluid under the porch; I remember there were five of them. And he would get the little kids down and give them Dutch rubs with his knuckles. But worst of all, he would drag us into the nansy patch if we disobeyed him. 'Fetch me a chunk of brown sugar from the pantry,' he'd order. Or 'Git me one of your pap's cigarettes.' After three or four draggings, all Burt had to do was look at you and you'd do anything he wanted. There was no arguing. You just did it.

My grandmother Virginia, on the other hand, loved the nansies. A rheumy woman with quiet, grey eyes and a chipped black cameo at her throat, she would trim off the dead leaves in summer and fuss over them each spring. There she'd be with her old-fashioned homemade sunbonnet appearing, then disappearing, in and out of the nansies. She seemed to be communicating with them, drawing them up from the earth. They grew to be huge.

The nansy patch is gone now, long since become lawn. When I look back on that patch, I realise that in my life I have witnessed the end of one America, one that would seem a nostalgic Carter Family country-music fable, or something for the Foxfire books, if I had not seen it with my own eyes. And only then because that America lingered forty years past its time along a road called Shanghai, ever changing yet unchanged in so many ways. Along its ditches the snakes still go blind while shedding their skins during dog days, writhing in their transfiguration in that place of the wild grape, the mountain laurel, and the now-collapsed world where I spent my formative years without ever having seen a black person, but nevertheless had seen a witch and a panther in a sycamore tree.

PAP AND MAW AND THE OTHER FARMERS ALONG THE road made their own world with their own hands. They held few 'jobs of work', as we called employment. Before World War II, most people's survival, even town people's, depended to some degree upon knowing how to do things that most of us don't know today—such as how to fix the broken accoutrements of daily life, add on a back porch, adjust tools properly, or fix the family jalopy. There is a deep pleasure in knowing how to take care of yourself and the people you love with your own hands, not to mention providing life's pleasant diversions the same way.

Once, while playing in the barn, I ran across a four-foot rounded club of sorts, narrow at one end and about five inches in diameter at the other. It took a moment for me to realise that this was a gigantic homemade baseball bat. So

I dragged it over to the house and asked my grandfather, 'What is this? It looks like a ballbat.' That's what we called baseball bats—ballbats. And that's what it was.

So I asked Pap, 'Whyzit so big?'

'Because I made it big.'

Pap had carved out that ballbat as a young man. He'd never seen a real bat, so he guessed. He grew up playing the kind of baseball they played back in the farms and hollers. Which meant that Pap had been playing baseball straight out of the tradition that emerged during the Civil War—a vestigial one that had rolled along in these hills entirely independent of the formalised national game which was already in existence when he was a boy. All his life he had made his own world with his hands, and fixed it the same way. I'd watched him and Nelson make hickory axe-handles, hoe handles, and oaken mallets, and watched them smooth out the hickory and oak wood by scraping the handles with large shards of broken glass, a practice that went back to pre-sandpaper colonial times. They were quiet and thoughtful as they worked—with their long, patient strokes, handle in lap, pulling the glass along the contours—in what I don't think it would be exaggerating to call a metaphysical, reflective space. After an hour or so, the result was a hard, glossy surface, same as the giant ballbat. Pap had learned it from his father, and Nelson had learned it from Pap, and, by watching, I learned it from them. Still, I cannot help but wonder what the homemade baseballs must have looked like. When I asked Pap, he said, 'Well, nobody ever hit one much past first base, I can tell you that.'

By today's notions, people along Shanghai Road

were poor and, in most cases, quite superstitious and ignorant of the larger world. Yet they were rich in human relationships, and very well fed. What we ate and the way we cooked it probably killed most of us in the long run, as it is killing me now via high blood pressure and diabetes, what with its salt, bacon grease, sugars, and fried everything from pork to okra and tomatoes. I'm not completely convinced, though, given that so many lived to see eighty. Maybe it was the 'healthy exercise'—a citified word if ever there was one. Farm folks back then were trying to avoid getting so damned much of it. To express relaxation and a let-up of toil, they'd say, 'Oh I'm doing pretty good—I'm staying off my feet.'

When it came to eating, the very scale of our meals would be considered obscene and hedonistic today. Maw's cooking was so good it would make you get down and pound the floor for joy. Everyone on the farm—which meant a bunch of us, because married aunts and uncles lived there half the time—ate meals together at a table about seven feet long and four feet wide. Often as not at breakfast, there would be a whole shoulder or a side of middlin' meat, along with three dozen biscuits, a couple of dozen eggs, half a gallon of sweet milk gravy, with three kinds of jam plus molasses on the side. Vegetables were fresh in season, and canned for the winter … simple fare, such as green beans and tomato pickles. If you'd handed Maw a head of broccoli, she wouldn't have known whether to put it in a vase or a pan. Meals were the heart of daily life, a rowdy family sacrament linking everyone. Childhood on this farm, and especially at that table, is the rootstock of my imagination. It is to this table and the faces around it that my mind returns to touch something near perfect.

Food was not yet an addictive substance, nor the subject of slick magazines or cooking shows for affluent foodies. Preparing it on an eight-burner woodstove was damned-sure not a hobby. In fact, there were no hobby crafts as such. Woodworking was just that: doing necessary work that involved wood. Having $3,000 worth of power tools in your garage simply to build a faux-Windsor chair would have had the old boys of Pap's generation winking at each other in amusement. Quilting, too. Buying new fabric to make a quilt would have been proof of insanity, or wifely incompetence at the very least—quilts being the primary way to make use of old clothing scraps.

To be a bit kinder, though, to the middle-class urban quilters and would-be Thomas Chippendales, a deeper desire drives today's overwrought and romanticised amateur efforts at high-craft woodworking. Few of these hobbyists are satisfied to create mundane things that do not draw attention to themselves, and they usually romanticise the woodworker's craft in high-art terms, or have $80 coffee-table books to that effect. But still there is the desire to regain something lost, some fugitive meaningfulness in a transactional, disembodied nation which demands that the quiet, productive satisfactions of the hand must be purchased.

America's vast white-collar plantation of clerks—and that's what most white-collar jobs are, regardless of the claptrap about being part of an 'information society'—leaves us disembodied. Eight hours a day of pushing the Empire's insurance and credit-card transactions around in cyberspace, even if pursued with utter diligence, can only add up to a pointless lifetime of tedium. Each task is only the movement of a symbol, which, like the bureaucratic or commercial transactions it represents, vaporises into the next one in a never-ending series. No matter how complex or valuable the work is supposed to be, the human being at the end of it is just a tracking mechanism attached to a stream of numbers and transactions. Only the mind is required to track the digital flow of zeros and ones through the circuitry of commerce, while the body slumps in the cubicle like some useless appendage. Work and life feel most productive and meaningful when the mind and the body are joined in a purposeful way. We can argue about the details of this remark later, but I've done both kinds of work separately and together—though not lately—and I'm convinced of its truth.

Employing the mind and body in a purposeful way was the only manner in which people like Pap knew how to be. It was an entire world and a way of being that was anachronistic even in the 1950s ... vestigial, charged with folk beliefs, marked by an ignorance of the larger world, and lived unselfconsciously under the arc of Jeffersonian ideals, backed up by an archaic confidence in the efficacies of God's word and grapeshot. I consider myself fortunate to have caught a glimpse of a more-purposeful and meaningful way as it went around the corner, only to be ambushed by an increasingly fancy and 'store bought' America—a slicker, glossier one with no handmade edges.

CHAPTER TWO

The Politics of Plenty

Politicised as the nation is today, I sometimes think about what the actual party politics of my family were then. Today, they are all hard-rightist fundamentalist-Christian Republicans. But for generations they were double-bottomed Democrats—though certainly not the kind of Democrats we know now.

Steeped in the wary Scots–Irish mountain ethos, they were not big joiners of parties or organisations. Pap had, however, joined the Ku Klux Klan, back in the Twenties. He quit after about a month when he figured out that the Klan was more than the Protestant fraternal group it publicly presented itself to be. He didn't reject the Klan so much for its racial philosophy, because that was not emphasised in a county where there were no blacks. He simply felt that Klan members were 'a bunch of windbags full of shit'. Nor did he much like the notion of wearing 'a white dress and a pilla' case with eyeholes in it'. During the Forties, Pap was also a member of The Patriotic Sons of Liberty, an Unger Store lodge group whose main function was to put on the local fair/public picnic down in the woods by the crossroads. The Patriotic Sons amassed a burial fund for members, a popular practice in those days, in which each of the group's fifty-odd members contributed fifty cents or so regularly to a kitty for the burial of any member who died. Very practical and efficient, dues were always pegged at a level high enough to cover a member's basic burial expenses. Ultimately, an insurance-company lawyer contacted the Patriotic Sons, informing them that they were running an illegal insurance company. The practice was abandoned.

Pap may have been a Democrat, but he felt free to cuss either party and its candidates with equal fervour, if he was in the mood. He didn't like Coolidge, and, though he voted for FDR twice, he was leery of parts of Roosevelt's New Deal. Particularly Social Security. He could not grasp how a man could get money in the mail at the end of the month if he had not worked during the month. The one exception to his distaste for the New Deal was the Civilian Conservation Corps camps, in which he and all of his sons spent some time. 'They worked 'em like mules for their pay, and that's how the taxpayers' money should be paid out,' he told me.

Not that he ever paid many taxes. Nor much Social Security Insurance in his old age. SSI came in later during his life, after he had held only a couple of wage-paying jobs—one briefly as a janitor at the Berkeley Springs Hospital, and one in a silica mine in the same town. Because of that work, he got issued a Social Security card, whether he liked it or not. Consequently, like others of his generation who'd paid little if any money into

Social Security, he got a minimum monthly cheque for something like $54, in his old age. After he died, a shoebox of uncashed Social Security cheques was found under his bed.

For the most part, though, he wanted nothing from the government, and gave it nothing in return if he could help it, in the belief that he could damned-well take care of himself, given enough land and enough kids to work it. For almost three decades, he had both.

Freedom, to him, resided in yeoman property rights — in farming and farmers. That put him in agreement with Thomas Jefferson's vision of an enlightened agrarian nation. Pap did not know the term 'right wing' or 'left wing' from a turkey wing. He didn't need to, and we might be better off now if we did not know either. In a county with only a couple of thousand inhabitants, every voter knew every local candidate. Those candidates didn't make campaign promises, other than to try to get the state to fix certain roads and maybe spend a little money on their village schoolhouse. When it came to state-level politicians, Pap did know that 'They fall in love with the farmer every October, they kiss 'em to death in November [the election month in the US], and skip town in December.'

Politicians, especially conservative politicians of 'The business of America is business' kind, have always loved farmers. And never more than today, when farmers buy all their food, purchase their chemicals, seed, and energy from them, and then sell the crop at the price that is best for corporate planners and speculators. Farmers along Shanghai Road were, for the most part, out of that loop, though they did buy a little fertiliser and certain kinds of seed on credit at the store, or the occasional gun for hunting. Pap bought an exquisitely balanced Harrington & Richardson double-barrelled shotgun in 1946 that became a family heirloom, of which we shall hear more later.

Politically correct and ecologically aware American liberals also love farmers. But they love them so long as they do not raise tobacco or clear land, or kill bugs with pesticides—and so long as they are the sort who display themselves in bib overalls and straw hats at the organic farmers' market on Saturdays. Pap had a foot in both camps. He never cleared any land; his was cleared a hundred years before he bought it. For the most part, he hand-picked bugs off the family garden. But he was a happy man when DDT and the earliest pesticides came along, because no man can hand-pick corn borers on a forty-acre stretch. In fact, he was so damned enthusiastic that, during the summer months, he regularly sprayed the inside of the house with his hand-pumped fly sprayer. That we were not all born with three eyes is a miracle. And toward the end, he was sort of his own farmer's market, as the ever-nearer Washington, DC suburbanites made autumn outings of driving over our way to observe the rustics and buy fresh sweet corn, tomatoes, and melons.

When it came to selling food to Yankees, for damned sure Pap made more money than his grandpappy Sampson Bageant made during the Civil War. Because Pap's customers were Yankees who paid on the spot. I have a copy of a Civil War-era receipt documenting Sampson's sale of 'one wagonload of bacon' (I've always marvelled at the number of hogs he raised to produce a wagonload solely of bacon) to the Army of the Confederacy, for which he was paid in Confederate bonds. More proof that Pap was right in that 'There's good money to be made off of folks from up north if you can keep them from picking your pocket while you're counting out their change.'

Among rural heartlanders, especially in the South, there exists a general mistrust of urban dwellers that stretches back two hundred years. This mistrust has been reinforced by thousands of little incidents between business people and farmers. Let me tell you about one that happened in 1950.

Pap never owned a car until deep into the 1960s. So he and Maw and their kids walked a couple of miles over the ridge to the store, not just to buy things, but to use the telephone in emergencies. The phone line ran only as far as the junction store. When my cousin Patricia (Teesie), the only child of Uncle Toad and Aunt Midge, died at age three of spinal meningitis, Pap walked over the ridge to the Unger Store, where he phoned the undertaker at Bumps' Funeral Home to come get the body. Owner Barry Bumps collected Teesie, did the embalming, and brought her back in the classic 'little rosewood casket' of mountain-ballad fame to Over Home, where Patricia was laid out in the living room for a day prior to burial. The day before the funeral service, her casket was placed inside the Greenwood church to await burial the next afternoon. At that time, it was discovered that the coffin would not fit into the child-sized concrete vault lining the bottom of the grave.

So Pap called Bumps again, and told him the vault was too small. 'No problem,' Bumps said over the store's phone receiver, 'I'll send someone out to install a larger vault.' Bumps' crew finished the job less than an hour before the scheduled funeral.

Maw arrived half an hour before the service. She took one look at Teesie's coffin, ran her hand over it, and exclaimed, 'My Lord! This is not the rosewood coffin we paid for!' Instead, the coffin was a cheaper thing, with fake gilt handles instead of brass, and rosewood stain over pine. 'It's been switched!' she said. During the installation of the larger vault, the funeral home had swapped the more expensive coffin for a cheaper pine version.

'We need to go down to the store and telephone Bumps, make him get up here with the coffin we paid for,' Maw snapped. She looked at Pap, and Pap looked at her, and both realised that was never going to happen. With the funeral less than a half-hour away, it just wasn't to be.

'You can't send everybody off and tell them to come back tomorrow,' Pap said.

'So we let Bumps get away with this?' Maw said.

Bumps knew all this, too. He also knew that nobody was going to challenge him, because he would just say, 'Sue me.' And lawsuits cost money. Besides that, no one in the family was irreverent enough to dig Teesie's body up again to prove he had switched coffins. The funeral proceeded as planned. Bumps went on to build a large regional funerary business that he sold for millions, amass commercial real estate, and hold political office.

Three generations of Bageants and not a few Unger Store folks know this story. And it is as good a symbol as any for the traditional rural suspicion of the American business community, which translates into the rural–urban divide today.

The county farmers particularly distrusted businesses in area towns — especially those in Winchester. For two hundred years, Winchester has been a mercantile town, first on the Great Wagon Road, when it hawked goods to settlers moving westward down into the Carolinas and Georgia, then later to the farmers and small communities of the surrounding area. Some older farmers still refer to Winchester's business community as 'town rats', because they always managed to gnaw away at the farmers' larders. To this day, there is widespread suspicion on the part of native rural residents toward Winchester's city government, to the point where county people will not approve of any joint efforts with the city, no matter the likely efficiencies or taxpayer savings involved.

Such latent distrust is national, and can be seen in the famous red state–blue state political map of the United States. It is the cities that are blue, not the vast stretches in between them. Essentially, it represents the long-term reverberation of the urban money-economy versus the rural values of a human work-based economy. Neither side any longer knows it consciously, or can define it clearly, but both sides still sense that it is about 'values' of some kind. Some are real; others are cooked up for political exploitation. But even with so much of the nation's heartland paved, overpassed, and strip-malled, in the strange suburb-like housing developments plunked in isolation and awkwardness in the heartland, and even though it is saturated by inane, homogenised consumer media, the divide remains.

THE CULTURAL VALUES MAY REMAIN, HANGING over everything political and many things that are not, but there are few if any remaining practitioners of the traditional family or community culture by which Pap and Maw lived—the one with the woman in the home, and the man in the fields, although Maw certainly worked in the fields when push came to shove. This is not to advocate such as the natural order of things. I am neither Amish nor Taliban. But knee-jerk, middle-class, mostly urban feminists might do well to question how it all started and what the result has been—maybe by getting out and seeing how few of their sisters gutting chickens on the Tyson's production line or telemarketing credit cards on the electronic plantation relish those dehumanising jobs that they can never quit.

It would do them well to wonder why post-war economists and social planners, from their perches high in the executive and management class, deemed it best for the nation that more mothers become permanent fixtures of America's work force. This transformation doubled the available labour supply, increased consumer spending, and kept wages lower than they would have otherwise been. National production and increased household income supposedly raised everyone's quality of life to stratospheric heights, if Formica countertops and 'happy motoring' can be called that. I'm sure it did so for the managing and owning classes, and urban people with good union jobs. In fact, it was the pre-war trade unions at full strength, particularly the United Auto Workers, that created the true American middle class, in terms of increased affluence for working people and affordable higher education for their children.

What Maw and Pap and millions of others got out of it, primarily, were a few durable goods, a washing machine, a television, and an indoor toilet where the pantry, with its cured meats, 100-pound sacks of brown sugar, flour, and cases of eggs had been. Non-durable commodities were vastly appreciated, too. One was toilet paper, which ended generations of deep-seated application of the pages of the Sears Roebuck mail-order catalogue to the anus (the unspoken limit seemed to be one page to a person at a sitting). The other was canned milk, which had been around a long time, but had been unaffordable. Milk cows are a wonderful thing, but not so good when two wars and town work have drained off your family labour-supply of milkers. So joyous over canned milk was my uncle Toad that he taught me this laudatory poem to evaporated milk when I was five:

Pet Milk, best in the land
Sits on the table in a little white can
No cows to milk, no hay to pitch
Just punch two holes in that son-of-a-bitch!

Amazing how stuff sticks in one's head for a lifetime.

The urging of women into the workplace, first propagandised by a war-making state, was much romanticised in the iconic poster image of Rosie the Riveter, with her blue-denim sleeves rolled up and a scarf tied over her hair. You see the image on the refrigerator magnets of fuzzy-minded feminists-lite everywhere. This liberal identity-statement is sold by the millions at

Wal-Mart, and given away as a promotional premium by National Public Radio and television.

Being allowed to manufacture the planes that bombed so many terrified European families is now rewritten as a feminist milestone by women who were not born at the time. But I've never once heard working-class women of that period rave about how wonderful it was to work long days welding bomb-bay doors onto B-29s.

The machinery of state saw things differently, and so the new reality of women building war machinery was dubbed a social advance for American womankind, both married and single. In Russia, it was ballyhooed as Soviet socialist-worker equality. And one might even believe that equality was the prime motive, when viewed sixty years later by, for instance, a university-educated specimen of the gender writing her doctoral dissertation. But for the children and grandchildren of Rosie the Riveter, those women not writing a dissertation or thesis, there is less enthusiasm. Especially among working mothers. The Pew Research Center reports that only 13 per cent of working mothers think that working benefits their children. But nearly 100 per cent feel they have no choice. Half of working mothers think their employment is pointless for society. Forty-two per cent of Americans, half of them women, say that working mothers have been bad for society on the whole. Nearly all working mothers say they feel guilty as they rush off to work.

Corporations couldn't have been happier with the situation. Family labour was siphoned off into the industrial labour pool, creating a surplus of workers, which in turn created a cheaper work force. There were still the teeming second-generation immigrant populations available for labour, but there were misgivings about them—those second-generation Russian Jews, Italians, Irish, Polish, and Hungarians, and their like. From the very beginning, they were prone to commie notions such as trade unions and eight-hour workdays. They had a nasty history of tenacity, too. You could gun them down at Ludlow and Haymarket, you could burn them up at the Triangle Shirt Factory, you could frame their leaders for murder and execute them, you could throw the National Guard against them, you could hire Pinkerton detectives to assassinate them, and still they kept right on raising Cain about liveable wages and safe working conditions. And then there were the 'coloured people', but not enough of them to worry about. And besides, if you hired too many negroes you riled up your Dagos, Kikes, Pollacks, and Hunkies, who didn't much care to work alongside them, having been successfully played off against the blacks to keep the price of labour down and to keep them from uniting under the banners of socialism, such as the Industrial Workers of the World (the Wobblies), and dozens of other emerging and even thriving people's organisations.

On the other hand, out there in the country was an endless supply of placid mules, who said, 'Yes, Ma'm' and 'No, Ma'm', and accepted whatever you paid them. Best of all, except for churches and the most intimate community groups, these family- and clan-oriented hillbillies were not joiners, especially at some outsiders' urging. Thus, given the nature of union organising—urging and convincing folks to join up—local anti-union businessmen and large companies alike had little to fear when it came to pulling

44

in workers from the farms.

Ever since the Depression, some of the placid country mules had been drifting toward the nearest cities anyway. By the 1950s, the flow was again rapidly increasing. Generation after generation couldn't keep piling up on subsistence farms, lest America come to be one vast Mennonite community, which it wasn't about to become, attractive as that idea might seem now. Even given America's historical agrarian resistance to 'wage slavery' (and farmers were still calling it that when I was a kid), the promise of a regular paycheque seemed the only choice. We now needed far more money to survive, because we could no longer independently provide for ourselves.

Two back-to-back wars had effectively drained off available manpower to the point where our family farm offered only a fraction of its former sustenance. Even if we tried to raise our own food and make our own clothing out of the patterned multi-coloured feed sacks as we had always done, it took more money than ever.

In her later years, weather permitting, Maw walked over a mile each way to our one-room schoolhouse to cook the school lunch, for which the state of West Virginia paid her a pittance. In winter, she rode the bus to school; and when school was out for the summer, she cooked for Camp WinWah, a youth camp for urban kids whose parents could afford to send them off to experience the glories of the mosquito bite and the burnt marshmallow.

By the mid and late 1950s, the escalating monetised economy had rural folks on the ropes. No matter how frugal one was, there was no fighting it. In a county where cash had been scarce from the beginning—though not to disastrous effect—we children would overhear much talk about how this or that aunt or uncle 'needs money real bad'.

Here's how much. During the winter, Maw would ride the school bus in the seat just behind the driver, Henry 'Pup' Brannon, so she could hold him upright during the mild heart attacks he sometimes suffered while driving. 'He needs the work real bad,' she said. One day the attack was not so mild, and Pup Brannon died after reaching home.

Riding the bus to school with Maw, I'd study her swollen, varicose-veined legs and her shopping bag full of fresh, woodstove-baked bread for the kids, which took her already-tired self hours to make each evening. And I'd wonder if old people should have to work that hard. But I also came to understand that she saw 'feeding the kids' as a civic part of farm life, too. And though she'd never have conceived of it in such terms, it was part of the independent Scots–Irish and German settlers' politics of self-sustenance and plenitude. Those politics are still part of conservative political culture in heartland America. They can be seen in the rejection of any government role in such things as nutrition programs and aid to single mothers, and the claim that community and religious organisations can do the job better than what they refer to as 'government giveaway programs'. Unfortunately, though, when they put this belief and their own money into practice, history shows that they tend to take care only of their own kind—Protestant whites.

WHEN IT COMES TO MONEY, I AM TOLD THAT BEFORE the war some Unger Store subsistence farmers got by on less than one hundred dollars a year. I cannot imagine that my grandfather ever brought in more than one thousand dollars in any year. Even before the post-war era's forced commodification of every aspect of American life, at least some money was needed. So some in my family, like many of their neighbours, picked apples seasonally or worked as 'hired-on help' for a few weeks in late summer at the many small family-owned apple- and tomato-canning sheds that dotted Morgan County. In the 1930s, 1940s, and 1950s, between farming and sporadic work at the local flour, corn, and feed-grinding outfits, and especially the small canning operations, a family could make it. Pap could grow a few acres of tomatoes for the canneries, and Maw or their kids could work a couple of weeks in them for cash.

This was local and human-scale industry and farming, with the tomatoes being grown on local plots ranging from five to ten acres. Canners depended on nearby farm families for crops and labour, and the farm families depended upon them in turn for cash or its equivalent. Like feed mills and crossroad stores, tomato-canning factories and tomato fields were an important fixture of life there.

Of the things grown and canned in the Unger Store area—apples, peaches, and tomatoes—the tomato is by far the most noble because the tomato, dear friends, is the most truly democratic vegetable in America. It has been anointed by Lady Liberty herself as the enemy of despotism and lifter of onerous mortgages.

You may point out—as any botanist surely will— that the tomato is actually a fruit, because it is developed from an ovary at the base of the flower. Ovaries be damned. Anything that is eaten with sausage gravy and biscuits is a vegetable. Nobody ever ate blueberries or bananas with meat gravy; at least, nobody in their right mind did.

Unlike Malaysian lettuce or bitter melons (just why good-ole garden lettuce and cantaloupes have become too pedestrian for today's foodie gardeners, I'll never understand), tomatoes are easy to grow and are enjoyed by both the rich and the poor. So let me fiddle-fart around here a bit and tell you how the tomato in Morgan County proved itself an ally of true democracy and a binder of community—a great leveller of men, transcending even religion and politics.

As with the recounting of any agricultural saga, this one begins and ends with dirt. In this case, four acres of the stuff, which Pap planted out with tomatoes. They were the traditional 'Mortgage Lifter' variety, and they basked in the sunny bottom land below the homeplace's ridge-top perch. From there, we could—and everybody was expected to—watch out for the deer and other critters back in the surrounding woods just waiting to pounce upon this four-acre buffet. An off-and-on war raged between the critters and the owners of the watchful eyes peering from the windows or front porch. Nearly every pair of them belonged to a hillbilly sharpshooter, as the army medals in the china cupboard attested, or to a kid who'd expended a few thousand rounds of ammo sharpening his or her skills (both women and men hunted deer around here, though far more men than women). No few possums, rabbits, racoons, and groundhogs gave their all for a taste of tomato in that bottom-land field. And once in a while, even a venturesome white tail deer ended up on the dinner table, thanks to the alluring American tomato. Not often, though, because deer browse high on the mountains in summer and autumn, and usually only come down in winter when the foliage gets scarce up there. Beyond that, deer prefer to browse at neck level so as to keep an eye out for predators. Tomatoes grow low.

This 'mater patch', as we called it, was one helluva load of work. There was the setting out of the plants in spring, hoeing weeds and plucking off bugs in summer, and then picking 17 tons (4½ tons per acre and upwards—something like 400 cratefuls altogether) of ripe tomatoes in late summer. But finally would come the excitement of the arrival of Jackson Luttrell's truck, and loading them up for the cannery. Some of us smaller fry would later miss having the opportunity to lay on the porch in a prone firing position with the barrels of our .22-calibre rifles poked through the railing like the defenders of Fort Apache holding out against its furred and clawed tribes of attackers. Pap, however, was happy to see the tomatoes off and away to Cotton Unger's little canning factory three miles over the hill.

Farm-transport vehicles were much scarcer then, especially anything bigger than a quarter-ton pickup truck. So the sight of Jackson Luttrell's one-ton Chevy truck with its high wooden sideboards was exciting in itself. In those days, farmers did not buy new $45,000 trucks to impress other farmers, or run to the nearest farm supply in one of them to pick up a couple of connector bolts. Every farmer had a farm wagon, whether pulled by horse or tractor, but almost nobody owned a truck. Common sense and thrift prevented them from spending big money on something that would only be used during one month each year at harvest time. Beyond that, farmers would not even think of growing those small acreages of tomatoes that the canneries depended upon if they had to buy a truck to transport them there—any profit made on the tomatoes would be lost on the truck. So, for folks such as Jackson Luttrell, who had one, ownership made more economic sense. He profited through its maximised use in getting everyone else's crops to the mill or processing plant. One truck served the farm community, at minimum expenditure to the entire group. They didn't even have to pay Jackson Luttrell any cash for the hauling.

That was because Cotton Unger, who owned the canning operation, was expected to get the tomatoes to his factory himself. As a businessman and entrepreneur, it was Unger's job to deal with the problems that came with his enterprise. Unger's job was to run a business; a farmer's job was to farm. These were two separate things in the days before the rigged game of agri-business put all the cost on the farmers through loading them with debt, and all the profits went to business corporations. Nor did Unger's duties as a capitalist end with getting the hauling done at his own expense. It was also his job to turn the local crops such as wheat, corn, and tomatoes into money, through milling or canning them for sale to bulk contractors elsewhere.

Cotton owned more than just the family store, which he'd inherited from his father, Peery Unger, and for which the community was named sometime after the Civil War. The store at the junction had gasoline pumps, a grinding mill, and a feed and seed farm-supply adjunct. It was also the official post office for that end of the county; and, just to be safe, Cotton Unger also farmed. The Unger family's store was a modest, localised example of a vertically integrated, agriculturally based business, mostly out of necessity.

Cotton never saw much cash, and never got rich by any means. Not on the ten-cent and fifteen-cent purchases that farmers made there for over one hundred years. Yet he could pay Jackson Luttrell for the tomato hauling—in credit at the store. That enabled Jackson to buy seed, feed, hardware, fertiliser, tools, and gasoline, and farm until harvest time with very little cash, leaving him with enough to invest in a truck. Unger could run his tomato cannery and transform local produce into cash, because he could barter credit for farm products and services. This was a community economic ecology that blended labour, money, and goods to sustain a modest but satisfactory life for all.

At the same time, like most American businessmen then and today, Cotton Unger was a Republican. He was a man of the Grand Old Party: the party of a liberator named Abraham, who freed millions of black men from the bondage of slavery; and the party of two presidents named George, the second of whom subsequently ushered Americans of all colours back into slavery through national indebtedness. Being of a Republican stripe made Cotton Unger a rare bird in the strongly Democratic Morgan County.

Today he would be even rarer, because he was a Republican with the common wisdom to understand something that no Republican has ever grasped since: he realised that any wealth he might acquire in life was due not only to his own efforts, but also to the efforts of all other men combined—men who built the roads that hauled his merchandise; men who laid rail track, grew crops, drilled wells, and undertook all the other earthly labours that make society possible. Whether they were Democrats or not, he needed the other citizens around him as friends, neighbours, and builders of the community. To that end, he provided transportation to the polls at election time for farmers without cars—and they were many, Pap and Maw among them—full knowing that nearly every last one of them was going to vote against his candidate. In his ancestors' time they had voted for Andrew Jackson, Martin Van Buren, James Polk, James Buchanan, Woodrow Wilson, Franklin Roosevelt, and Harry Truman—all Democrats.

The old-timers say that Cotton always looked kinda weary around election time. And well he must have been. On election day, Cotton chauffeured around Democratic voters, people who would vote against his interests, vote in favour of higher business taxes or to increase teachers' pay to the point where the school-marm could almost make a living. But Cotton also understood that his personal interests resided more with his community and neighbours than with his political affiliation. Republican politicians in faraway Charleston took the back seat to his face-to-face daily life with his neighbours. Cotton, like his father Peery, and his grandfather, C.J. Unger, before him, knew that when you depend directly on neighbours for your daily bread, you'd damned-well better have their respect and goodwill. And you'd best maintain it over generations, too, if you plan to pass the family store down to your sons and your sons' sons. We may never see that level of operative community democracy again.

Jackson Luttrell, the man who hauled the tomatoes for Cotton Unger, was a successful farmer by Morgan County standards. He was never rich, but he was successful because his farm was a model of common sense and productivity. Over his life he won awards for his farming practices. Jackson's farm was better than most, partly because he was one of the rare ones with a modest, formal agricultural-school education. But mainly because Andrew Jackson Luttrell practised thrift as a high art form, yet never as mere stinginess. Jackson was a generous farmer when it came to those in need. When he stopped his truck even for a short moment to talk to a passer-by, he cut the engine to save gas. He wore the same heavy-canvas barn-coat three-quarters of his life, and never once threw away an empty coffee can or a bent nail that could be straightened and used again. Over the years, he expanded his holdings beyond grain and vegetable crops to include cattle, hogs, orchards and, later, a small tomato-canning operation of his own. Throughout his life he also cut men's and boys' hair on his back porch for ten cents a head. He was a fair barber, a very good farmer, and a thoughtful Democrat. He was a straight-up Methodist and a hauler of the tomatoes of democracy, in a system where everyone benefited through an economy of labour, with the small money of small farmers supplying the grease for the common-sense machinery of community sustenance.

Like sustenance farming in Morgan County, the

tomato-canning sheds are no more. Today we see only their rusting, ramshackle roofs pushing above the surrounding overgrown sumac and wild blackberry vines. The faint peeling signage of their abandonment whisper names such as 'Little Miss Tomato' and 'Ruby Star' in the rustling foliage, as if to say, 'Here, good people once earned money, though not much, and with it they bought shoes for their kids, and paid the taxes of their county and republic. What money they needed, I issued forth each Friday. On Saturday they went to town, and on Sunday they prayed, thankful for such fortunate things as I, a humble canning shed, enabled them to do, such as to put money in the church collection-plate, honestly grateful for the enoughness of their world. All this I did before I was murdered by a distant hand.'

'YEP, THIS USED TO BE PRIME TOMATO COUNTRY,' said Vernon Krauss, whose family once owned a small tomato cannery. 'So good, some city folks who drove out here to buy vegetables nicknamed this county "Tomatoland".'

Vernon, a bearded, portly fellow given to wearing suspenders with brightly striped T-shirts and work-stained second-hand dress trousers, eased himself down onto the plastic Pepsi crate that serves as his garage-shop chair. 'And, in fact, and I'm gonna tell you straight out, my friend, that this here's *still* good tomato country,' he declared. 'About as good as t'maters get.'

Vernon shitteth us not. Quality-wise, the meaty, vine-ripened tomatoes of this county are a source of pride.

Take it from a Southern soul: native Southerners are to tomatoes what French grape-growers are to Bordeaux. We do not eat nor even bother to pick poor tomatoes. Not that there are many in this part of the country. If you can't grow decent tomatoes in our hot, sunny climate and soil, then God has definitely cursed you with the blackest of thumbs. Or tomato hornworms, if you haven't got enough sense to rotate your garden patch.

'What happened to all those places, those small canning outfits?' I asked Vernon.

'Well, sir, the big dogs wrung their necks like chickens. You know, Campbell's, Hunts, Dole … Oh, there was some middle men involved, brokers and all, but that's what it come down to. We got middle-manned right out of business by the big guys. We shoulda seen it coming. But I doubt there's anything we coulda done anyway. Progress and all that happy horse-shit.'

Interestingly, the big companies often got the end-product of the little operators anyway. 'Our operations sold some to the local grocery stores, but we sold canned product to the big companies, too,' Vernon said. 'We'd even slap their label on the cans for 'em. They'd sample-test for quality before they paid us.'

Much to the ire of the big companies, though, local canners had a small leverage in setting their prices. 'Very damned small,' says Vernon. No thorn is too small to be borne by the elephant's foot of industrial capitalism. Food corporations made short work of the little tomato operations, through numerous tactics and with the co-operation of the US government, new industrial taxes, and FDA legislation that allegedly created safer, more sanitary, and standardised canned tomatoes.

A tomato blight finally struck Morgan County near the end of the 1950s, finishing up what the corporations had started. While government subsidies soon led to the development of a blight-resistant tomato, the US Department of Agriculture was not at all interested in developing a corporate-resistant food supply. So it was goodbye to the men hefting cases of cans onto the trucks. Goodbye to women in hairnets and rubber gloves along the canning lines, who would return in a few weeks to the full-time family life of the homemaker. Goodbye to Jackson Luttrell's magnificent red truck, whose appearance over the ridge was like that of the Roman God of reaping, Saturn, flashing in the sunlight and proclaiming the harvest. Soon would come the rewards of the field, and then the frost.

THE FROST WAS UPON THE PUMPKIN ONE MORNING in 1960 when Jackson Luttrell dropped the wagon bolt into the tractor hitch, then stepped up onto the tractor's axle, easing himself into the cold, iron seat. He'd done it ten thousand times, but this day it took him three tries. Sixty Novembers in the fields exact their rightful toll, and he was more than feeling his age. Five minutes later, Jackson was down in his bottom land loading corn shocks onto the wagon. (You don't waste a big truck on light loads.) A skiff of snow covered the dark soil around the corn stubble, or 'stobs', as he called them. Every remaining stub of a cornstalk represented one whack of a hand-held corn cutter—all fifteen acres, some 300,000 of them, wielded by either Jackson himself or neighbours with whom he'd exchanged such work for forty years. So now he dragged each shock to the wagon, rolling it up the sideboards and dropping it onto the bed.

Twenty years ago he'd have heaved them over in a single motion. Between shocks he'd catch his breath, surveying the fields and woods around him with a squint that looked as far into the past as it did the landscape. The bottom field's right-hand corner was where he'd killed his first buck at the age of eleven. And beyond that was a hillside where mountain laurel sprang up each year. It had been a secret trysting place for him and Audrey when they were courting. Years later, they still laughed together about 'the blanket in the laurel'. To his left lay what was once a farmed-out, washed-out gully he had slowly filled in over the decades with stone and earth until it was now level ground upon which he had planted trees — walnut and hickory, with a few butternut trees thrown into the mix. He thought of it as sort of a wild nut-grove. The squirrels, mice, and deer saw it as their winter larder, once they were done with his summer corn crop.

Jackson pulled his canvas barn-coat up around his neck, and snapped the ear covers of his red woollen cap under his chin. The wind was beginning to bite at the back of his neck and make his bones ache. How many hundreds of wagon loads — thousands, really — of corn and hay had come out of this field since his grandfather had started farming it in 1859? How many corncribs had it filled with burnished ears? How many tons of oats had been hauled from this earth into his barn's granary?

During spring, this bottom field had always made

him feel good because it was dependable and had been well cared for. Always it was a producer, bursting forth each spring with the season's promise. You could get two hay crops here in a good year. And later, during wheat-threshing or hay-mowing season, when the rivulets of sweat cut their way through the thick layer of face-blackening hay dust, the metallic taste of cold well-water guzzled from the galvanised bucket with the tin dipper went down like bright wine.

But now, in the late autumn, it stirred the reveries known only to old men. In his mind's eye appeared a younger, shapely Audrey coming down the hill toward him in her home-made cotton sunbonnet with the fresh, cold well-water. And it was for that vision, and a thousand others like it, that he kissed her on the neck each evening when he got home. Not on the mouth, though, because that kind of affection at their age might cause suspicion that he'd been taking a nip of whiskey out there in the field. And he surely did that if the weather was right. But he'd judged it not yet cold enough on this day, which would be the coldest of his life. The wind kicked up flakes of snow as he bent over his last corn shock.

When old farmers fail to show up for dinner, old farm wives all share the same sense of dread. Audrey called their son, who found Jackson's body slumped over the steering wheel of his old John Deere. The wagon was fully loaded. In the middle of a heart attack, Jackson had shut the engine off to save petrol.

CHAPTER THREE

An Empire of Dirt

When the tomato canneries were still running, the term 'farm credit load' had not yet been invented. As the idea of indebtedness came to be accepted as part of 'farming as agri-business', debt mounted. About the time that Pap paid off his farm, America reached the point where its very best farmland was not able to pay for itself. We're still stuck there. Suffering from extreme scale-overshoot, and the paper value of land going through the floor, agri-biz is looking hopefully toward the approaching world food crisis caused by global warming and desertification. All American agriculture is dependent on petroleum-based herbicides, insecticides, and fertilisers, heavy fuel-eating tractors, petroleum energy for truck and air transport across thousands of miles, refrigeration, plastics for packaging and for shipping ... The assumption seems to be that Mother Nature will grant American farmers an exemption from having to face up to sustainability problems. We shall see if American exceptionalism can be stretched that far.

If the benefits of a return to smaller-scale farming seem obvious to you, pat yourself on the back. Because that makes you an agricultural genius akin to Luther Burbank. The best minds in agri-biz have yet to discover this concept. Their solution is to 'loosen credit'. In other words, to perform a rescue of the same credit and loan-based system that keeps collapsing like a 400-pound drunk on the dance floor. Charging into the dance hall, Congress, urged on by agri-biz institutions (as in, 'Here's ten million for your next campaign'), insists upon resuscitating debt-based American agriculture. Because, as we are told from birth, Old Bloat Butt there on the floor is supposedly the only dancing partner in town. Bankers wink at one another in the sidelines and divvy up the bailout loot.

Thrift is anathema. Consequently, bankers have seen to it that American farmers can never return to the sustainable farming that Pap and his generation knew—the one in which thrift was admired and waste was abhorred. There was one car more or less for the whole extended family, if that, and little food was bought at the crossroads store because we grew and preserved our own. A man owned one suit, often passed along from some other member when the original owner became too old and fat, or was deceased. (Never shoes, though. Wearing 'dead man's shoes' was considered bad luck, a lure for certain misfortune: 'When old Charlie Ritter died, his wife pitched his work shoes on the trash pile. A hobo come along and took 'em and, doncha know, that hobo got run over by a train the next day. Killed deader than Dolly's goat.')

Likewise, children's clothes were passed along. In summer, we kids did not even wear shoes; they were considered unnecessary in good weather, and best saved for school. Shoelessness is a symbol of world poverty for Americans, although it is hard to accomplish nowadays, with the avalanche of cheap sweatshop footwear crammed into every market in the world. (Exactly when did shoes become 'footwear' anyway? 'Shoes' has worked pretty well since the eleventh century when they were dubbed 'shoos' in Middle English.) Anyway, I can't say that we were terribly scarred by the experience of having our feet actually return to the touch of the earth each spring. We looked forward to it.

Not that money was unimportant. Money has been important since the first Sumerian decided it was easier to carry a pocket full of barley shekels than hump a four-foot urn of barley down to the marketplace on his back. And it was certainly important 5,000 years later to the West Virginia hill country's subsistence farmers. But in the big picture, money was secondary to co-operation and the willingness to work hard. A considered ecology of family labour, frugality, and their interrelationship with community *was* the economy. And the economy was synonymous with their way of life, even though that would have been a pretentious term to Pap and his contemporaries. He always said, 'You just do the next thing that needs doing. You keep doing that, and everything gets done that needs to be done.' When I'd ask him what to do next, he'd say, 'Just look to see what needs doing, dammit!'

Understanding what needed doing was the glue of subsistence farming's family-work ecology, which was also ecological in the environmental sense. Knowledge was passed along about which fields best grew what produce, the best practices to maintain fertility, and what the farm could sustainably produce year in and year out. It was a family act.

Those farm families strung out along Shanghai Road could never have imagined our existential problems or the environmental damage we now face. But, after having suffered such things as erosion from their own damaging early-American practices, they came to understand that nature and man do not stand separately. The mindfulness involved in human-scale farming demands such. To paraphrase Wendell Berry, we should understand our environmental problem as a kind of damage that has also been done to humans. In all likelihood, there is no solution for environmental destruction that does not first require a healing of the damage done to the human community. And most of that damage to the human world has been done through work, our jobs, and the world of money. Acknowledging such things about our destructive system requires honesty about what is all around us, and an intellectual conscience. And asking ourselves, 'Who are we as a people?'

'Hah!' replies Sammy Slick, great-grandson of the old Uncle Sam, the one with his sleeves rolled up, fists clenched, ready to duke it with the enemies of democracy. 'Bageant, you flatulent, nostalgic old fraud! You *know* the answer to that question, the answer I've been kicking up your arse ever since we saved the entire world in The Big War … ever since you were in grade school. The only acceptable answer is, "We are the American people!" Which means your arse, too! Now get this through your thick head: Americanness is now the national civic religion—being American!'

This answer does not suffice. But we are forced to accept that nationalistic identity message, thanks to the absence of any genuine opportunity to live amid and experience the particulars of one's own family or clan heritage, and especially community identity. For this we may particularly thank the industrially imposed migration of family members all across the nation for 'good jobs' or, these days, any job at all. The American exhortation to 'follow opportunity' is birth-to-grave and relentless. In other words, if you want to work, you will work where the hell the company tells you to work, and do so from the minute you graduate. You're a human asset now, kid! So pack your grip—you're moving to Buffalo.

TO SOME DEGREE, MY PEOPLE HAVE ALWAYS BEEN 'human assets' for 'the big-money boys', as Maw called them. Even the 18th-century settlers along Shanghai Road served as profit centres for the powdered-wig set, the owning-class elites in England. The culture and families along Shanghai began in the 1730s with pre-colonial squatters on the lands held by Lord Thomas Fairfax. Very little is known of these original settlers. A few decades later, though, settlers constituted one of the only two resources that the place offered Fairfax. The other resource was dirt—six million acres of the stuff. The mixture of dirt and human sweat has ever been the mortar of colonial empires on every continent. The sweat of the lowly born had made the fortunes of a thousand kings and wealthy noblemen, and would do the same for Fairfax—but only if he could convince enough colonists to produce it for his financial benefit. Few settlers were likely to do so for sheer love of his royal title (Thomas Lord Fairfax, Sixth Baron of Cameron and Proprietor of the Northern Neck of Virginia).

Fairfax's only option was to sell the dirt to the settlers. Some of it lay on the fertile green floor of the Great Shenandoah Valley. Other parts were on slopes or steep mountainside, with poorer soils and harder to work—as was the case along Shanghai Road, thus named because, if you followed it up into the mountains, it delivered you to the ancient settler-village of Shanghai. Two hundred and fifty years later, it's still up there, though smaller, and still called Shanghai.

Located on abandoned Shawnee Indian hunting grounds, the village got its name from the Scots–Irish Gaelic term 'Coli-shangi', meaning a jubilee or noisy celebration or, more colloquially in America, a Scots–Irish brawl. Fairfax couldn't care less what they named the place, so long as they paid.

Fairfax conducted his real-estate enterprise with the help of a young distant relative named George Washington. Their selection of settlers was by no means random. Farming successfully in isolated hill country required a certain cultural conditioning and traits such as tenacity and inurement to toil. The Washington–Fairfax selection process helped set in motion essential community, society, and religious and political beliefs still to be found throughout our Allegheny portion of the Blue Ridge Mountains.

The Blue Ridge mountain chain stretches some 1,400 miles from North Carolina to an indefinite point in Pennsylvania. The Indians called it 'the long divide'. White settlers named it the Blue Ridge because of the blue haze shrouding the mountains, the fog of water transpiration by millions of acres of trees, pine, pin oak, maple, honey locust, dogwood, and redbud.

By the late 1700s, these mountains were the stronghold of self-sufficient Celtic and German farmers who were immensely independent and more than proud of it. Our people lived entirely by their own labour, the labour of free men. Our state motto to this day is: 'Mountaineers are forever free.' Mountaineers looked down, both figuratively and literally, on the wealthy lowland plantations that were completely dependent upon African slave labour to grow their broad-acre crops of cotton, tobacco, and peanuts for export to Europe. The more slaves, the more could be grown and sold by the lowland 'Planter Society', who shunned both labour and the mountain folk. They lived by the monetary wealth economy, usually in debt to English banks for their affluent, imported, commodity-rich lifestyle of fine china, wines, expensive libraries, and fashionable wear.

Meanwhile, as settlers migrated down the Great Valley of Virginia, as they called the Shenandoah Valley toward the fertile southlands, the poorer among them kept seeping westward into the uncleared Blue Ridge, where land was cheapest and work was hardest. When they settled on Fairfax's land, they may have become human assets to his holdings. But they were not slaves and they were not employees. The overwhelming portion of the fruits of their labour were directly their own. They could not be fired. They could not incur oppressive financial debt. And if their farms were isolated specks in the blue Appalachian fog with their split-pine log floors, they were nevertheless specks located in a great, shared commons called nature.

In contrast to Fairfax and the planter society's money-based economy of wealth, these settlers lived by a family-based economy of labour. Not that they had a choice. Any kind of coinage or currency was rare throughout the colonies. Their economy depended on the bartering of labour and sometimes goods between themselves. Dr Warren Hofstra, an eminent historian of the area, tells me this system was so complex that they kept sharply detailed ledger books of goods and services bartered, even of small favours done for one another. In essence, this was an economy whose currency was the human calorie. Be it a basket of apples or a week's labour hauling stone for a house, everything produced (which was everything in their subsistence world, there being no money), was accomplished by an expenditure of human energy. Calories burned could only be replaced by an expenditure of calories to plant, grow, and preserve future calories for sustained sustenance. This was a chain of caloric expenditures or barter going all the way back to the forging of the iron hoe or plough that made subsistence possible at all. Keenly aware that both time and their own human energy were finite, they measured, balanced, and assigned value to nearly every effort, large or small. Wasting these resources could spell hunger or failure to subsist.

This attitude lives on today among the descendants

of the settlers. When outsiders move into this area, they often comment on what they perceive as the miserliness of the natives. Or the fact that they will not let you do them even a small favour, lest they be obligated in return.

A lady new to the area, a physician who hails from Delaware, told me: 'I went shopping with Anna at the mall last week. We went in my car. She tried to give me three dollars for "gas money". I told her that was very kind, but we'd only driven two miles at best and that it wasn't necessary. She kept pushing the money at me, saying "Here, take this", getting more and more insistent each time. I kept declining until I noticed that she was becoming honestly and truly angry with me. It was so damned strange, I've never seen anything like it. So I took the three dollars.'

I explained that many natives are like that, and told her about the early settlers' rigid barter-and-favour economy, and how these attitudes have unconsciously come down through our cultural history, remaining as deeply instilled social practices and conventions. It can work the other way around, too. Some people will unexpectedly do something very nice for you, or give you something — maybe an antique or whatever.

'Don't let the Southern charm fool you, though,' I said. 'In the back of their mind they have marked it down as a favour or a social debt owed. And they'll expect you to recognise when to pay it back. Maybe volunteer to feed their dog or water their lawn when they are away. At the same time, you should feel somewhat honoured. It's a down payment on developing further friendship. If they hadn't judged you to be a worthy, reliable, and reciprocating person, dependable in a friendship, they wouldn't even bother to know you at all. In fact, that's why so many outsiders perceive some natives as snotty and cold.'

'Amazing,' she said. 'I'd never guess their behaviour had such deep cultural roots.'

'Neither would they,' I replied.

As the hill-country population grew, their isolation lessened. Farmers grew more connected in a community network of seasonal mutual efforts, such as threshing, hunting, hog slaughtering, haymaking, clannish marriages, and birth, burial, and worship. These conventions were still being observed into the 1950s as I was growing up there.

Family and community life in that early, non-wealth-based economy is impossible for us to comprehend. No man can fully grasp a life he has not lived, or for that matter completely grasp the one he is living. But we Blue Ridge folk most surely live subject to the continuing effects of that dead culture which is never really dead.

For example, the old agrarian culture of reserve, frugality, and thought-out productivity translate as political conservatism today, even though few of its practitioners could identify a baling hook if their lives depended on it. At its core stood—and still stand, for the most part—'family values', which meant (duh!) valuing family. Valuing family above all else, except perhaps God's word. Grasping the true meaning of this is to understand much of the conservative American character, both its good and its bad qualities. I dare say it also holds some solutions to the dissolution of human community, the destabilising of world resources, and the loss of the great commons, human and natural, all sacrificed to the monstrous fetish of commodities, their acquisition and their production through an insane scale of work and round-the-clock commerce and busyness.

OK. I'LL SAY IT SO YOU WON'T HAVE TO. There ain't no goin' backwards. We certainly can't all take up horse farming or go to sowing lespedeza hay and oats. Of course not.

But the underlying theme here is loss, and that loss poses some big questions.

Is it at all possible to regain a meaningful, positive, and satisfying expression of character while working in such a monolithic, non-human scale of 'production?' Anybody else feel like America is just one big workhouse, with time off to shit, shower, and shop? Or is it just me? Must our jobs necessarily to be the most important thing in our lives?

Yeah, yeah, I know, them ain't jobs. In America we don't have jobs — we have careers. I've read the national script, and am quite aware that all those human assets writing computer code and advertising copy, or staring at screen monitors in the 'human services' industry, are 'performing meaningful and important work in a positive workplace environment'. 'Performing?' Is this brain surgery? Or a stage act? If we are performing, then for whom? Exactly who is watching?

Proof abounds of the unending joy and importance of work and production in our wealth-based economy. Just read the job-recruitment ads. Or ask any of the people clinging fearfully by their fingernails to those four remaining jobs in America. But is a job—hopefully, a good one—and workplace striving really everything? Most of us would say, 'Well, of course not.' But in a nation that now sends police to break up the tent camps and car camps of homeless unemployed citizens who once belonged to the middle class, it might very well be everything.

In one of those divine moments of synchronicity that writers pray for, I just got reinforcement of the above. Checking my email web browser, one of those annoying ads masquerading as advice popped up. It read: 'Doing good work is no longer enough! Ten tips to keep from being laid off your job.' Shown was a cheerful young woman at a desk, apparently feeling deliriously safe about her job, judging from her hysterical, bug-eyed smile, thanks to those reassuring tips from a commercial jobs agency. When personal-employment fears, job terror, and insecurity can be captured and turned into a job for someone else, there's not much room left for the general spirit of commonality, or a sense of a shared commons in the nation's work-life. Not when any of us could become indigent at a moment's notice.

But you won't hear anyone complaining. America doesn't like whiners. A whiner or a cynic is about the worst thing you can be here in the land of gunpoint optimism. Foreigners often remark on the upbeat American personality. I assure them that our American corpocracy has its ways of pistol-whipping or sedating its human assets into the appropriate level of cheerfulness.

HARD AS IT IS TO APPEAR CHEERFUL WHEN WE ARE terrified, most of us in America still manage to appear so, because we fear what will happen if we do not. Our main fear, of course, is of losing something. Or everything. Nor is the fear unjustified. In a nation as monetised and hyper-propertised as America (and, let's face it, when the ownership rights to the genes of humans, plants, and even the right to generate toxic pollution can be bought and sold, you have to call it something like 'propertised'), you also acquire an unimaginable fear of losing something. Anything. Maybe everything. But especially physical space.

Aside from the tent camps for the homeless underneath bridges and overpasses, every habitable space has been made private. Each has ironclad boundaries, surrounded by a force field of suspicion of strangers, and guarded by a state of hyper-vigilance directed at unknown dangers. This force field of fear extends to outdoor spaces designated as public commons: our national parks have police SWAT teams in them, designated to rescue campers should they be snatched by psychopaths, national-park killers, or rapists with a love of the outdoors.

America's rural countryside is the same. Some Morgan County residents who occupy twenty acres in the woods presume that meth addicts will drive 100 miles to violate home and hearth while they are commuting 50 miles to pay for that twenty acres with its artificial log chalet. And so, all along the roadside edges of the county's sun-dappled deep-green forests and meadow fields, the warnings slap you across the eyeballs: KEEP OUT! ... NO TRESPASSING — VIOLATORS WILL BE PROSECUTED! ... WARNING! POSTED — NO HUNTING ... PRIVATE

LAND — KEEP OFF! ... PRIVATE ROAD — DO NOT TRESPASS! You see this bold, black-and-white signage stapled to venerable pines and weather-silvered fence posts everywhere, often placed there by Washington government employees who've bought a hundred acres of bucolic peace, which they visit a few weekends a year. Their first act is to get a free stack of NO TRESPASSING — NO HUNTING posters from the sheriff's department (always a good political handout, as these people will retire here someday, and especially prized because the second line is 'By Order of the Sheriff's Department'). They nail them to every tree in plain sight and quite a few that aren't. Property rights are more touted and enforced in America than in any place on earth. In an interesting twist, our Supreme Court has ruled repeatedly that property belonging to corporations is inviolate, and that millions of dollars in corporate money generated by that property is equivalent to free speech! For the ordinary citizen, the right to defend private property may be violent if need be.

Consequently, the younger generation of my native redneck brethren often have fierce dogs guarding the premises while they are at work, lest someone steal their guns or flat-screen televisions or all-terrain vehicles (not that it doesn't happen sometimes).

It wasn't always this way. When it comes to property rights, twelve generations of folks in Morgan County have held them as dearly as anyone else. But the old farmers did not post such signs because they recognised that the land as a whole was a natural commons. Access to its fish, game, air, and waters, and rights of egress, were assumed to be a common right. There was no need to ask permission to hunt, say, squirrels and rabbits on another man's fields and woodlands.

Deer were a different matter. Farmers hunted in organised, mutually informed groups. That way, they always knew each other's locations in order to prevent accidental shootings. One group walked the wooded mountainsides, causing the ever-skittish deer to move downhill. A second group shot at what deer might come by their assigned deer-stands. Every hunter knew the locations of the others, so the direction from which a gunshot came told all parties which of them had just gotten a shooting opportunity at a passing buck or doe. If he missed the animal, someone else down the line might or might not get a chance to can some deer meat for the winter. I can hear the animal-rights and anti-gun people gnashing their teeth, but we're talking about an important source of food here, and keeping deer herds thinned back to healthy levels. Deer get small, hunchbacked, weak, and gnarly when overpopulation outstrips their food supply. Then, too, there is the devastation that an overpopulation of deer—and I've seen herds unnaturally large as a hundred—will wreak on a corn or bean crop in a single evening. It's a good case for keeping a couple of night-barking dogs, even if you don't hunt. Real dogs; preferably, hounds.

I wish I could say I had a real dog. But every night my wife and I go to sleep with a miniature cocker spaniel named Brandy in our bed. I suspect the Bageants of previous generations must be thumping a mouldering knuckle of protest against their coffins at the thought. By their reasoning, dogs were supposed to live under the porch, or in the barn, where they could guard the granary from raccoons, deer, or even corn rats, providing they were willing to sink to the level of a barn cat. And when the dogs got too old to walk or feed themselves, they retired to a soft spot behind the kitchen stove—assuming they didn't get run over limping across a road, or just dropped plumb dead somewhere in the woods. Usually, though, they came home to spend their last hours on a pile of barn straw or on the back porch before that happened.

All in all, farm dogs had about as much old-age security as modern Americans have today. And certainly a more dignified death—no catheters, feeding tubes, radiation-treatment sickness, or $100,000 medical bills for their final weeks' stay in the intensive-care ward of Conglomerated Medical Arse-Jammers Incorporated. A farm dog's life may not have had adequate health and elder-care coverage, but this was not a bad trade-off for a life spent doing what dogs were designed to do—smell the exotic pissing spots of wild animals and canine neighbours. (Well, I'll be durned! Old Spike is back, and pungent as ever.) Or cock their heads watching a squirrel or a bird for a solid twenty minutes, before taking their third nap of their day. Or run in the fresh air and chase anything that moved except livestock, children, and higher-caste pure-bred bitches—which should be kept locked up by any responsible man who cares about fine canine bloodlines, anyway. Or as Joly Vernon, up on Sleepy Creek Mountain, used to put it, 'If we bred people with half the sense we breed dogs, there wouldn't be no Republican Party to put up with. No lawyers, either.'

And then there were the dog felonies, stuff a dog could

get the chair for—such as killing chickens, sucking eggs, biting people, and 'running stock' (chasing cows, horses, sheep, etc.). That included running deer. Deer were supposed to be left alone until deer season so they could mate, give birth, browse, and grow fat. And even during hunting season, dogs were not used because, among other reasons, it was illegal, and deer killed with high adrenaline-levels always taste like crap. Otherwise a dog could piss anywhere he chose, eat anything he found, no matter how disgusting, and live as God designed dogs to live.

How your dog behaved said much about you. The dog happily roamed the surrounding neighbours' fields and streams as an ambassador representing your family and farm. If the dog betrayed this high office he was disappeared, as it were. You never saw a dog run stock or chase a neighbour's chickens—or not more than once, anyway. If they did, they were immediately blown away by your neighbour. And maybe thrown to the hogs to eat. Neither the dog's owner nor the offended neighbouring farmer ever mentioned the dog again. A man who owned a destructive dog either cured the animal of its habit, and kept it in constant sight or contained, or destroyed the dog himself. For a dog, the rules were in black and white: 'Suck eggs and die', or live by the rules and remain free to say, 'Piss on the world.'

All of which is my own way of getting around to telling you a little story about Joly Vernon's dog. Joly lived up on the side of Sleepy Creek Mountain. An ageing bachelor, he stayed on his parents' farm and took care of his elderly widowed mother who, in true Vernon fashion, lived to be almost one hundred. The Vernon place was a modest picture of perfection, well kept and with tractor-tyre planters in the 'front yard' — 'lawn' was a pretentious city word then — from which hydrangeas and columbine greeted visitors in riotous colour during their season.

Joly Vernon kept one of the best hounds in the county, maybe the state: a Redbone coonhound named Ranger. Redbones are devoted animals who love to run alongside their masters day and night, and are never happier than when serving their owner, especially during the excitement of the hunt: Ranger would track a raccoon all night, swim creeks, and run along fence lines sniffing upward toward the top rail — something only a smart hound will do. You see, Brother Coon is a sly critter who'll travel via creek waters and walk the top of a fencerow to throw dogs off his scent, or swim out into rivers, luring the dog in so he can jump on the dog's head and drown it. Ranger was way too smart to let that happen. Ranger also had a beautiful 'bugle', a bay that carried a mile, which let Joly know where the dog was at all times during the hunt. For the most part, Joly sat by a small campfire waiting for Ranger to bark 'treed', meaning that the coon was finally cornered up some pin oak tree. A small night fire under the stars, with maybe a couple of buttered yams baking under the coals, and the sound of a good coonhound at work is one of those utterly American experiences that cannot be duplicated.

One summer, Joly got a new neighbour, a retired Air Force colonel, a DC beltway refugee from Washington's suburbs. The colonel had purchased 75 acres and a picturesque 1790 stone house adjoining the century-old

Vernon farm. The Colonel, as he seemed to enjoy being called, was a nice-enough guy. He smiled and waved at every passing car, just like everybody else did. He pulled his new truck over alongside the road for passing funeral processions and took off his hat until it passed, like everybody else.

But the Colonel did have some 'funny ways', as we called them. For one thing, he wore alligator cowboy boots all the time, and kept expensive Arab horses, fancy feed-burners of the kind that put veterinarians' children through college. For another, he shaved his head clean and sported a precise, pencil-thin moustache. Vernon, for one, didn't think much of the Colonel's tonsorial handiwork: 'If you're gonna go to all the trouble to shave your whole head and your jaws every day, why would you take so much extra time to carve out that useless little cookie-duster under your nose? It don't make sense at all.'

One day, the Colonel showed up at Joly's front door with a complaint. 'Your dog has been roaming around on my property. In fact, I believe it's been shitting on my lawn. I'd like to see an end to that.'

Joly thought about this for what seemed like a long time. As far as he was concerned, a dog could shit anywhere it felt like shitting, except in the house—which Ranger was never gonna see the inside of anyhow. Secondly, Joly's dog did not roam. Ranger stayed by his side all day, whether Joly was ploughing, hunting, or in the outhouse reading a third-hand copy of *Farm Progress* magazine. Ranger spent his nights on the porch under Joly's bedroom window, waiting for Joly to awaken. It was pure devotion, although anticipation of the morning-breakfast scraps Joly tossed out the kitchen window may have been a factor.

Finally, Joly spoke.

'I wouldn't want to dispute a fella,' Joly said, 'but my dog never roams unless I set him on a scent. That's how I trained him. So it musta been somebody else's dog. And besides, around here, dogs that make no trouble are free to roam. What makes you think my dog's been on your "lawn"?'

'Well, yours is the closest farm to my farm.'

Joly was getting madder now, not only at the accusation against his dog, but at the assumption that proximity equalled culpability.

The Colonel said, 'I don't keep dogs on my farm because ...'

'Now, lookee here,' Joly interrupted, 'I wouldn't call that one-man dude ranch of yours a farm by any means. And you can kiss my arse and get the hell off my propity!'

'Mr Vernon, if that's the way you feel, I don't have any other course than to take action.'

Next day, Joly looked out the kitchen window to see the Colonel coming up his driveway again. Apparently, the Colonel was ready to take action of some sort, though Joly wondered just what kind of action a man takes against an anonymous dog turd. But if the Colonel wanted a fight, then, by damned, he'd get one. Joly picked up his shotgun and let it hang discreetly just behind his overalls pant leg, and then stepped onto the porch.

'Mr Vernon, 'the Colonel said, 'I might possibly have been wrong about your dog. I'm not yet saying I was or was not. But it would be settled if you chained your dog up, wouldn't it?'

'Colonel, there ain't going to be no chaining up my dog. And we're gonna settle this thing right here.'

Ranger circled eagerly, hoping to catch the scent of another dog on the Colonel. Or at least get petted.

Joly raised his single barrel, pointing it toward the Colonel's crotch. 'Ever kiss a dog's arse, Colonel?' Joly asked.

The Colonel blanched. Then his face warmed up into a smile.

'No, but I've always wanted to,' the Colonel replied.

And, with that, he shook Joly's hand, went back to his truck, and drove off laughing. The Colonel had proven himself a man of reason after all.

They were civil to one another forever after. Good neighbours, even. Over the years, they came to share fence lines. Joly coon-hunted on the Colonel's place. And, for many years, Joly sold the Colonel hay for his fancy feed-burners. Old-timers swear that the story of Joly's dog is the wood-splitting truth. If it ain't, it should be.

Once in a while, a city slicker 'gone country' does come to understand hunting, America's most ancient tradition of the commons. And the freedom that God and man grants good dogs. But not often, as those black-and-yellow POSTED signs attest. They tell me that a few of the signs are put there by farmers who fear city hunters who cannot tell a cow from a white-tail deer. I don't know a single real farmer there who posts such signs, and, despite folklore to the contrary, I've never known even a city hunter who mistook an 800-pound cow for an 80-pound doe. I suppose it's possible. On the other hand, suburban hunters sometimes plug one of their hunting buddies, so who's to say?

Today, the Colonel is gone. Ranger, too. And, of course, Joly. But, after Joly's mother died, I'll be damned if Joly didn't up and marry a younger woman—a Yankee Unitarian, no less—move to Charleston, and adopt a Peruvian earthquake orphan. Renaming the boy Kenneth, they eventually sent him to the state college of forestry, spawning what must be the only Inca forest ranger in the state of West Virginia. Kenny worked somewhere down near the Kanawha River for thirty years before he retired to Phoenix. He rents the 'Old Vernon Place' to a couple of ageing hippies who keep goats, raise organic vegetables and, rumour has it, seem to have a bit of herbal assistance with their decidedly mellow and reflective attitudes. Not that anyone cares. They are good neighbours, with a well-behaved Chesapeake Bay Retriever named 'Dutch'.

And there is not a POSTED sign on the place.

CHAPTER FOUR

Behold the City!

I put to you that the United States is without doubt the greatest show on the road. Brutal, indifferent, scornful and ruthless it may be, but it is also very clever. As a salesman it is out on its own and it's … a winner.
— Harold Pinter, in his 2005 Nobel Literature Prize lecture

In contrast to the media's national storyline, my feral research tells me that most heartland people had strong mixed feelings about leaving rural America. The human experience they lived in the flesh is not easily quantified, sliced, and diced to fit into research tables and indices. Even so, recorded evidence indicates that tens of millions in this exodus—which spanned three generations before it was over—never wanted to leave in the first place. Government surveys of soldiers taken near the war's end showed that the overwhelming majority of white soldiers planned to return to live and work in their home communities. Black soldiers were a different matter—they had a damned-good reason to continue their flight from the racist environment of the South where they were concentrated. That most white rural natives wanted to return to home and hearth after a bloody and gruelling war makes sense when you think about it, especially considering that provincialism and rural distrust of urban life was much stronger then than it is now. After all, how logical is it that a southern-born rural American would say to himself: 'I've waded the blood and foam of Normandy's Utah Beach to protect home, hearth, and sweetheart, so now I'm taking my sixth-grade education and my deer rifle and moving to Philly, where I don't know a soul.'?

Like everyone else, rural dwellers wanted 'modern progress'—a venerable American sound byte dating back before the turn of the century—and a better future, too. Who would not? But most would have been quite happy to see a few advantages such as an adequate education, liveable wages, community-scaled industry, and some modest social guarantees simply being made more available outside urban areas.

That's not to say that the perceived virtues of city life over life on the farm were not attractive to many rural young people. As part of the first true movie generation in America, they saw rural life represented by such movies as the Ma and Pa Kettle series, in which the lazy, slow-witted Pa and his slightly smarter wife and dozen kids demonstrated bumpkinism on their ramshackle farm while city folks were having romantic candlelit dinners. Looking backward, they saw the Great Depression, which was only ended by the advent of booming corporate wartime production in the cities. There, the 'American people' were saving the world from untold horror and doing so while, by the grace of God, putting money in their pockets at the same time. 'The American people at their finest', declared newsreels and the print media.

The phrase, 'the American people', took on a new and more potent meaning after the war, and became the absolute stock feature of every speech by every president and politician afterward. Again, Harold Pinter:

> Listen to all American presidents on television say the words, 'the American people', as in the sentence, 'I say to the American people it is time to pray and to defend the rights of the American people and I ask the American people to trust their president in the action he is about to take on behalf of the American people.' It's a scintillating stratagem … The words 'the American people' provide a truly voluptuous cushion of reassurance. You don't need to think. Just lie back on the cushion. The cushion may be suffocating your intelligence and your critical faculties but it's very comfortable.

Our national narrative of such things as the 'Greatest Generation' is full of holes, and the stuff of much hubris. My generation, 'The Greatest Zygotes', as it were, the progeny of the Greatest Generation, were brought up on post-war propaganda from the time we were in the womb. From the beginning, we were fed television shows such as *Industry on Parade*, which extolled the wonders of working in mind-numbing factories. These shows were indistinguishable from the Russian *Glory of the Soviet Worker* films of the same period. One episode so effectively sold us the virtues of an industrial soda pop bottling-works that, after watching it, my cousin and I wanted to work in a Coca Cola bottling plant when we grew up. But first we'd have to move to town, of course.

'Organising for war' had taught industrialists and government agencies the best ways of organising the American population and its resources toward heavier and more profitable production, both of which lay in worker aggregation and concentration. Consequently, the post-war migration was pushed by planning decisions made by the nation's industrial and financial power-holders, and was made policy by the US government in the drive toward maintaining its status as a capitalist industrial super-state. Such policy also solved another problem. Historically, farmers tended to be some of the most hardcore populists, and had often sided with the Wobblies and other socialist movements during hard times.

In the winning of World War II, along with increased industrial capability and profits, US capitalism had accumulated an immense amount of another kind of capital with the American public—moral capital. The Soviet communists had gained the same in Russia. Both spent that capital industrialising their nations at the expense of traditional farmers, though to different degrees. Stalin starved and shot Kulaks who did not produce enough grain to finance his communist state's industrial goals. We caused ours to move where they could be more directly manageable and profitable to the interests of a rapidly emerging corporate state.

The US post-war rural out-migration was initiated—though in a different way and for different reasons—by the same corporate-financial powers that caused the earlier tragic migration of workers in search of work during the Great Depression. Endless footage of the Dust Bowl has subsequently made it synonymous in American minds with the Great Depression, even though they were two separate events. The Dust Bowl affected only a portion of the country. But, according to the average American's grasp of the history—to the degree that we have one at all—those ten million Americans 'riding thumb' and hopping rail cars all came out of Oklahoma, which had a population of about two million at the time. We never see documentaries or movies about the corporate malfeasance of unregulated stock markets and commodity speculation, banking, and other enterprises of the already rich that ruined more rural Americans and farmers than the Dust Bowl ever did. But we do see and read about those very few urban investors who jumped off the twentieth floor during the 1929 stock crash. The recklessness of the financial elites and the layer of speculators that cushioned them blew away millions of Americans—folks who never saw a stock certificate in their lives. As Depression-era migrant Grace Pample told me in one of the most poetic summaries I have ever heard from the mouth of one of my own people, 'It was the big-money men, it was them who made us to rise and blow across the land like the Russian thistle, like gypsies in the dust.'

Unlike the Depression and the Dust Bowl, the post-World War II rural out-migration was driven by a good economy—too good to give up, if you happened to be a wartime corporation. America emerged from the war with vastly increased manufacturing capability, and was the 'last man standing' after its traditional competitor, Europe, lay in smoking ruins. Super-expanded wartime corporations

85

that had cranked out planes and tanks had become very rich, and were not about to downsize just because they'd run out of Dresdens to bomb. For instance, there were America's gigantic munitions plants, making ammonium nitrate for explosives. How would they hang on to their massive profit-levels with no industrial-scale warfare to sustain them? In one of those brilliant industrial–economic decisions so often made by corporations and governments working together, it was decided that the stuff could be dumped on millions of acres of corn and other crops at a profit. After all, plants need nitrogen, right? Why not short-circuit the cumbersome processes of nitrogen fixing through photosynthesis and carbon exchange? Thus was set in motion the frying of the heartland's soil, and the destruction of our waterways and estuaries through run-off, and the creation of acid rain through evaporation. In a similar move, agri-biz built a new industry called pesticides from the poison gases developed for the war. There was no use in wasting good killing power: bomb the bugs and weeds.

And so the military-industrial complex managed to keep up, even increase, its head of steam, despite the loss of that all-time champion booger-devil, Adolf Hitler. Such serviceable Great Satans just don't come down the pike every day, and we've had to manufacture them ever since — the Soviet Union/the Cold War, the communist Chinese, Saddam Hussein, Fidel Castro, Hugo Chavez — to maintain the complex that Dwight Eisenhower so presciently feared. Incidentally, Eisenhower included not only the military and defence-industry corporations in his definition, but also the news media and the research establishments, the public and private universities that had flourished in the fertile soil of the war's technological drive.

Millions of decent, urban, blue-collar workers—people whose lives had hung on jobs, or the lack of them, since the destruction of the tradesman and craftsman culture at the turn of the century—still remembered the pre-war soup lines in the big cities. They were thrilled to participate in the wartime rise of corporate industrialism and the money it generated. Studs Terkel quotes a retired worker commenting on the wartime boom economy in *The Good War*: 'The war was fun for America. I'm not talking about the poor souls who lost sons and daughters. But for the rest of us, the war was a hell of a good time … That's forgotten now.'

In any case, the trick at hand for post-World War II corporations was to keep American workers mobilised to produce goods at the same pious levels that had whipped Hitler and Hirohito, and then increase upon that. There would have to be mass production of hitherto unimagined commodities, and legions of new customers to consume them. Not to mention a cheap labour force to produce them at maximum profitability. The answer lay out there in the sleepy hinterlands.

SO HERE WE ARE, A COUPLE OF GENERATIONS SINCE the last serious buckwheat crop was hauled in from the ridge fields of Morgan County—back when a man smelled like sweat at noon, Lava soap at dusk, and Old Spice aftershave when he was courting. The very mention of that life and aesthetic deems anyone who can remember it a nostalgic coot. So be it. Damned few of us grasp how the loss of traditional aesthetic and foundational values, the yeoman agrarian tradition, are connected with so much modern American tragedy.

We have been paid back for our disregard of that tradition and the uprooting of its souls in surprising and often chilling ways. Creating an underclass of throwaway labourers, and sub-prime mortgage and credit-card debt slaves has its blowback—in the form of inexplicable heartland school shootings, backwoods and trailer-court meth labs, or Timothy McVeigh's Murrah Center bombing in Tulsa.

Timothy McVeigh as blowback? I'd say so. Having known a number of McVeigh types, I agree with Gore Vidal as to the democratic, agrarian roots of McVeigh's misguided actions. Despite the horror he caused, unforgiveable by any standard, the Bronze Star-decorated Gulf War veteran acted out of an essentially rural Jeffersonian patriotism. Contrary to the media image of a psychotic misfit, McVeigh's letters to Vidal reveal a literate, complex man who understood the Constitution much better than most US senators do—few if any of whom keep a copy of that document in their offices. McVeigh understood that whatever democracy once reigned has been subverted by corporations and bought politicians, and believed that America had become a corporate-backed police state consisting of only two classes—the elites and the rest of us—regardless of the party in power. If he was paranoid, he certainly was not alone. Millions of us wonder why the government funds the training of our local police force in armed tactical 'emergency population control', or why they are supplied with specialised equipment to collect data for federal intelligence agencies. Hesitant as we are to admit it, we have the same severe doubts as McVeigh did about things like Waco and the Branch Davidians.

McVeigh chose the second anniversary of the Waco Siege, in which the federal government killed 76 people, including twenty British nationals, twenty children, and two pregnant women. The officially manufactured version of both Murrah and Waco offers us a Great Satan, with McVeigh as a crazed redneck psychopath, and the Waco's Branch Davidians as a cult led by a child molester. This was untrue in both cases, but the government versions have since displaced all other facts about these events.

Another disease currently eating the soul out of the heartland's white working-class's futureless young is the meth epidemic. This epidemic, with almost 120 million casual users and 1.5 million known addicts, is a profit centre — especially if its victims end up in places like Montana Correctional *Enterprises* [italics mine] in Deer Lodge, where they will be contracted out to the private sector as telemarketers at the minimum wage. The prison manager there says that the convicts constitute a dependable workforce: they never come in late, and they stay the full shift. They get to keep a little over one dollar an hour of their earnings, so a guy pulling five years in a lock-up can earn almost six thousand bucks for five years of labour. What's not to like?

Statistically, nearly all of these imprisoned young men are but a generation or two removed from traditional farms or farm communities and their agrarian values. They are the white underclass's good ole boys who landed in jail, mostly for committing non-violent offences — stupid offences like growing pot, screwing 18-year-old jailbait when they were drunk at the age of nineteen, writing bad cheques for child support, car theft, and thinking they could outrun the state cops and avoid a speeding ticket, three times. This is completely irresponsible, falling-down-stupid stuff, but not evil stuff like committing drive-by killings or rape. They are part of an America tradition that accounts for so many country songs about prison: *Folsom Prison Blues, Mama Tried, Doin' My Time, In The Jailhouse Now, Tom Dooley, Draggin' Shackles, I Heard that Lonesome Whistle Blow, Cold Cold Bars …*

The tragedies of these whites are at least in part due to their marginalisation, displacement, and their underclass cultural ghettoising, just as are so many of the tragedies of African–Americans who went north only to be trapped in underclass ghettoes. Workplace throwaways on the trash heap of no-longer-useful or wanted Americans, they are reduced to inhabiting thin-walled mobile homes in trailer courts behind decaying strip malls, or sub-prime mortgaged paperbox modular homes. The result: graveyards of yokels and hicks stacked generations deep, with cowboy and combat boots sticking out of the grave still defiant, still ready to kick the Devil's own arse.

The rural–urban divide is real, and rural defiance still simmers beneath the surface of American politics, morals, and values, although it can be hard to discern — what with all the materialism, cell phones, high-definition TVs, and the rest. The populations in our big urban commercial centres are still the drivers of demand and the transactional economy, and consequently they rule the fate of rural people they never see. We've been pretty well wiped out or captured. As David B. Danbom said in *Born in the Country*, the battle between city life and country life may have even been over before the war, 'but the victorious cities continued to take prisoners'. Yet the libertarian, fiercely independent Jacksonian hog-and-hominy culture of the subsistence farms dies hard. Parts of it — some good, others not-so-good — endure in many forms.

One of them is conservatism. Another is stubbornness. In fact, because of the inherent toil and the years it took to build a good farm — one that would sustain generations — caution and stubborn endurance may be the chief hallmark of the culture. Redneck culture (the term 'redneck' is not a pejorative to us rednecks, just to urbanites who think we all chew tobacco at the dinner table and nurse our babies on cheap beer), western cattle-ranch culture, logging, even traditional West Virginia coal-mining, in some respects, all share the same characteristics.

And if that culture happens to be at the core of your values, your inner identity, part of a chain of blood and heritage that is your cultural DNA, the result is alienation. If, when we look around us in the world, we do not see ourselves in society, nor does society see itself in us, we come to feel the sustained, unutterable pain of aloneness. And we wish for the return of at least some part of the material and psychic order of the world as our people have known it. The knowable one that sustained us. Even for subsequent generations raised in the cities, it lingers, however inchoate.

STANDING BACK FROM THE SUBJECT FOR A MOMENT, here's the backstory.

Given the 15,000-year-long history of agricultural practice, the destruction of America's agrarian culture was so swift as to be virtually instantaneous. It was quick even by our national historical measure: beginning about 1937 under Roosevelt, it had been accomplished by the mid-1960s. According to our national storyline, however, the death of our agrarian society was unavoidable—just part of our onrushing national vitality. In the official version taught in schoolrooms everywhere, America arrived at the industrial age by means of the raw strength of a younger nation endowed with can-do spirit and vigour; at the nuclear age by sheer brilliance; and at the consumer age because God wants his anointed people to own iPods, a DVD player in every room, and at least one salad shooter per family member. We became what we are as a result of the purest form of destiny—or, for the more articulate, by way of those 'historical trends' that pundits and ponderers of such things are always talking about.

Consequently, the migration of millions of American families during the post-war era was 'part of a necessary economic trend' away from the farms, villages, and small towns. After all, we could not remain a nation made up entirely of farm families and the small communities that served them in a symbiotic relationship. According to the American storyline, the malling of the countryside and the application of every American's labour to the manufacture and distribution of commodities was in the 'highest purpose use of labour' and in 'the people's best interests'. And that's true, if our best interest and highest purpose lies in employing every man or woman in the production of salad shooters — or, now, pizza delivery, since salad-shooter production has moved to Taiwan. Now we are reduced to the service industries, fast food, finance, and debt collection.

What has been overlooked is that every human system begins somewhere in the earth's soil or under it, and is either proven sustainable or not. We chose to abandon a proven system for a high-risk one — getting apples from China and hamburger steak from Argentina, feeding our crops petrochemicals, and frying the dirt for more profitable yields. The system of human proximity to the farms that produced the food, fibre, fuel, and medicines, and a host of other civilisation-sustaining commodities, had worked for 10,000 years. You'd have to call something like that a well-tested system. Especially considering that our venture in industrialising the earth in defiance of Mother Nature's product specs (such as inventing space-saving square tomatoes that do not freeze in winter because of the whale blubber DNA that has been inserted in them) has led to the ecological catastrophe underway.

Because the proven system was land based, not to mention that it had millennia of trial-and-error learning behind it, agriculture got pretty good at what it did both in the dirt and for human civilisation. An agrarian economy evolved that let the small, sustainable communities up and down the ladder thrive as the products coursed through the villages, to market towns and on to the cities, where the money was generated. The money then travelled back down through the system to nourish the smaller communities and villages that supplied the farmers, who in turn sustained the small communities and the cities. This was a neat, comprehensible circle, with each stage and link a direct human-to-human bond. There was no 'trickle-down effect'—just the coursing commerce of a 5,000-year-old natural, human economic system of trade, commerce, and agriculture.

The system was still working even as the Industrial Age rolled to new heights in America. During the first half of the twentieth century, the vendors in Philadelphia's Ninth Street Market or the butcher shops in New York City were still selling vegetables and fruits that came primarily from nearby farms outside the city. 'Ya wanna Long Island duck, buddy?' Strawberries flowed in from New Jersey, and beans and sweet corn, potatoes, and onions from every direction. For a minute analysis of this, read *Five Acres and Independence*, written in 1935 by Maurice Kains, who, like tens of thousands of small farmers then, raised a flourishing family on a sustainable and profitable farm, growing produce for sale in a nearby big city.

As US industrialisation continued, locally owned factories and businesses sprang up along the chain, offering employment to those of each succeeding generation whose numbers exceeded the ability of farms to support them. A finely veined nationwide system of farms, cottage industries, small manufacturers, and businesses offered the assurance that, if you chose to, you could still live, love, and die in your community. You could live out an entire lifetime within the connective tissue of family and community.

But a floater always makes its way into the pool to foul the water for everyone. Increasingly, local factories came to be owned by absentee industrialists—very rich industrialists and families who had amassed unprecedented capital, with no small thanks to two profitable worldwide wars and the non-regulated American-style capitalism that had prevailed. The top of the food chain was theirs, and they were determined to fully maximise that position.

These absentee holdings were aggregated and expanded in a proliferation of facilities producing petroleum-based goods. Oil was abundant, and looked to be endless at the time. Synthetic products were in direct competition with farmers' output, with petro-textiles replacing locally grown cotton, wool, and flax for linen with highly profitable nylon and polymer clothing. Not to mention the onslaught of plastic commodities being mercilessly hammered into the populace as modern miracles Those small-to-medium-sized local factories, originally acquired by industrialists to utilise cheap rural labour, began to be concentrated into the monoliths and ultimately the 'industrial parks' (parks assumedly because of the island of foot-high shrubbery in the middle of their two-acre parking lots) that we see today. Surrounding farm communities withered, leaving thousands of village placenames (locally, Bloomery, Siler, Whitacre, Star Tannery, Iron Furnace, and, rather sadly, New Hope) with few or no inhabitants.

That the absentee owners were corporations made them more dangerous than any robber baron had ever been, because they were deathless. The corporations and trusts replaced mortal thieves such as Rockefeller and other robber barons, and capital was continuously aggregated on an unimaginable scale.

In a human-focused economy, a periodic redistribution of wealth makes eminent sense. Even Adam Smith acknowledged the necessity of periodically levelling wealth so it could continue to flow as the lifeblood of the system through communities and generations. Unfortunately, he felt that wealth should generally move toward the already-rich in these redistributions, as they were God's preferred financial managers.

But now the corporations were many, bigger than ever, and they endured through the generations. Powered entirely by balance sheets, and dedicated solely to the accumulation of more wealth, the notion of parting with assets—much less reinvesting in people—was antithetical to their purpose: the enrichment of their stockholders. Most of their managers were members of an elite whose main accomplishment was commandeering some portion of the medium of exchange, then deriving more wealth simply by withholding capital from those who had created it—working people and farmers. Corporations skimmed off much of the worker–farmer-produced wealth, then rented their own money back to them. Capturing and controlling the economic lifeblood enabled corporations and the stock market to suck up nearly every dollar that was available in the old field-to-market, town-to-city relationships.

This occurred at different rates in different places, but eventually gobbled up everyone. My people just happened to be caught in the first waves, but the culmination has been worldwide. Any thinking person recognises the global corporate serfdom of sweatshops and information services, and even the shipping of cheap, warm bodies around the planet for construction work.

If they had been reliant purely on their own merits, the corporations that came to dominate America probably would not have survived the 1930s. By then, America's wildly fluctuating economy was already demonstrating the folly of overly concentrated capital—which equates to over-concentrated power. What was needed, said the big players who'd wrecked the nation's economy with uncontrolled speculation and greed, was—lo and be damned—a controlled economy! One controlled by corporations.

The problem was, the only entity capable of such control was the government. The capitalists needed government authority to survive. But the constitution of the United States of America was founded on a separation of business and state to the same degree as the separation of church and state. If the big corporations such as E.I. DuPont were going to undermine the nature-based and labour-based agrarian economy and replace it with a synthetic, petroleum-based commodity economy (toward which they had invested heavily since the early days of John D. Rockefeller's Standard Oil, just after the turn of the century), government authority by constitutional sanction would be necessary. As a 1937 shareholder's report of the E.I. DuPont company put it, 'the revenue-raising power of government [taxation]' had to be converted into 'an instrument for forcing acceptance of sudden new ideas' and a 'social reorganisation'. Uh oh! Just *whose* sudden new ideas? And *what kind* of social reorganisation?

The report stated bluntly that for DuPont to realise further extensive profits from its wartime investments in products such as nylon for parachutes, tyres, tents, and ropes, the government had to be the primary tool. While this plan was put into the shareholder's report, it was never to be publicly discussed.

The chance to pull it off came, ironically—or maybe not—with Roosevelt's New Deal. FDR was, contrary to the legend that has grown up around him, first and foremost a capitalist determined to save capitalism. Given his affluent background and times, he, like everyone else, could not imagine anything but capitalism as the nation's preordained economic system. His lifelong circle of friends and associates consisted entirely of the elites of family and corporate wealth, which meant that it also included some of his enemies. But together they created a host of 'emergency legislation', in much the same fashion as 9/11 let George W. Bush get away with so much under the excuse of a national emergency. Even allowing for the resistance of some wealthy elites and corporations, FDR favoured the capitalist corporations' plans to commandeer the national economy.

The Supreme Court, however, did not. Elite and capitalistic as the justices were, their job description nevertheless had given them only one designated responsibility—adherence to the US Constitution. And it would have taken a rewriting of the Constitution for the government to crawl into bed with the corporations. When your job has only one clearly stated responsibility and the whole nation is watching, it's hard to get out of doing it. On the other hand, you can just let it pile up and pretend you're getting around to it. Every piece of legislation that FDR and his cohorts created somehow got snagged in the Supreme Court and just kept on piling up.

Even at the time, many rural citizens didn't like the smell of things, and ever since then they have been portrayed as conservative hicks who resisted FDR's benevolence and compassion. Urban citizens, on the other hand, accustomed to the complexities of commerce and complete dependence upon the wealth economy, and desperate for relief of any kind, were more enthusiastic. A job's a job, dammit, no matter who is in control — so long as the paycheque doesn't bounce.

The key for Roosevelt and the money men was taxation. You can't engage in societal management without controlling individual behaviour. The Constitution denies government that power, but does grant it certain other exclusive ones, such as imposing taxation, coining money, and declaring war. Cotton Unger couldn't print his own money. Nor may a common citizen make war on, say, Canada.

Throughout the 1930s, the public watched FDR and the corporatists duke it out with the Supreme Court. Because the Constitution sets no specific number of Supreme Court judges, FDR decided to add six new justices to the court. Then, as today, despite their manufactured air of gravity and aplomb, Supreme Court justices hate sharing the limelight with any larger cast than is necessary.

Now, dear reader, the spectacle of nine dignified, white-haired men in black robes on a stage (OK, we do now have a couple of white-haired women and representatives of minorities to help the institution's public image), people said to be in possession of the greatest constitutional knowledge in the land … well, it is the very picture of national gravitas. Which is why we never see a photo of a justice taking out the trash or kicking his dog. Or hear about how the court was plagued with drunkards from the outset. Our first Supreme Court caused so much public outrage with its boisterous drinking that the justices vowed not to drink when the court was in session — except when it was raining. Chief Justice John Marshall observed that since the court's jurisdiction was the entire country, it must certainly always be raining somewhere in the republic. The six justices resumed drinking.

While the public was engaged in the debate over FDR's threatened stacking of the court, the president and the titans of capitalism accomplished their agenda of controlling unwelcome social behaviour — by taxing it to death.

In changing American social behaviour through taxation, two stages must be gone through: the first tax must be a very logical one, and the second one must be created of whole cloth, a manufactured tax to counter a manufactured threat. So, after the Supreme Court knuckled under to FDR's threat to divide up the judicial limelight, a more compliant court happily passed a $200 tax — the equivalent of $3,000 today — on machine guns. (This same tax, incidentally, later allowed the Bureau of Alcohol, Tobacco, and Firearms and the FBI to invade the Branch Davidians at Waco, on the grounds that they had not paid the machine-gun tax — which they had not, because they owned no machine guns.)

The court understood that the machine-gun tax was unconstitutional, but the court also understood public relations. What kind of deranged bastard needed a machine gun? Well, let's see ... there was John Dillinger (whose penis was 14 inches long, according to folk legend of the day, which was either threatening, or vastly intriguing, depending upon one's sex or moral perspective in life). There was Seymour 'Blue Jaws' Magoon, Bonnie and Clyde, Pittsburg Phil, Baby Face Nelson, Al Capone ... And if there was further doubt, members of Murder Incorporated were Jewish, Italian, or Irish. This was proof to the Anglo–Americans majority of naked immigrant depravity. So two hundred bucks per tommy gun it would be under the 1937 Machine Gun Tax Act.

The next tax that the court upheld was the beginning of government control of farmers. At first blush, the 1937 Marijuana Tax Act looked like a drug law. Most Americans knew that hemp was the stuff that rope was made of, so outlawing hemp after centuries of its use would have seemed ridiculous. But they had never heard the word 'marijuana', so the tax act adopted a little-known Mexican street-slang term as its name, in order to demonise it and to differentiate it from the thousands of acres of hemp being grown for naval ropes, canvas, etc. Never mind that in the entire previous year, fewer than a couple of pounds of the stuff had been seized by border police. A $200-per-gun tax had worked on machine guns, so a $200-per-ounce tax was placed on hemp cultivation without a permit—and no permits were issued. The synthetic-fibre and plastics industry had handily eliminated its most threatening competitor, hemp, from which both fibre and plastics could be readily made.

Henry Ford showed what could have been when he began developing hemp plastics for automotive bodies and chassis in the mid-1930s. In 1941, he demonstrated the durability of an automobile made mostly of biodegradable hemp and soybean-derived plastics by attacking it with a sledgehammer. In now-famous footage, the sledgehammer bounces off and goes flying into the air. Unfortunately, industrial-hemp production had been outlawed by the 1937 law.

In one of the hundreds of coincidences by which the law served the interests of many corporatists, DuPont was enabled to eliminate hemp as competition in one of its biggest markets—paper production. DuPont had a monopoly in the market for chemicals used in the manufacture of paper from trees. If hemp fibre, which required none of those chemicals, could be eliminated, DuPont's monopoly within the heavily chemical-dependant wood-pulp paper-manufacturing process would expand geometrically—as would the need for tree farms and associated insecticides, herbicides, and other chemicals used in silvaculture. DuPont was by no means alone among giant corporations in manipulating government policy and law, and consumer options, behind the scenes. DuPont just happens to be the best documented. (See Gerard Colby Zilg's *Du Pont: behind the nylon curtain*, a 1974 National Book Award nominee.)

Thus it was that, in 1937, America was at last made safe from an epidemic of 'Reefer Madness', and the planting of the evil fibre that, according to public-service films, made young girls throw off their panties in the throes of crazed lust, and young men suddenly purchase switchblades and go roaming the 'angry Negro streets at dawn' in search of the nearest opium den. And for the first time in the history of the United States, the corporatists could use the government to control what seeds farmers could and could not put into the earth.

In short order, by way of the New Deal's provision of crop subsidies and various pieces of agricultural legislation, corporations gained control over the land without having to own it or pay taxes on it. The small farmers were now under direct threat: they were the chief competitors to the industrial food giants and to synthetic producers of thousands of formerly natural goods and raw materials. The farmers' natural cotton and wool threatened the new petroleum-based synthetic fibres; and natural corn for animal feeds and silage was being grown on small farms spread evenly across the nation, inhibiting the domination of the corporations' animal-feed products. The result was inevitable: small producers were eventually taxed or regulated out of existence.

In another happy coincidence, subsidies for big agri-biz producers began snowballing, and have never stopped. Government-subsidised railways and roads were built into the Midwest to serve the ever-expanding corporate-scale farms. Corporate corn became the basis of the vertically integrated corporations' processed American diet.

As per plan, a nation of consumers of synthetics—such as artificial cheese, diglyceride ice cream and salad dressings, corn-based pet foods, beer, and even the ink on food labels—was cultivated in the next generation.

Counting all the meats, sweeteners, and additives, more than a quarter of the American diet is now corn based, thanks to federal subsidies. I can remember when Maw would buy King golden corn syrup for our hotcakes, in a one-quart tin that lasted the whole family for a month. I'd sit at the table marvelling at the broad-faced wild lion on the label, trying to imagine a world in which such lions roamed. But nobody then could have imagined a world in which Americans consume over sixty pounds of corn syrup per person each year.

(We can see the results of it all in those corn sugar–obese Americans wearing acrylic clothing emblazoned with corporate brands, and guzzling synthetic soft drinks—Americans who've never once considered that the pizza crusts they gnaw at start out as a grain crop. Nowhere can we see this more clearly than in my poor, beloved West Virginia, statistically the fattest and most unhealthy state in the most overweight and unhealthy nation in the developed world—but only by a narrow margin over a dozen other states. We have mortally obese high school students dying of heart attacks, an epidemic of obesity-induced diabetes, and double-wide coffins being lowered by small cranes into graves occupying double plots. A state built on raw-boned miners and mountain farmers is now one vast reservation of cheap labour that is fed on cheap food.)

Ten thousand years of agriculture was synthesised into money. The soil-to-city chain of small farms, villages, and towns linked to the great city markets was destroyed. Those ever-more-profitable compressed gobs of humanity in the cities and suburbs could be cultivated for maximum productivity and profit as corporations increasingly dominated the national needs hierarchy. If you made a movie of all this, swapping the humans for some sort of large, intelligent rodent or insect, and left everything else as it really is in American life, people would call it chilling science fiction.

Lately, we have come full circle. Now there is a popular movement to put the farms and the people who eat their products back into closer proximity, through local farmers' markets, etc. The advantage is food with few or none of the petro-chemicals required to preserve them for transport; no industrial-scale storage at massive depots; far less fuel consumption in transport; few or no agri-chemical inputs and no industrial-scale farm machinery involved; and, of course, healthier, fresher foods—for the better-heeled middle class, or those willing to cough up more money for reasons of health or ecological idealism. You don't see many ghetto blacks, blue-collar mooks, poor whites, or Salvadorean dishwashers munching organic apples at a buck a pop.

Personally, I eat beautiful, unblemished apples flown in from China. They are gorgeous looking because they are so pesticide laden that any bug which gets within 50 feet of them is instantly croaked. Also, because the new Mandarin capitalism—not exactly a pillar of worker rights—has its ways of dealing with pickers and handlers who bruise apples. Here in Winchester, Virginia, acres of apple orchards stretch away into two surrounding states. God knows where they are sold, because they aren't sold here.

Last autumn, I stopped at a local farmers' market,

where the apples looked good. Too good.

'Where do you get your apples?' I asked.

'Oh, I get 'em from a distributor in Baltimore. They get 'em from China.'

To cut a long story short: the bastards won. This distillation of how they won, this little piece of feral scholarship, is bound to make some people apoplectic. Especially academic hairsplitters in political science and history departments. The 'Oh but ...' crowd. Which is OK with me. Everybody needs a job. But mine is the view from here in the cheap seats among the non-players, in the game of big politics and bigger money. We call 'em like we see 'em. But no matter how you connect the dots, or which dots you choose to connect, it comes out the same: our parents' lives were displaced; our own have been anxious and uncertain; and our children's are sure to be less certain than ours. And nobody grows apples and tomatoes along Shanghai Road anymore, because that requires an abidance in, and caring for, a specific place. A nation is nothing but a place, a piece of dirt, that people either do or do not take the time to contemplate, to care for, and care about.

DRIVING ALONG SHANGHAI ROAD TOWARD MY childhood church in Unger Store, Morgan County, West Virginia, I crest the hill just above our old family farm, and spot something that makes me stop and turn off the truck motor. Ahead of me in the Sunday-morning sunlight is Ray Luttrell, an old farmer I've known all my life, meditating on his hayfield, standing on the very spot by the road where I've seen his late father stand countless times, just looking at that hay, motionless for many minutes.

Before him is his most familiar place on earth, his native ground. And I feel that for a moment, at least, I once again know that same home ground, again feel the personal sense of eternity in its very 'itness'. Before us is a tableau profoundly exclusive to this place and its people, so specific in its fabric of detail and history that it cannot exist anywhere else on earth.

When you are born and raised in one ancestral place and, like Ray, accept that you'll die there, you know it intimately, specifically, and forever. Just as those before you knew it. All your early memories, all the voices inside your head, come from there, and you know it and its community in a way other people never will. The geographic arch and trajectory of a life can be so specific as to know its precise beginning and ending spot. While squirrel hunting with Pap as a boy, we stopped in the woods at a pile of leaf-covered stones that had once been a chimney. 'Right there,' Pap said, 'is where I was born.' And all his life he knew exactly where he would be buried, too—behind the church for which I am heading, where we may find him today, next to Maw and all his children. Right there in the Greenwood Methodist Church cemetery.

On this late-April morning in 2009, the sun raises steam from the dewy lawn of Greenwood Methodist Church, up on the hillside bend in the road. Inside, about fifty people, most of them above that same number in age, listen to the minister, a young woman in her thirties, tell about how the Lord does provide, followed by the group recitation: 'Be guided by God's word, that you may bear good fruit …' Then, as living proof of that good fruit, Ray Luttrell's fresh-faced 10-year-old granddaughter is called up front to be recognised for her recent accomplishment: a prize-winning social-science school essay entitled 'Why We Are In Iraq.' For that, she earned a story and a full-colour picture in the local newspaper, *The Morgan Messenger.*

This is followed by a lilting version of 'Easter People Raise Your Voices'. The window-tinted rays of coloured light flash on the spectacles of the congregation and choir. I count four people not wearing glasses, which says something about the church's ageing membership. Toward the end comes the time when church members express any 'Joys and Concerns', as the moment is called. A tall fellow aged about seventy stands up, looking firmly into the congregation's eyes and, in an accent similar to that of many who've retired here from Washington, DC, says, 'Did you know that California has passed a law against children using the words "mother" or "father" in public schools? They must now use the word "parents". And the American Civil Liberties Union says it will sue any community that observes the National Day of Prayer. Wake up, America!'

As background for foreign readers, America has had a National Day of Prayer since the Continental Congress called for the first one in 1775, asking the colonies to pray for wisdom in the creation of a new nation. In the 1980s, America's fundamentalist Christians commandeered the holiday for their own political purpose, through the National Prayer Committee, focusing on events specifically for the evangelical community. Ever alert to opportunity, the Hallmark Card Corporation issued a new line of National Day of Prayer greeting cards to capture the 100-million-strong patriotic evangelical market (which has since been replaced by the 9/11 Patriot Day card).

When it comes to waking up America, the little church at Unger Store may not have been the best place for the ex-Washingtonian to start. Only one woman nodded in agreement, and so fervently that it led me to think she might be his wife.

Personally, I have serious doubts about California schools outlawing the words 'mother' and 'father', which sounds too much like far-right Internet propaganda. Yet, having known Californian gay and lesbian parent activists, such a ridiculous agenda is not out of the question. I grew up observing the National Day of Prayer in the public schools, although the observance has soured for me over the years. But I'd guess that I am the only person in this church house who feels this way.

Several expressions of concern and calls for friendship prayers follow, mostly regarding sick members, people about to undergo cancer surgery, a family that had suffered the death of an elder …

The music begins again, and the church's brass offering-plate is passed down the aisle. On this same spring Sunday in 1905, the church offering amounted to 21 cents. And on this Sunday in 1873, many of these people's ancestors were worshipping in a tiny log church on this same spot. And about a month from now, the Greenwood Methodist Church will celebrate its annual 'homecoming', welcoming people back who grew up in this church. The congregation will celebrate its 137th year and its 7776th Sunday service.

'Anyone have any joys they would like to express?' asks the minister. This elicits the heartfelt testimony of an 82-year-old woman: 'I was forty when I got saved. When I found Christ. So by now I've spent more than half my life in His service. It has been a happy life and a better life. And I don't need anything more than what He has given me. But I would like to ask for one little thing, for Cindy Hill [the pianist] to play "Oh How I love Jesus." Would you do that, Cindy?' And she sat down.

During the music, I thought about my father, grandparents, uncles, and the other family members buried just outside those thick, stained-glass windows. The past became present, and I found myself looking around for a girl, certainly an old woman by now, who I'd had a crush on in the little one-room schoolhouse we attended then. Up front is Ray Luttrell again, this time in a green-and-gold choir robe. His son Dallas stands beside him in the choir, and in the pew in front of me I see the back of the Luttrell grandchild's head, the precisely parted white scalp hairline down the middle, with its odour of peach-scented shampoo.

The Doxology rolls around, signalling the end of the service. Perhaps for the first time in my life, I hate to leave a church. It is so peaceful here. I see what we rarely see anymore—a humble willingness to abide by the forms that have held the community together for generations. Each person is an individual, but travelling together like a flock of arrows toward a mutual destiny, always somewhere Over Home.

Because abidance has been so continuous here, it's hard to walk a few steps in any direction without bumping into a reminder of previous abiders. You remember the dead, and in doing so you have access to all they ever did that was right and all that was wrong — what worked or did not work for those people and that community. You know that, even if you don't know you know it. In this way, places own us and we belong to places. A community with no memory of its dead is no real community, because it has no human connectivity grounded in time — just interaction. It's merely a location populated by disassociated beings. A community's inherited memory from its dead provides its spiritual and moral animation, its posterity. This is because we are humans, not aggregations of marketing or employment demographics, and are more than just a bunch of people who happen to be in the same place at the same time.

More than any other people I have met, Americans fear the loss of their supposed uniqueness. Yet none of us is in the least way unique. Just because we come from the manufacturer equipped with individual consciousness does not make us the centre of any unique world — private or public, material, intellectual, or spiritual. 'Oh, but we have unique feelings and emotions that are important,' we say. Yet I venture that none of us will ever feel an emotion that someone long dead has not felt, or some as-yet-unborn person will not feel. We — you, me, the child in Bangladesh, and the millionaire frat boys who've run our financial and governmental institutions with such adolescent carelessness — are swimmers in an ancient, rushing river of humanity. All of our lives will eventually be absorbed back into the river of time without leaving a trace.

Still, there is the restless inner cultural need to differentiate our lives from the other swimmers. Most of us, especially educated people in the Western world, will never beat that one. Certainly not as regards the material realm. The truth is that we will seldom, if ever, make any significant material or lifestyle choices of our own in our entire lives. We will buy whatever corporations choose to sell us. We can 'think globally', but we necessarily exist locally, regardless of where we choose to be. Americans, in particular, find it hard to grasp that there's no 'better place' left to run toward, geographically or economically. No frontier other than the present, upon which we can choose or not choose to begin building a more resonant and meaningful place in the world through abidance.

That is what endures in Ray Luttrell and a few remaining others along Shanghai Road. Watching Ray makes me feel fortunate to be connected at least in some fashion to a known and knowable chain of lives lived entirely in a distinct place, even if mine has not been. And I like to believe, vainly perhaps, that as long as they endure, I endure, even as departed friends and ancestors endure in me. All I can do in testimony is windrow these words like hay; with providence, they will be as orderly, and make as much earthly sense, as Ray's long streaks of clover hay under the coming June sun.

And so they come to me again—Maw, Daddy, all of them—and then they evaporate. Somehow, only Nelson, the last to fall, holds most steady, remaining an almost corporeal old friend. To the end, we could see that in each other's faces. Nelson, do you remember the spring day when we climbed the barn gable so we could see the seagulls that mysteriously blew into our clay hills—swept from an ocean neither of us had ever seen, though it was scarcely a hundred miles away, each bird a genuine miracle high above the green barley? The time we saw that panther in the sycamore tree and Maw said it was the sign of war? Nelson, I am sixty-three years old, the same age that both Maw and Daddy were when they died. I have written this in testimony. With this book, I presume to be done now with such remembrance. But somehow I suspect it will go on, this peering down old wells, this excavation of memory and its shades.

CHAPTER FIVE

Mama's People: whiskey, blood, and prayer

Fifty-five winter suns have arched low across the horizon on their journey toward spring since Nelson and I watched those seagulls blow across Morgan County. Today, this particular winter sun falls so weakly into my office here in a magazine-publishing complex that it casts no shadow. I've begun to answer my emails, replying in that careful way which protects one from workplace-career assassinations. Outside my office door, flitting like fashionable birds of urbanity, a handful of editors and managers gab mindlessly about money, Microsoft, movies, frequent-flyer miles, and fresh salmon. They speak with the voluble consumer fluency of the management-class culture. An hour from now, their day's work will begin—but not until they've had their double lattes and studied the dismal stock-market report at their terminals.

Even after having worked for thirty years in the magazine editorial world, these people—my colleagues, not my friends—seem so weak and pitiable. They would, and do sometimes, crawl and beg to keep their jobs, cry like babies to remain in their kingdom of relative comfort. They understand that most of the work in this world completely sucks shit. At least 75 per cent of Americans out there spend all day long sucking that shit, making the world go around, holding things together so that people like us can pretend that pushing ideas around on paper is real work. I've done both kinds, and know that this is the truth.

Such thoughts sound arrogant. I know that. But, to be more accurate, it's the blunt repugnance for such temporal indulgence coming from a Southerner raised poor and Pentecostal.

Their discussion has turned toward a recent wedding. It was an affair of 'flawless greenery with designer bows', followed by an extravagant 'honeymoon trip through four countries'. By comparison, we Bageants are such a long and unbroken line of peasants; I cannot but think how my Shenandoah Valley family was nine generations in America before the first of us had a honeymoon. Even then, it took me three wives to do it.

I'm sure a honeymoon never crossed my daddy's mind when he came back from Japan in May 1946 with a khaki service cap cocked over one eye and that same handsome grin he left with. The fighting sons of Uncle Sam Slick had whipped the evil kraut and the yellow heathen, just like John Wayne in *The Sands of Iwo Jima*, a movie that Daddy would watch a dozen times through the years. Now it was time to cut corn, hunt deer, and raise a family. He'd come back with a bride: Gladys Jewell, a petite, very pretty girl he'd met at a Baptist servicemen's revival—one of Billy Graham's, in fact. She was sixteen years old, and arrived on Shanghai Road with me already in her belly. When the couple walked through the front door, Maw took one look at my mama's condition and said: 'Well, Joe, you sure got your arse in a sling, didn't you?' It was no eloquent welcome. But then, the Bageants were not eloquent people. Maw wasn't angry; just blunt.

'But how do you think that made me feel?' my mother remembers. Maw ordered the couple to 'sit down and eat something', and started cooking, which was always her usual way of making an offering or escaping an uncomfortable situation. In this case, it was a little of both.

The men in the family were unabashedly ogling this pretty new female member, who was so obviously more beautiful than any squat, short-legged, thick-lipped, broad-faced Bageant in the house. Thanks to Maw's genes, most of the family faces—including my own, but excepting my father's—very much resemble jack-o'-lanterns, even more so as they get older. Many hill people were like that at the time, crude in etiquette; and though their behaviour was certainly crass, it was also akin to the naive staring of children, though with the sexual undertones of adults living in relative hill-country isolation.

'The Bageants scared the bejesus out of me,' my mother said. 'I'd never seen anything like those people. Especially Maw. She could do every damned thing in the world, and do it all better than me. She wouldn't let me do anything because she was a perfectionist. Then she'd call me lazy because I wasn't doing anything.' And I was thinking to myself, she was a teenager at the time, for chrissake.

'Still,' my mother continued, 'when I married Joe Bageant and moved Over Home, it was more of a home than I'd ever had, and I'd never seen such a place. I grew up in a two-room shotgun house down near Greensboro, North Carolina. Soon as any of us was old enough to git, we got. But these Bageants, they was always around there even after they was married. And when they'd eat, they'd come down like wolves. Hungry as I grew up, I loved seeing people eat like that.

'Sometime later, Pap made a pass at me while Maw was out. I told him to go to hell. Well, he started crying. I think he suddenly realised what he'd done—what an awful thing it really was. And he cried, and he said over and over how sorry he was, and he begged, "Please don't tell Maw, please don't tell Maw." And you know, I never did. Young as I was, I would have been scared to death to tell a woman like Maw. Besides that, I didn't come from perfect people myself. I knew people could be weak sometimes, do things they'd regret the rest of their lives.

'And so I became his favourite daughter-in-law. Not because I had something on him, but because he was honest-to-God sorry and he felt I had forgiven him. And over the years I came to love that old man like he was my own daddy. And Maw, too, once she softened up and seen that I was good to Big Joe and really did love him, no matter how we came to be married.'

Indeed, Mama did not come from perfect people. She seldom spoke of her previous life, and I never asked. Somehow, I feared terrible things that I did not care to know. Not until over fifty years later, when I set about writing this, did I take the time to read all the old letters and the thick but incomplete life history she'd hand-written over the years. The thing starts with the memory of her father ... what little there was to remember.

Her mama had had a couple of husbands, but her real daddy was a man named Reynolds Miles. His family referred to him simply as Miles. Mama knew her father for only three weeks when she was six years old. That was when he briefly drove a grocery delivery-truck as a prisoner trustee for the Guilford County jail.

The local Jehovah's Witness Church of Greensboro, North Carolina, had organised to have him jailed for his intense alcoholism. The same church also arranged for the court to order my mother's mother, Beulah, or 'Little Mama', to work at a slave-wage cotton textile factory. That left ten kids to somehow be cared for while Little Mama worked long shifts. In its unending mercy and love of community good, the court issued a solution. The courts ordered an indigent mulatto woman named Ola to take care of the children in exchange for room and board and five dollars a week, to be paid by my grandmother Beulah, who earned $18 a week. For most of the rest of their lives, the children referred to her as Aunt Ola, their 'nigger mammy', though it was later softened to just 'mammy', and visited her up until she died, just the same as they did with any other relative. Contrary to popular mythology, you didn't have to be a rich plantation-owner to have a black mammy. Often as not, it was an alliance of mutual misery.

In any case, Guilford County, North Carolina, didn't hand out money to people, no matter how miserably poor, if it could be avoided. And it could indeed be avoided through court orders to force folks to work, as the Good Lord intended poor folks to do. Single men were sometimes ordered to work twelve hours a day for nothing more than food and a place to sleep in some tobacco farmer's barn. In Little Mama's case, it happened to be mighty convenient that the 'cotton factory' to which she was sent was rounding up scab labour to break a union. Then as now in the US, courts, churches, and capitalism work together through the hands of God and Adam Smith, both of which are said to be invisible. We may assume that God's invisible hand is catching the fallen sparrow, but Smith's has been more debatable. One thing I do know is that Smith's invisible hand put Little Mama in the workhouse and sent Ola back into the slavery of her ancestors.

Pappy Miles got jailed, alright. But he could have had it worse as an inmate, such as working on the road gang, instead of driving the jail truck on grocery and supply runs. This allowed him to stop at his home and skim off groceries for the family, or sneak away from the truck to pick turnip greens for them to eat. On delivery duty, he'd slip away to visit his family, even if only to sit in his rocking chair by the fireplace, dipping snuff. The last time he ever visited, the kids tied him to the rocking chair and begged him not to leave. Mother's life journal says, 'He did love us kids. He didn't say so but thank God I told him I loved him when he left our place.'

Miles, who'd only finished the third grade, was by no means naturally given to indolence. He was—among many other things I would later discover—a master carpenter who'd managed to build two houses for his family during the Depression. But depending upon whom you believe, each of his two sisters cheated him out of a house, or he gambled them away. Given the evidence, the odds are good that his sisters, both Bible-thumping Pentecostals—one raised tobacco, and the other worked in the textile mills—stole the houses. According to my mother's journals, 'What he built with his own two hands and scraped together during the Depression, even with all those kids, they took from him. My daddy had a lot of help in becoming an alcoholic.'

Even so, some of my mother's best childhood memories are of the summers and the entire third-grade school year she spent with Miles's sister, Maggie, the obsessive perfectionist sister, memorising Bible verses, seeking earthly perfection.

One of those perfections was the disciplined use of God's resources. Mama was issued a school pencil, which she displayed to Maggie each day to show how much it had been sharpened. Sometimes Maggie's husband, the henpecked Lonnie, who suffered equally under Maggie's religious obsession and frugality, hid a pencil along the road to school for my mother. Once Maggie noticed that my mother's pencil was not of the same type that she issued, and accused her of having stolen it. Mama took the rap for the terrified Lonnie; but, at least, writes my mother, 'Maggie did not beat us with a strap like Little Mama did. Her way of punishing me and Uncle Lonnie was degrading us and making us feel like scum.' Child self-esteem is never a problem for Pentecostals—since, like evolution, they do not acknowledge its existence. In the eyes of God, we are all born unworthy pieces of shit of His own making and design. Yet strive for perfection, we must.

'We went to church every Wednesday night and twice on Sunday,' my mother recalled, 'and read the Bible out loud for an hour each evening before bedtime. It was no big deal. She was a pretty woman, very expressive, and could really make the wars and cruel kings of the Old Testament come alive! I had nightmares gasping for my breath in the river of blood, and sat straight up in the feather bed, screaming. But she could not hear from where she slept in her own distant bedroom sanctuary, where even Lonnie was not allowed to enter.' It was 'a perfect place with dainty lace curtains, a desk and oil lamp, an easy chair, fine clothes hanging in the closet, and an organ.' Even a Persian rug. 'I always wanted to sneak in there and feel that rug,' my mother wrote. But she never did. Manifest perfection so reigned in that room that it overflowed through its lone window. The view from Maggie's room window was onto the front porch, which was painted and waxed to a high gloss, where no one was allowed to walk, and which was appointed with fine porch furniture upon which no one was allowed to sit.

My mother never did understand why, out of the nine kids, Maggie took in what she called her 'no-good brother's daughter'. 'Maybe it was guilt from stealing the house, but she never worked me like Aunt Jennie, Miles's other sister, did on her tobacco farm. We worked the entire summer, sun up to sun down, and came home with one silver dollar.'

Maggie's religiosity and especially her obsessive cleanliness may have had something to do with the third sister, the frowsy, unkempt Dovey, who lived up the road in a small shack. She had ten children, most of them out of wedlock, some of whom slept in the well house. Dovey read all day, six days a week. She did her entire week's work in one day, and that day was Saturday. On Saturday, she cooked anything that would keep, in huge pots—sweet potatoes, biscuits, collards, and corn bread. For the rest of the week, everyone served themselves on tin plates, and drank cold milk and buttermilk stored in the well house. Each family member was responsible for washing and keeping track of his or her eating ware, such as it was. All parties except Dovey fed hogs, milked, and gathered eggs—more as a matter of life's ways than as chores or work. The same went for laundry, and the bathing and grooming of smaller children, while Aunt Dovey would read. She'd give my mother good books to read, which Maggie would promptly burn in the fireplace.

SIXTY-NINE PER CENT OF AMERICANS TOLD ZOGBY International's pollsters in 2006 they believed that if Darwinism was to be taught in schools, 'the evidence against Darwinism' and 'intelligent design' and creationism should be taught alongside it. This is what happens when the industrial state's fanatical belief in science comes up against the religious institutions' flaying of the people's minds with superstitious fear of an unseen, omnipotent, and unquestionable, wrathful God. No one should suffer those two forces in tension within the one mind and soul. In her later years, my mother once said of her religious upbringing, 'How any kid is supposed to grow up knowing anything as an adult, without ever being allowed to ask a question, is entirely beyond me.' Outwardly, the Pentecostal fanatics of her childhood failed to convert her in any significant way. But, inwardly, they would later affect my family deeply through the viral transmission of terrifying Old Testament fundamentalism to an already-religious family.

Harsh Christian fundamentalism has been part of the American fabric since it arrived with the Scots–Irish, German, and English religious reformers of the 18th century—though few could have predicted, or even imagined, that it would eventually take on the political potency we see today. The rise of Billy Graham and Oral Roberts during the 1950s and 1960s on television was an indicator of its growing mass appeal, a national acknowledgement of a widespread following that had always been there, just not so public. The media evolution and political consequences of fundamentalism now comfort millions of Americans, and scare the crap out of millions more.

Christian fundamentalism is still morphing, shape-shifting to suit new political agendas, as it has done since the 'evangelical movement' of the 1960s and 1970s, under which umbrella the Jimmy Swaggarts, Pat Robertsons, James Hagees, and subsequent power-drunk charlatans slipped into the nation's religious mainstream. Religion is, among other things, an industry in the United States. Every church, no matter what type, wants to grow—just like any other business does. The church business is built upon the faithfulness of America's under-educated and neglected whites, who trust their preachers more than they do their politicians. The preachers, at least, lie to them face-to-face, eyeball-to-eyeball, from the pulpit. In a sense, they trust 'the devil they know', and overlook the many sexual and financial scandals of their fundamentalist Christian leadership. At the very least, their preachers are mouthing the word of God, which is right there for all to see in the Bible.

For some reason, hopeful American progressives at this writing seem to believe that the thin majority of educated Democrats now in Congress, led by the clearly educated and articulate Obama, can somehow affect the hearts and minds of tens of millions who honestly believe that one of Noah's chores was feeding the dinosaurs on the ark. But the ignorance and superstition of American fundamentalism goes back a long way, and is rooted in the lack of real education in heartland America. As long as we purposefully refuse to fully educate the hardest-working class of Americans, or allow any development of their intellectual and philosophical vistas, simple-minded fundamentalism will be back on our nation's political front porch, and scaring the rest of the world. Especially those godless, unarmed Europeans with their free socialist healthcare and their liberal educations.

Regardless of its negative intellectual and political impact—and you sure gotta describe wiping its arse on the US Constitution at every opportunity as 'negative'—fundamentalism has also done cultural and social good for the white American underclass. The hardening of Protestant fundamentalism is in part an attempt by ordinary working-class people to replace the sense of community life that was lost in the second half of the 20th century. It established new human networks not unlike those of the early-settler communities, with household-centred values and the communal spirit of yeoman goodwill. A good, old-fashioned American-style church supper or children's event touches my heart like nothing else; I would gladly attend more of them, were it not for the abysmally ignorant conversation that accompanies them. And I blame that on our system, which purposefully and consistently rejected universal and free higher education, leaving the bulk of the citizenry in frustrated ignorance and incomprehension, clay to be kneaded into outrage by political potters.

But underneath fundamentalist Christian outrage, and despite its misdirection by demagogues, one can find their adherents in common cause with progressives: there is much the same disgust with the cheapening and trivialisation of society. For example, both sides abhor the debased sexuality of advertising and entertainment; the destruction of familial intimacy; monetary greed; infantile materialism; the fraudulence of American politics; and—particularly among working-class heartlanders—the media mockery of America's traditional, rural-based values. Even fundamentalism's obsession with 'the end times' can be seen as a variation on the ecological movement's eco-apocalypse being delivered by global warming. Biblical apocalypse or planetary ecocide: either way, we're talking about the end of the world, with one camp assembled under the tent of technology and 'rational science' (unable to grasp that technology is by no means neutral in destroying the natural world), and the other in the shadow of the cross waiting for the Last Days.

There are also a growing number of in-betweeners, most notably the Christian Greens. American political strategists don't know what to make of them yet, but both camps want them inside their tent. The Christian Green fundamentalists in my home state grew out of the anti-mountaintop-removal movement in Appalachian coal country, aligning themselves with eco-movement politics in the spirit of earth stewardship.

Although they get a small splash of media coverage, mostly due to their political novelty, they are getting nowhere in this age of increasing coal-energy dependency. 'Mr Peabody's coal train' still hauls away my native mountains to fuel the national power grid, to run electric toothbrushes for those without enough stamina to move a one-ounce object up and down, and to run all those 'non-polluting' electric lawn mowers ... to smelt metal, make plastics, and provide electricity to recharge the batteries of 'green' hybrid cars, which, for all intents and purposes, run on coal. When it comes to American self-delusion and denial, the difference is mostly a matter of type.

AS I'VE SAID, CHRISTIAN FUNDAMENTALISM HAS undoubtedly created millions of intact families and a sense of community. In other cases, however, fundamentalism has split families, and continues to do so, dividing their members sometimes violently, more often quietly. Although my family and the Shanghai community were always essentially religious, two camps began to emerge in the mid-twentieth century: the fervidly devout, who proselytised at every waking moment, and those who felt

that 'What's between me and God is just that—private.'
Everyone was nevertheless shaped in the American
Christian tradition, which isn't exactly a light-hearted
one, even before the cast-iron version came in with the
evangelical movement of the 1970s to pound us first into
acquiescence and then submission. You could not argue
with 'The Word of God'. Most of us couldn't remember
when had we ever tried to, but it seemed best not to
take any chances, given His omnipotence and propensity
for floods, scourges of boils, and the like. Getting saved
seemed like common sense.

At the same time, life for the emerging post-war
white underclass was getting more difficult and stressful.
Decent, hard-working folks on both sides of my family
turned to 'Our Lord' for solace and guidance—which
required only about a quarter-turn, as it were. There no
longer seemed to be any dependable rules for surviving
in America's newer, more virulent materialism and the
wealth economy's shift in values. But at least their rules
were written down in black and white by God himself for
all to see in the 'Good Book'.

Those written by man seemed not only unclear, but
as deceptive as the Devil himself. For example, once,
when I was in my twenties, my father asked me to read
a document he'd received from the bank. It wasn't that
he couldn't read it on his own, but because, reprobate
as I am, my family nevertheless acknowledged me as
its most literate member—for what that's worth in a
family whose members care only to read the One Book,
over and over again. Anyway, the payment on a tiny
modular home that Daddy had managed to buy had been

127

raised by a considerable amount—with no explanation given—during a time in the late 1970s when 16 per cent and even 18 per cent mortgage rates had become common. At these levels, the monthly payment had jumped so high that he could no longer afford it.

There we stood together, at the far end of the backyard he'd carved out of the brush and hand-planted in the hard, red clay. He was wearing his battered straw hat, standing next to his beehives (he loved watching the orderliness of the apian world), where no one else could hear us. A light summer wind rustled the papers as I read them.

'Joey, can they do this to me? Is this legal?'

Reading the terms, I could see that it was an adjustable-rate mortgage, of which I'm sure he had no concept. In fact, amortised, the rate hike effectively wiped out the entire four years of payments he'd already made.

'Daddy, I'm afraid they can.'

His face locked into that hard set, the kind you see on bronze Confederate statues on Southern courthouse lawns. But his eyes could not hide the confused pain and insult he felt. Redneck men have a way of crying inside that manifests itself as a rigid, faraway look, a combination of pain, outrage, and fatal resignation. Daddy had known the banker, who had a reputation for being a good ole boy and a man of the people, for 25 years. He'd known the salesman—from whom he'd purchased both the plot and the crappy modular house that was already beginning to fall apart—from boyhood. Betrayal is the only word for these sorts of things, and Judas is the rightful name for those men who knew full well he did not understand the terms of the loan. Both of those men are now retired and affluent.

In awkwardness, my father and I looked away from one another for a while, mostly at the ground or the fence line running into the pine woods. Then he said: 'Well, Maw always said that "paper will lay still for anything".' We went back inside the house. Whereupon he went into 'Daddy's room', a tiny sanctuary, filled with religious tracts and books, hunting rifles, and his country-music records. When he entered that room, we knew not to bother him. (Grandchildren excepted — they could bother 'Papaw' any time they wanted.) There he read his annotated New Testament Bible into the night. Whatever can be said about fundamentalist Christianity, the word of Jesus Christ sought in honest, humble solitude never betrayed any man.

On the other hand, there is no end of misery that God will lay the heathen. So early on, at around age five, as a prophylactic to a 'heethern' life, as my dad pronounced the word, it was deemed best that I attend those half-day summer-season indoctrinations held in church basements across America: Bible School. This was thrilling news to me. In Bible School you got to draw and colour pictures, sing, and do all sorts of handicrafts. I did not yet know the limits of the curriculum. Students drew and coloured pictures of Jesus, sang songs about Jesus, and glued together pre-cut paper puzzle shapes that — surprise, surprise — turned out to be Jesus, with only a rare occasional break, such as Noah's Ark. After more than a week of this repetitive theme, I asked the handicraft teacher, Mrs Roach, if I could whittle, promising to be real safe with the pocket knife. (We carried pocket knives from about age six back then. I still do; it feels unmanly not to.) I wanted to carve a wooden Indian, like the one in the Hank Williams song, 'Kawliga'. Mrs Roach was, as they say, not amused.

'I think you're missing the whole point of being here. Show some respect for Our Lord. Now you go sit in the cloakroom and think about it. Come out when you can tell me what you've learned.'

From inside the dark cloakroom, I could hear the choir in a practice session upstairs:

Were you there when they nailed him to the boards?
Were you there when they nailed him to the boards?
Sometimes it causes
My sinning heart to tremble,
Were you there when they nailed him to the boards?

After an appropriate period of trembling, which seemed like forever but was probably about five minutes, I emerged cautiously from the cloakroom. Mrs Roach let me stand there while the rest of the Bible Schoolers finished up the next tune, the standard off-key rendition of 'Yes, Jesus Loves Me.' She turned in my direction.

'Out already?' she said. 'I could hold a bear in a bathtub that long. What have you learned?'

'That Jesus don't like whittling?' I speculated.

'Not in His church, He don't. Now sit back down with the rest of the children.' Embarrassed to death, I rejoined the other, more earnest God-seekers, who had set about rendering Calvary's holy emblem in the preferred three-dimensional medium of children of that day: popsicle sticks.

I dived with a new-found fervency into the project

at hand, in the full knowledge that 'God is everywhere and He is always watching.' Then, after finishing up on a fine, multi-dimensional, four-layered cross, complete with pedestal, I blew it again. Apparently, somewhere in that leather-bound Good Book there exists a passage regarding such things as the popsicle-stick rendition of Our Saviour's sorrow and the proper use of construction paste in Jesus' name. I'd attempted to liven up my cross with the tempera paints from the craft-materials shelf. Whereupon I was informed by Mrs Roach that we were not allowed to do this.

Me, timidly: 'Why not?'

Mrs Roach: 'Because only Catholics worship gaudy crosses.'

Bible School is sort of the gateway drug to getting saved, which ultimately everyone in my family did at some point. Getting saved was permanent in most people; temporary, in others. But getting saved was a rite of spiritual and moral passage for all. Inoculation with the goodness of Christ, however, didn't have any effect with some folks. When I consider my moralistic take on life, I can't say it didn't work at least somewhat in my case. But I'm still a sucker for the cross of gaud. Given that Mrs Roach has long ago departed with the angel band, I can confess to having stood around in any number of European cathedrals gawking at some particularly ostentatious representation of the 'nailin' boards'.

IT WAS NOT LONG AFTER MY UTTER FAILURE TO obtain redemption through Bible School that the most mysterious and seldom discussed figure in all our extended family came hobbling from out of one of those corners of my mother's past that were almost never talked about. Beyond my mother's few and bitter recollections, I knew little of Pappy Miles, other than what I'd gleaned from a picture of him in a white-linen suit, wearing a rakish straw hat and leaning on the Ford coupe with a 'don't you dare cross me' look in his eye.

Then, in the summer of 1957, Pappy Miles, the escaped jailbird who'd vanished, showed up at our house in Winchester. He was making the rounds, making amends with his children before he died. Apparently he was successful enough, because I was allowed to visit his home in North Carolina that summer, while Mama was hospitalised for one of her periodic severe—read suicidal—depressions. Daddy was driving trucks, and simply couldn't afford to stay home with his kids for an indeterminate amount of time, so the plan was for my brother and sister and me to stay Over Home. Then Miles offered to take one of us. Mama was too depressed to be allowed an opinion, and my old man was making a run to Greensboro anyway. Why Miles was trusted to care for me, I will never know; they must have been desperate. As for me, I particularly wanted to be as far away from home as possible, and Greensboro, North Carolina was farther than I'd ever been.

It turned out to be one of the best summers of my life, mostly for three reasons. The first was that, now, at the age of twelve, I had become an absolute book addict, and old Miles, despite only having had a third-grade education, proved to be extremely literate by even the most formal measure. I'd been reading everything in the local library, randomly and crazily. I had even read Céline and Genet, though of course I didn't really understand them—I hadn't the slightest clue as to their context. Existential? Did it have anything to do with the drive differential on a car? The words sounded alike. Ah, but the exotic flow of the words and the thoughtful world they implied: 'Life is a classroom and Boredom's the usher, there all the time to spy on you; whatever happens, you've got to look as if you were awfully busy all the time.' (Louis-Ferdinand Céline) Given my age and provincialism, I rather believed that their world was imaginary. A summer with Pappy Miles later convinced me that the literary world was very real.

The second reason was that Pappy Miles lived in an unpainted, old plank cabin at the edge of a swamp ... a whole swamp of my very own, beginning at the front porch. Which leads to the third reason: Miles had a small, boy-sized .22-calibre rifle, which he put at my complete disposal.

So I'd sit with the old man on the front porch of his shack, and plink away with the rifle at whatever critters crawled out of the swamp. Sometimes, if I got lucky, it was a water moccasin snake. But more often it was a feral cat, a plain old housecat gone wild in the swamp.

The swamp (which the old man pronounced to rhyme with 'stamp') was a nearly supernatural place wherein the water turned a different colour each morning. A textile mill dumped its waste dyes upstream. Some days, it was blood red; other days, it was electric green or cobalt blue. Miles would take his coffee out on the porch in the morning, before the day got hot. Sitting on the worn wooden steps, with his suspenders hanging loosely at his sides, he'd comment on the view.

'She's damned-near purple today (slurp)', he'd say, with a bit of amazement showing in his puffy, red face. It *was* kind of miraculous.

Later, with his feet propped up on the porch rail, Miles would read Voltaire, sometimes aloud, while I plinked away with the 'cat rifle', as Miles called it. The self-educated son of a farmer, Miles particularly liked Voltaire's *Natural Laws* and almost anything written during the Enlightenment. Pages would be turned and the cat rifle would crack, each sound measuring the hours of an old man and a boy spending time together.

Come dusk, Miles would wash up in the kitchen basin, put on his straw hat, and hobble up the gravel road to the country grocery-store a quarter-mile away to get his whiskey. You weren't supposed to be able to do that, because North Carolina was a dry state, and Guilford County was a dry county. In 1934, the good Christian people of North Carolina had first voted against the sale of 'spirituous beverages', and had subsequently done so at every opportunity. But, as Pappy Miles observed, 'As long as the citizens of North Carolina can stagger to the polls, they'll vote dry.'

Half an hour or so later, he'd return with a bottle of Old Crow and a new box of cartridges. The sun would drop from the sky as if it had finally been maimed by the cat rifle, and the kerosene lanterns would come on in the cabin. After that, he'd cook some hominy and pork, or beans and cornbread, and then read silently until we both fell asleep. Years later, I'd realise it had been the stuff of Southern novels.

Meanwhile, where had he been all these years? It turned out that he'd run off to live with the Seminole Indians, where he opened a small grocery store. Then, at the age of seventy, he'd come back and bought a shack conveniently located between the swamp and the edge-of-town grocery/liquor store so he could sip cheap whiskey and read for the rest of his life.

'So why'd you run off and leave Little Mama with all them kids?' I asked.

'Well, my little running buddy', Miles said, 'I left for somethin' better'n Greensboro, North Carolina. Folks that's left behind can only see a man running off. If they ain't willing to run alongside, they cain't see what he's running toward, which might be somethin' finer than their small minds can imagine.'

This touched me somewhere inside because he always called me his 'little running buddy'. I liked the old man even more after that. And I like his memory especially now, when I stop to consider that I stayed away from my family for more than ten years after I left home at the age of eighteen. A couple of wives, thousands of books, and a cotton sack full of troubles later, I suspect I got a little of his blood somewhere in the deal.

Miles had once been a bookkeeper on a big cotton plantation, had owned a smart-looking white Ford coupe, and had made a good living. He knew how to 'turn a dollar' when he wanted to, back before he became a drunk (which some would deem genetic, because all five of his sons became alcoholics). There was a 'whole 'nuther story' to his life with Little Mama before my mother was born. In his prime he was fast and wild, and definitely had

135

a mean streak when he was drunk. He'd left Little Mama years before he was jailed, on a drunken night when he spat tobacco juice up against the woodstove. Older aunts and uncles say he spat it directly into the pot of beans on the stove; but then, I've watched family folklore grow before my eyes, so I have my doubts. (I also know that spitting your tobacco juice up against a red-hot stove is an ancient rural Southern tradition, which I have practised myself—you aim for the reddest hot spot, and the juice is cleanly vaporised.) Whatever the case, without his supporting income, Beulah and all ten of those kids had to move into a two-room pine-board shack you could see daylight through.

Worse still, they had to pick cotton—every able-bodied one of them—for a penny a pound. Now if you've never torn up your hands on the hard, rough pod of a cotton bol under the unforgiving Dixie sun, you ain't missed much, no matter how romantic it looks in the movies with all the black folks singing 'Go Down, Old Hannah.' It takes a damned-lot of cotton to fill a 100-pound sack, and when Old Hannah does finally go down behind the tight, flat line of the horizon, you're ready to sing out of pure gratitude that you didn't drop dead in that cruel, red dirt. So it's no wonder my mama always said, 'Maybe I ain't give my kids much, but by God they never picked cotton.'

Given what Miles' disappearance had reduced them to, you can see why some of the older kids—the ones who could remember him—hated Miles for the rest of their lives. Of course, by the time the old man came back, 'just so we'd have to bury his sorry arse', as one uncle put it, there weren't as many of his kids left to hate him. One got killed in World War II's South Pacific campaign; one froze to death in Korea; and one, Uncle Garland—who was as wild and fast as Pappy Miles—got his head snapped off as clean as a green bean when he ran his Indian motorcycle under an oncoming truck in 1941. But most of his surviving kids said he was one mean son-of-a-bitch.

And the truth was that my grandfather could be meaner than a snake on a griddle. I once saw him smack a neighbour's dog across the head with his cane. He killed that dog deader than a canned codfish.

'You outright killed that dog,' I said, shocked. One of the dog's eyes had popped half-out of its socket. 'I meant to,' Miles said. Then he proceeded to get blind drunk and bust things up in the yard. I stayed out of the shack until the old man lapsed into the cruel, black sleep of the rightfully tormented.

Miles died when a car struck him during one of his dusky walks along the rocky road to the liquor store. He went down, quite literally, with a 'splash of Old Crow on the rocks'. So there he was, a battered, linen-clad lump, face down, with his jacket turned inside out and up over his head. There was just the amber whiskey running from the broken bottle inside his jacket pocket. He'd been 'killed deader than a saw log', as Uncle Johnny unsentimentally put it, adding, 'He was so mean, he never even bled.'

The county cops came. Neighbours came. Before he was even on the cooling board, the foot-washing Baptist women from up the road were muttering how awful it was, the way that mean old man died, 'soaked in liquor like that'. But when I look back on that summer and my knocking a cottonmouth snake off a cypress limb with the cat rifle, his way of dying seemed fitting enough to me. If he was indeed mean, he was no meaner than the sisters who stole his houses; no meaner than me shooting those harmless swamp cats. And if he had a weakness for alcohol, well, I've been there, too. And, besides, wasn't it Voltaire who said, in *Natural Laws*, 'Our errors springing in no wise from malice, but being the natural consequence of human frailty, we hope that they will be pardoned to us in this world and the other.'?

I've always told myself that someday, when I don't have a boss riding my arse and a woman riding my heart, someday near the short end of my candle, I'd have time on my hands just like he did. Time to publish Miles' name in something other than the 'jail notes', as newspaper lists of court convictions were called in his time. Time to write about old Miles and pour two slugs of better whiskey than he ever drank—one for me and one for him—and then drink the two shots myself. Now I've done both.

CHAPTER SIX

Son of a Blue Goose

Aunt Ony Mae sat on the front porch glider adjusting her blouse, which is to say, adjusting the dish towel stretched under her huge Bageant tits to absorb the sweat brought on by the heat of what I am guessing was the summer of '57. Between adjustments, she picked the clots of pine pitch off her arms. We—meaning Ony, her tall, mountain-skinny husband, Uncle Belmont, and I—had just come in from cutting pulpwood, where I had happily been working the 'jimmy-john', the narrow 12-foot pole used to tip falling trees in the proper direction, and running the home-made measuring rod that ensured each stick of wood was exactly four feet long (or was it five?), lest it be rejected by the pulp mill.

Uncle Belmont had sawed, and Ony and I had carried and loaded, with Belmont picking up our slack when he got too far ahead of us. For a long day's work of cutting, loading, hauling, and unloading a three-quarter-ton truck with high sideboards and piled high, they'd made seventeen dollars—minus petrol and oil for truck and chainsaw. About seven or eight bucks each, which made it a top-dollar day. If the cutting conditions were good enough, if you could drive the truck close enough to the trees, if there wasn't too much brush and bramble, and if the right-sized trees weren't too far apart, you could make a load in a day. Some days you did, and some days you didn't.

I got no pay for my labour, nor expected any; being allowed to work with adults was pay enough. The little kids looked at me with envy. I was damned proud of myself, sitting on the front-porch steps listening, keeping my mouth shut for a change, so as not to blow this crowning moment. Faking that natural, manly weariness of farm-and-hill-country menfolk, the wry, quiet wisdom in the face such men so often show, I mopped my brow with a red work hankie, and looked off into the hills as if perceiving worldly truths that only a grown working man could know. The only part I can be sure that came off was the weariness. I didn't need to fake that.

Cutting and hauling pulpwood was the labour of last resort in the new, permanently cash-strapped rural economy. Not that other work paid any more. The minimum wage was one dollar an hour, if you could get anyone to pay it. One of the few businesses that did was the Little Miss Tomato canning factory—one of several locally—where Ony and Belmont had tried to get hired on. They wouldn't have made a penny more than they did in the pulp fields, the minimum wage being what it was. In fact, an eight-hour day on the steamy canning line would have paid a few dollars less than what Ony and Belmont had just earned. But it was easier work, and there were fewer associated costs involved. Momentarily, I was about to see a graphic example of those associated costs.

Belmont passed by me on his way up the steps, and said to no one in particular, yet to everyone at the same time, 'Dammit, the truck's got a crack in the engine block.' Which meant that there was radiator water mixing with the engine oil, and tomorrow the truck probably wouldn't make it to and from the pulp fields nine miles away, most of it up and down steep hills.

Belmont was perfectly capable of rebuilding an engine block himself. But, even with the busted knuckles and endless cussing that came with doing the job, he and Ony would still have to come up with at least $60 to pay for a used engine block and parts. And they would be unable to earn money for at least a couple of days.

Belmont stood there for a moment, wearing a gaunt, indecipherable expression, and then said, 'If we'd a got on at the canning factory, this wouldn't a happened.' He went back to the truck, gunned the motor, and drove off, cracked engine block and all. Everyone knew where he was headed: either up the road to Unger's Store to spend the $17 on beer—lots of it—to drink in the woods (Maw and Pap didn't allow drinking at home if they could stop it), or to Buck's Tavern, to drink the money up at the bar. Belmont duly came back at midnight, stumbling and hollering and singing to himself. And if Ony Mae was mad, it was only because he hadn't taken her with him.

Their kids—cousins Clayton, Kenny, and Carole, all under six—heard the ruckus upon his arrival, but never got out from under their single quilt. This was not a sign of poverty, but merely the way you 'slept kids' in those days: in the back room, where they were living until Ony and Belmont could find a place to rent. Belmont was already out cold he before his head hit the pillow. In fact, he was knocked cold from the moment his finger wiped that oil water off the engine block. In my childish logic, I attributed all this—their misery and the tragic conclusion of my first manly day in the pulp fields—to them not getting hired at the canning factory.

Having been an adult now for over forty years, I have watched alcoholism of the kind that plagued and eventually destroyed Uncle Belmont and Aunt Ony's life come to be labelled 'a disease'. And I've watched it grow into a $100 billion recovery-and-treatment industry, with a 3 per cent success rate. I've watched us go through the 'alcohol gene' crap (genes do not cause behaviour), just so genetic scientists could get a piece of the action. Both the disease and genetic theories have since been thoroughly disproven. What has been proven, though, is that social category and class are by far the best predictors of substance abuse—an activity in which Americans lead the world. There is more substance abuse in Los Angeles alone than in all of Europe, and nearly all the victims come from the underclass. Hopefully, someday, Americans will look at the system that creates such a staggering number of substance addicts, and the industries and profit centres built around them.

Uncle Belmont never had a secure day throughout his life of relentless hardship. Any suffering that might have caused ... well, that was just an associated social cost of American paper-pulp production—the kind that never makes capitalism's balance sheets.

CONVERSELY TO AUNT ONY AND UNCLE BELMONT'S situation, that same year saw the beginning of a brief period of prosperity for my parents: their 'two good years'. After working as a farm hand, driving a taxi in piss-poor, catch-as-catch-can jobs, and getting off-and-on work, sometimes as a local truck driver, my father caught a break. He found himself owning a semi-truck and hauling for Blue Goose produce—a Teamsters Union job. He bought a modest home (for $8,000), this man who'd quit school in the sixth or seventh grade—he was never sure which one it was, which gives some idea how seriously he took his attendance at the one-room school we both attended in our lifetimes. Daddy was making more money than he'd ever made in his life—about $4,000 a year. The median national household income was $5,000, mostly thanks to America's unions. At last, we were getting our piece of the rainbow pie. And if it was not a very big piece, we had no way of judging and were happy enough.

This was the golden age of trucking and of unions. Thirty-five per cent of American labour, 17 million working folks, were union members, and it was during this period that the American middle class was created. One-third of working folks, the people who busted their arses day in and day out, making the nation function, were living better than they ever had. Or at least they had the opportunity to do so.

From the Depression through to World War II, the Teamsters Union had become a powerful entity, and a popular one, too, because of such things as its pledge never to strike during the war or a national emergency. President Roosevelt even had a special designated liaison person assigned to the Teamsters. But power and money eventually attracted the usual assortment of lizards, and by the mid-1950s the Teamsters Union had become one corrupt pile of shit at the top level—so rotten that even the mob enjoyed a piece of the action. (Actually, the reason the unions turned to the mob for support dated back to the 1930s, when unions needed to get their own muscle to counter the hired goon squads that management would throw at the picket lines. Even the goon squads were an improvement, however, over the 19th-century practice of owners calling the business-friendly governor to have the guard come and shoot down strikers.)

The membership—ordinary guys like my dad—were outraged by and ashamed of union corruption, but were rendered powerless by the crooked union bosses in the big cities. No great follower of the news or current events, my dad tried to keep up with and understand Teamster developments. This was impossible, since his information sources consisted of anti-union Southern newspapers, and the television coverage centred on the Teamsters' few top criminal figures, and their courtroom trials.

All this left him conflicted. His Appalachian Christian upbringing defined the world in black and white, with no grey areas. Inside, he felt he should not be even remotely connected with such vile things as the Teamsters were associated with, and he sometimes prayed for guidance in the matter. On the other hand, there was the pride and satisfaction he felt in providing for his family in ways previously impossible. He'd built a reasonable working-class security for those times and that place in West Virginia. Without Teamsters Union wages, that would not have been possible.

I doubt my old man ever went to a union meeting. There was no local office I know of, so there were no meetings held within a reasonable distance. (I could be wrong there, but I don't think so. I've asked old truck drivers, and they cannot recall one.) But since Blue Goose was nationally organised, he got the benefit of other drivers' union struggles in the cities and larger towns. This may sound ridiculous, but I'm not quite sure he fully associated the liveable wage he was getting with his union membership. Daddy had little knowledge of American history, and certainly no knowledge of the century of struggle that had led to unions and worker rights. Heartland America was and still is a strange place, where poor education and purposefully managed information vacuums prevent social understanding. Things, good or bad, just sort of happen to you, and a passivity reigns for working-class people, as if all things larger than their families are beyond their control (and may be, given what we've been reduced to). So they believe that Jesus, providence, or plain luck, or any combination thereof, govern their fate. And they believe that God wants to see everybody working at all times—the harder the better.

So Daddy drove his guts out. There were rules, and log books, and all the other crap that was supposed to ensure that truck drivers got enough rest and reasonable working conditions to keep them safe on the roads. Rural-heartland drivers saw it for the bullshit it was, but it was much better-paying bullshit. For a little guy hauling produce from Podunk, USA to the big cities, it still came down to heartburn, haemorrhoids, and longer hauls and longer hours than most drivers' falsified log books showed. And sometimes way too much Benzedrine, or 'bennies'.

Bennies were a type of speed commonly used by truckers back then because of the gruelling hauls. As a former doper who has done bennies, I can tell you that they are gritty, nerve-jagging stuff. Their only virtue is their ability to keep you wide awake and jumpy, and—after you've been awake on them for a couple of days, which many drivers were—crazier than a shithouse rat. Nearly every truck stop sold bennies under the counter. So it was overworked and wild out there on the roads at times. Once, while hallucinating on bennies, Daddy nearly wiped out a roadside joint. He recalled 'layin' on the jake brake, down shifting, and watching hundreds of the witches like in *The Wizard of Oz* come down out of the sky in the dark'. Somehow he got 30,000 pounds back onto the road while several folks inside the diner were pissing themselves in their window-side booths.

My daddy ran along the eastern seaboard in a 12-wheeler (there were no 18-wheelers then). It had polished chrome, and bold letters that read BLUE GOOSE LINE. When it was parked alongside our little asbestos-sided house, I'd marvel at the magic of those bold words, the golden diamond, and the sturdy goose. And dream of someday 'burning up Route 50' like my dad.

Old US Route 50 ran near the house, and was the stuff of legend if your daddy happened to be a truck driver who sometimes took you with him on the shorter hauls: 'OK, boy, now scrunch down and look into the side mirror. I'm gonna turn the top of them side stacks red hot.' And he would pop the clutch and strike sparks on the anvil of the night, down shifting toward Pinkerton, Coolville, and Hanging Rock. It never once occurred to me that his ebullience and our camaraderie might be due to a handful of bennies.

Yessir, Old 50 was a mighty thing, a howling black slash through the Blue Ridge Mountain fog. It was a road famed for its treacherous, widow-making curves, back in the time when truck stops and cafes bloomed in the trucks' smoky wakes. A roadmap will tell you that it eventually reaches Columbus and Saint Louis, places I imagined had floodlights raking the skies, heralding the arrival of heroic Teamster truckers like my father.

I have two parched photos from that time. One is of me and my brother and sister, ages ten, eight, and six. We are standing in the front yard, three little redneck kids with bad haircuts, squinting for some faint clue as to whether there was really a world out there, somewhere beyond West Virginia. The other photo is of my mother and the three of us kids on the porch of that house on Route 50. On the day my father was slated to return from any given run, we'd all stand on the porch listening for the sound of airbrakes and the deep roar as he came down off the mountain. Each time, my mother would step onto the porch, blotting her lipstick, Betty Grable style, her hair rustling in the breeze, and say, 'Stand close, your daddy's home.'

And that was about as good as it ever got for our family. Daddy's heart later gave way from a congenital defect, and he lost everything. He was so scrupulously honest about debts that he could never recover financially. Unable to borrow money, uneducated, and weakened for life, he set to working in car washes and garages. After his trucking days were over, we were assigned to the margins of America, a million miles from the American Dream, joining those people never seen on television, who are represented by no politician and never heard from in the halls of power.

I know it was only a little house by the side of the road with not enough closets, ugly asbestos shingle-siding, and a red-clay yard that refused to grow grass. But it was ours, just like the truck and the chance to get ahead that the truck offered us. For a while, at least, we felt as though we were some small part of America as it was advertised. All because of a job acquired during the heyday of unions in this nation.

Sure, it was also a period of Teamsters Union corruption. Yet the criminal history of the few top lizards on the national rock of greed is not the history of the people. If a few pricks and gangsters have occasionally seized power over the dignity of labour, countless more calculating, bloodless, and malevolent pricks — the capitalist elites — have always held most of the cards.

Which is why in 1886 the railroad/banking tycoon Jay Gould could sneer, 'I can always hire one half of the working class to kill the other half.' And why the speaker at the US Business Conference Board in 1974 could declare, 'One man, one vote has undermined the power of business in all capitalist countries since World War II.' And why that same year *Business Week* magazine said, 'It will be a hard pill for many Americans to swallow — the idea of doing with less so that big business can have more. Nothing in modern economic history compares with the selling job that must now be done to make people accept this new reality.'

Well, we must have swallowed the pill and bought the sell job, because 1974 was the last year that American workers made a wage gain in real dollars, despite staggering increases in productivity since then. The 'new reality' is now so old it's part of America's cultural furniture.

Only about 12 per cent of American workers are unionised, and half of them are members of fake 'house unions' run by the company. Unions are still fighting to exist (although 36 per cent of government employees are unionised, because the Empire allows some leeway for its commissars). For instance, in 1978, when I was working to organise the local newspaper, the management was not even allowed to speak to the workers on the matter until after the union vote results were in. Today, employers can legally force employees to attend anti-union presentations during the workday. At these captive-audience meetings, union supporters are legally forbidden to speak under threat of being accused of insubordination.

Things are changing, though. Union membership climbed 12 per cent in 2008. Twelve per cent of 12 per cent per cent ain't much, but at least it's forward motion. At this rate, it will only take us a decade to get back to the 1956 level of union membership, while globalised sweat-shopism is progressing geometrically. You'd think that, given the way things are now, union membership should be at an all-time high. But so are the impediments, starting with the very people doing the organising. Nowadays, the sons and daughters of the college-educated commissariat get degrees in union organising without ever having done a lick of real work, or ever having touched a drill press or any other tool, or having experienced the kind of work they are supposed to be organising. So we can expect no miracles from top union leaders among the Empire's elites. The new union elites and their minions are lawyers and marketing professionals and the soft little sons and daughters of college professors and CPAs, who grew up at the mall while their daddy was 'on sabbatical' from the university. They've never come down off the mountain with both stacks red hot, or gathered on the porch of a crappy but new roadside bungalow, proud because they owned it, and stood up straight because, 'Boys, your daddy is coming home.'

So it will be up to us, just like it always has been … up to the Nicaraguan janitor, the forty-year-old family man forced to bag groceries at Wal-Mart, the pizza-delivery guy, the writer, the dancer, the welder, the certified nurse, the long-haul trucker, and the short-order cook. Some people are bound to get hurt in the necessary fight. In fact, people need to be willing to get hurt in the fight. That's the way we once gained worker rights, and that's the way we will get them back.

And if somehow we get our act together and do that, they will snicker at us from their gilded roosts on Wall Street and Pennsylvania Avenue. What else is new?

CHAPTER SEVEN

Class Rules

Home of the brave, land of the free,
But I get mistreated by the bourgeoisie.
Lord, it's a bourgeois town.
Uhm, a bourgeois town.
Got the bourgeois blues.
Gotta spread the word around.
— American folk-blues singer Leadbelly, in 'Bourgeois Blues'

After my father lost his small trucking business, we bounced around the area from one rented house to another, before moving to town for good. The sixth-grade school year was half over, and already I'd been in two schools when my parents moved permanently to the old Shenandoah Valley town of Winchester, twenty some miles down the pike. Though we didn't know it then, Winchester was the ancestral home of all the Bageants in America. Our original ancestor, John William Bageant, arrived in Winchester in 1755 with the English general Edward Braddock's army, to keep the French and Indians at a safe distance. Consequently, we still had many kinfolk in town, people who we seldom saw because they were in a higher social class. One was a successful undertaker; one, a grocer; and another owned commercial orchards. They were business people in a mercantile town. Most were Masons and civic-minded joiners, whereas my father and mother had never joined anything in their lives. But we were about to join what the Department of Commerce's PR tracts called the post-war nation's 'burgeoning new and willing work force being deployed across the nation'.

And so they were deployed on such fronts as Martinsburg, West Virginia, and its Dow Corning plant, in Winchester, Virginia, where factories such as O'Sullivan Rubber Corporation, American Brakeblock ('The Breakshoe' we called it), or the numerous garment factories exploited cheap, non-union local labour. One executive speaking to the Winchester Chamber of Commerce at the time described these people as 'very hard working and docile', a phrase that can be often be found in slave advertisements of the pre-Civil War South. Having been well conditioned for uniform industrial behaviour by the all-consuming war effort, men and women alike went from the 'war defence plants' to the defence of corporate capitalism's hometown fronts, large and small. (There is not one damned word in the US Constitution that designates capitalism as the nation's official economic regime, but somehow we always seem to find ourselves fighting for it under the banner of patriotism.)

Given the influx from farms to towns and their surrounding counties, many local merchants made modest fortunes. Even the little dogs in the Chamber of Commerce were pissing themselves for joy over the prospects for bourgeois capitalism, as the bumpkins-turned-plant workers and their families swarmed downtown on Fridays after payday. But it was the big dogs of crony capitalism that really cleaned up. Bank owners and large landholders, in particular, amassed what would become true fortunes in the tens of millions. A sociologist friend of mine aptly calls their dominance of these two vital resources—land space and the availability of money—'wolf leverage'.

Born of genteel planters who could never balance their books, and speculators who despised the notion of trade, southern capitalism is and always has been crony capitalism. It is still the only type known to the descendants, who constitute the new oligarchy—the people who finance political campaigns for city and state governments. They eventually created what came to be called 'The New South', in places such as Atlanta or Raleigh–Durham, North Carolina, and drove it to stratospheric heights thirty years later when they discovered the credit opportunities in Old Dixie. This was pretty much the Old South revisited, but with an added ingredient of 'white niggers' from the upland farms.

I use the n-word here because some of 'our betters' used it privately about us, and because it fits the times and sentiments. Common practice in Winchester was for the well-heeled-area's business people—plant managers' wives and those of the local gentry—to shop downtown during the week so as to avoid the labouring white underclass they employed. A few stores, particularly men's clothing stores and ladies hat and dress shops, were obviously more upscale, with even mundane items purposefully priced high to keep the ever-price-conscious riff-raff out. Their customers didn't mind that they could have purchased, say, white cotton socks at half the price.

Stores like these held me in thrall. For me, peering into the window of Bell's Men's Clothing Store, with my hands cupped around my eyes, the display of smooth-flowing gabardine dress pants and seersucker suits, silk ties, and polished leather belts seemed to exist in a marvellous dimension of their own. I couldn't resist going inside, where it smelled like leather and exotic aftershave, and of the Windex used on the glass display-cases.

Once through the front door, though, it was as if I had suddenly broken out in warts. My clothes and even my skin seemed dirty under the clean, fluorescent lights (and maybe they were, given that we had to stoke a coal stove in the middle of our living room to stay warm). I could smell myself polluting the air of this sartorial temple. And I could see the clerks eyeballing me as a potential shoplifter.

Thirty seconds later, my father, who'd come down the street and seen me enter, appeared behind me. We'd come downtown to get a wrench set from Sears and so he could jaw with one of the salesmen, an old friend from the sticks.

'Come on outta here! Did I say you could go wandering off?' Daddy said, loud enough so the clerks could hear. Actually, he had, tacitly, when he'd said to me, 'Don't go more than a couple of blocks. Be back in fifteen minutes.'

Outside Bell's, he told me, 'You don't need to be going into places like that.' I got the point.

Another instance of classism in practice involved Uncle Joe, a visiting uncle from my mother's side, who had married one of my mother's sisters and made good money working in the naval shipyard in Norfolk. We considered him rich; his daughter had a pony and a cowgirl outfit, for chrissakes! Uncle Joe asked to try on a pair of $40 Florsheims at a shoe store in downtown Winchester. That was big bucks for a pair of shoes in late-1950s' working-class Winchester—about a week's pay, or close to it, in our household. (Uncle Joe looked like a redneck during the week, and was indeed one at heart, but he had good taste, and always dressed to kill on Saturday nights, and on Sunday mornings when he bothered to go to church.) 'I had the damnedest time making that clerk let me try them on,' he told us. 'He went and got the manager, and I had to raise hell with both of them. You'd a thought I was a nigger.' As a Southern white man of those times, he wouldn't have wanted to try on shoes that had been on a black man's foot.

That's what I mean about being a white nigger in the eyes of the town's 'leading families' we read so much about in the *Winchester Evening Star*, which published their every little move—such as having a visitor from a foreign country, or getting yet another award for business leadership or civic involvement.

Much later, as a middle-aged man, I came to know the shoe store's owner, Bill Shendell. Bill turned out to be a very progressive man. A member of the city council at the time, he helped me immensely when, as a news reporter, I took on a crooked city government. I can see now that his store's clerks were as much a product of the same classist American culture as I was. This is not just a Southern thing; it's an American thing. You can drop me in any American community, and I can show you a hundred examples of it in a day. We grow up with the stuff in our bones, and it just leaks out of our pores in one form or another for the rest of our lives, either as enforcers of classist culture or as victims of it. Or both. My father was certainly an enforcer of it when he made it clear that people like us were not to ogle, much less touch, the garments of the higher castes. I look back now and realise how much of the class system is enforced through the culture of shame. Shame about money.

Once class-system rules are in place, behavioural patterns become set, and roles are played out that create an ecology based upon unacknowledged, mostly unconscious, class recognition. Those pissing downhill and those at the bottom of the hill are equally oblivious to their roles in preserving class lines. In the end, both upper and lower classes, liberal or conservative, are dancing partners at the same heartbreaking ball, where the same melody has been playing for two centuries. The lyrics may change to suit the national moment, but the dancers go on in their hopeless embrace, unwilling to leave their familiar, windowless American ballroom, never stepping into the light of day, simply because they do not know it is out there.

Even as I was peering into that window at Bell's, America was well on the path to becoming the mountain of meaningless discarded stuff that has made us one big landfill site for China. We could already feel the rising tsunami of goods all around us: bigger refrigerators, home freezer-chests, Melmac dishes, Corning ware, console TV sets, hi-fis, air conditioners, lawn sprinklers, TV dinners, 'sportswear', multiple family cars, vacuum cleaners that doubled as everything imaginable, crock pots, blenders, hair sprays, electric hair-dryers, automatic washer-dryer combinations, power lawn-mowers, instant potatoes, pancakes, biscuits, and coffee. It was a steadily building avalanche of wonders that no modern American family could do without. Cranking out these time- and labour-saving devices required massive amounts of time and labour. Tens of millions of American women now worked forty hours a week, and needed a dishwasher because they no longer had time to do the dishes. Men needed powered everythings for the same reason. The time available to conduct the quiet family labours called 'home life' shrank, and then shrank some more.

Madison Avenue was trumpeting all this as the new, more affluent, sophisticated middle-class American life that everyone else was deliriously enjoying. Seeing is believing, and we could see it right there on the television screen: city people wearing bow ties were sipping martinis. I was so impressed by the snappiness of Gary Moore's bow tie that I got hold of one—a clip-on bow tie—and wore it to school. Naturally, I was laughed out of the joint for looking like Alfred E. Neuman of *Mad* magazine, which I did. Unfortunately, I was wearing that bow tie in the only school yearbook picture I ever had taken. Thus my contemporaries from those days are still laughing.

Television's urban sophisticates also cracked jokes, which we rural peasants didn't quite get, about 'taking a spritz' and traffic on 'the freeway'. Shapely women in matador pants threw up their hands and widened their eyes in near-sexual delight at the sight of Dad's sizzling meat on the newest rage, the backyard grill, as he stood there in a barbecue apron and a ridiculous chef's hat. Television, we knew, didn't lie. Somewhere out there were smiling men who actually wore aprons and such contraptions on their heads. And, to be certain, a record number of Americans were owning more stuff than ever in history.

The closest resemblance on TV to the households in which we lived came from the show *Lassie*. And even then, Jeff's mum, Ellen, never seemed to work very hard and, as my mother observed, 'She definitely gets her hair done every week.' Not to mention that the dog was smarter than the entire human family that owned it. But lest we felt inferior when our own family mutt pissed on the rug, there was always Jeff's obese, dim-witted playmate, Porky, and his hopeless Bassett hound, Pokey, who ate dirt and slept through farmhouse burglaries.

Forgive me for being so anecdotal as to cite a television show. I cannot help myself—I'm an American. TV owns my brain as much as it does anyone else's. Americans were the first to feel TV's full impact upon culture; the first to become fully saturated and mutated by the medium they had created, and in turn to be recreated by the medium itself. The only reason I have some idea of TV's effect on America is because I am among that dwindling older minority who started out in life without it. And they don't care to discuss it at the moment because they're too busy watching television.

Anyway, while Jeff's mum, Ellen, was getting her hair done, my own mum was on the night shift at one of Winchester's woollen mills or garment factories, and my brother, sister, and I were watching commercials for Swanson's TV dinners while we ate Swanson's TV dinners with gusto. Having a TV dinner to eat was our best-case scenario. At worst, it was mayonnaise sandwiches and 'coffee bread'—white bread soaked in coffee—because there was nothing else in the house to eat. I've laughed about this with many working-poor whites and blacks of my generation who ate those same things. 'The secret to a good mayonnaise sandwich was relish,' says my black friend George. 'If you had some pickle relish to scrape out of the jar onto the bread, you had a pretty good mayo sandwich. But you couldn't let the little kids see that, or there'd be no relish for your next sandwich.' We laugh about all that now because there's no use crying over it.

WE MAY HAVE COME TO SETTLE IN WINCHESTER, but we never came to settle in any one particular place. There was North Kent Street, Cameron Street, Boscawen Street, a different rented house or apartment every year or less, on a street named for some lord in England, always in the part of town nearest the railroad tracks. I can't remember a time in Winchester when the late-night trains' whistles didn't blow near our home, and it got so I would wake up at 11.10 p.m. if the Chesapeake and Ohio Railroad engine didn't blow its long, mournful airhorn. To this day, the sound is comforting to me.

Always these residences adjoined one of the two black neighbourhoods. The line between lily-white and black was clear to us because we were on the line—the redneck mongrels along a single street dividing white and black.

We were usually next door to other once-rural families similarly displaced after two centuries out on the farms ... the McKees and Brannons, the Braithwaites and Caves, the Campbells, Yosts, Luttrells, and McIlweees. And since we didn't much fit into the world of our neighbours on either side — blacks didn't even walk on the white streets in our neighbourhood, and white people on 'the right side of the railroad tracks' stayed out of our neighbourhoods — the very closest neighbours' children constituted our friendship groups. We had no trouble recognising each other on sight, or recognising new arrivals in town or at school, with their plaid-flannel Sears mail-order shirts and work shoes.

Another way that kids from the sticks knew one another was our special status in the school system. In what would now be called middle school, many of us were put in what was openly called 'the dumbbell room', a special classroom for sub-intelligent and back-country kids. I arrived in the sixth grade reading well above my pay grade — popular authors such as Pearl Buck, Bennett Cerf, and no few classics, simply because I couldn't differentiate as to types or levels of literature. All of it was marvellous stuff to me, whether *Moby-Dick* or Betty Macdonald's *Please Don't Eat the Daisies*. Yet here I was in the dumbbell room with so-called retards, fist fighters, and drooling crayon-eaters. The usual stated reason was 'behavioural problems'; although, given my timidity, I can't imagine having acted up in class. After a few weeks, I was back with the 'normal kids'. Ultimately, we little crackers came to see being in the dumbbell room simply as pulling your time in this new, citified system. According to Beaky

Anders, so named for his prominent nose, 'Aw, they're just seeing if they can crack ya.'

When a kid would make parole from the dumbbell room to regular class, there would be a hearty round of congratulations from the parolee's friends. Not all made it, though. I remember some who, despite the truancy laws, just disappeared — simply never showed up in school again. The official story was that they had moved.

Here we were, poor kids from poor families. We had cleared the first hurdle. Next year we would be seventh graders entering Hadley High School (which then also contained what we would now call middle school). At Hadley we would be told by the school superintendent, in an annual school 'boys' assembly' session, that we were legally free to quit school at the age of sixteen, reminding us that quitting would allow us to get jobs and make money. And that in only one more year we would be eligible to join the military. Lots of boys got up right then and walked out through the doors. I myself would later drop out of school and enter the US Navy. In a scant five years, many of us would be fighting in the jungles of some place called Vietnam. We were twelve years old.

HADLEY HIGH SCHOOL LOOKS BETTER THAN MANY of America's state capitols. It should. Hadley's 40-acre campus was designed by the Frederick Law Olmsted family of architects who designed Central Park. With typical Olmsted sensitivity to the natural beauty of the site, the school's long, tree-lined vistas and greenways lead the eye toward its cascading wide steps and up into the massive, white-columned portico. This viewscape was recently violated by a local real-estate developer's million-dollar gift to his alma mater, an outdoor sports facility on the front lawn. But based upon the architecture and remaining landscaping, it's obvious why Hadley is the only high school on the Register of Historic Places. Hadley is a rare bird in another way, too, because it is a 'privately endowed public school'—a public school with millions in an endowed trust. The endower was a Civil War–era judge named John Hadley, who left the equivalent of a million dollars in 1895, since grown into more millions, 'for education of the poor'.

After years of squabbling by local contractors, businessmen, and town leaders anxious to get a piece of the endowment-money action, the school was completed in 1925. As education went in those times, it represented the state of the art in both curriculum and facilities. To local business-class whites and elites, Hadley represented another opportunity beyond any piece of the trust money they might chip off for themselves—the opportunity to quit paying private high school fees, as was the common practice then. In the estimation of the high bourgeoisie steeped in the classist American South, the unwashed spawn of the poor were not capable of appreciating, much less benefiting from, such a school. So they appropriated it for themselves, and made it a bastion of Old Virginia traditions. The school reeked of heritage and dignity with its polished, hardwood-floored halls lined with busts of Confederate generals, founding fathers, and rolls of honour that listed graduates killed in war. It was a grand setting. Undoubtedly, the afternoons spent by the light of its eight-foot mullioned windows raised high to the summer's air while conjugating Latin verbs had some cultivating effect on young minds. But not much, and not on most of us.

To understand an American public school like Hadley, and its role in preserving class barriers, one has to understand a bit of American social history, and how long our republic has struggled to assure an adequate supply of dumbed-down proles for American labour—especially in Southern climes like my native Virginia/West Virginia. Dominated by an aristocratic upper class, state-supported public education arrived in our region nearly 100 years late. When a fund for public elementary education was finally established, it was to supplement teacher pay only, at five cents per student. Anyone who wanted their children to attend school free had to publicly declare themselves to be destitute and a pauper. Most working-class people had too much pride to stomach such grovelling. Beyond that, county commissioners would not approve children for school anyway, preferring to let the designated money accumulate in county coffers, a surplus always being a sign of their good management. Common citizens in small communities sometimes built 'field schools', the traditional little red schoolhouse, run by people with perhaps a high school education, but untrained as teachers. State and local elites did not want to pay the taxes associated with real public education, so the public went uneducated.

In the first quarter of the twentieth century, while judge Hadley's money was still sitting in trust, there was growing pressure for public education from an emerging business middle class. They wanted free public schooling for their children. By 1914, Virginia's political clique, dominated by descendants of the old aristocracy, finally accepted that some sort of state-supported public education was going to be unavoidable, even in the rural counties. That year saw sixty of Virginia's 95 counties organise rural school-aged males into 'boys corn clubs', wherein each boy planted, ploughed, weeded, and harvested an acre of corn in the name of education, which is still hailed in our state's education history as an era of staggering progressiveness. Not a penny of state money was spent; the federal government paid all the costs. Meanwhile, the children of the gentry continued to attend what were known as academies or 'classical schools'. Today, they attend even more exclusive Virginia private schools such as Powhatan elementary school (with fees of $17,000 per year) and Foxcroft high school ($40,000 per year).

So here I was, entering this fine high school endowed with what had grown into a multi-million dollar trust, and through the doors of which no black child was allowed to pass, on the grounds that a privately endowed school did not have to accept blacks. (High courts later ruled that, endowed or not, anything calling itself a public school and accepting public tax money had to accept blacks along with the money. With that, the school superintendent resigned.)

Back when the school was appropriated by the business class and town elites, they set in motion a continuing spirit and set of practices called 'the Hadley experience', an experience that back then did not include the sons and daughters of gas-station attendants and warehouse workers, or the labouring class of any sort. We were encouraged indirectly to drop out of school at the earliest legal age, and, as I said earlier, once a year directly by the school superintendent himself. Now elderly and retired, most of the teachers of that time swear there was no such bias. But a few of those still alive are not afraid to say otherwise. 'Those teachers, including me, were afraid to fall out of the middle class,' recalled Mr Dee, an elderly Hadley English teacher (since departed). 'That was a class-manufacturing system if ever there was one.'

'I never in my life thought I would be sitting here on your lawn talking about this subject,' I told Mr Dee. 'I'd never have guessed you ever thought about it.'

'Well, Joey, a few of us did. And, once in a while, one would speak out, and they wouldn't be back the following year. Me, I had a wife and a new baby and a new house, and was earning $4,000 a year. I had responsibilities to my family. And, you have to admit, you could get a good education at Hadley if you tried hard enough.'

'Ummm … I suppose so, but I don't think most adolescents are well enough equipped to get over such social hurdles,' I said.

'Those were not times when people considered sociological implications. It was a different system then.'

Soaked in my old man's aftershave and self-doubt, I walked into that high school system at the age of thirteen. And there was ole Beaky with his flattop haircut and buck teeth, sitting alphabetically in the desk in front of me because his last name began with the letter 'A'. We were no longer in the grammar school penitentiary; we were in the Big House now, by his estimation. He looked to be right. Senior high jocks scowled threateningly at you, or bumped you hard in the halls for laughs; the poorer-neighbourhood kids you already knew seemed to have turned surlier over the summer, some even challenging male teachers to fistfights in the classroom; pretty girls with genuine tits instead of wadded Kleenex looked at you like you had lice; and in the principal's office was a cricket bat used on your arse. It was labelled 'The Board of Education'.

'The best thing to do around here is to lay low,' Beaky advised. 'Blend in and look like a dumb fuck.'

That didn't seem too difficult. We dumb fucks were by far the majority. And, besides, there were some benefits to being a dumb fucker at Hadley High School. We had our own designated cigarette-smoking area under the school's front portico. I didn't smoke yet, but I bought a pack of cigs so I could hang out down there because in smoking there was a sort of weird class-solidarity.

In every classroom there were three or four of the kids for whom the school was meant. They dressed well, and made good grades without question, or even effort, as I later found out. One former classmate, now the inheritor of a large engineering company, said, 'I seldom opened a book, and would have flunked out, but there was always enough "extra credit work" for me, like taking down the set after a school play, that I got good-enough grades to get into college. And in college (at the good-ole-boy network called the University of Virginia), I was good at sports, and there was enough of a social network that I got by and even learned enough engineering to keep this company together.'

He was one of those fortunate few who played football, who went to away games with parents and friends, had money for milkshakes at the drugstore after school, lived in the brick houses up behind the school where there were no broken bottles in the dirt yards, and whose mothers and fathers attended school functions in cashmere sweaters or ties. These are all clichéd images, but true. It was the waning of the Fifties and the cusp of the Sixties—which arrived in Winchester, partially at least, in the Eighties.

School life offered a combination of insecurity, sexual longing, and continuing adolescent cruelty. It might be the 'Highland Gang', poor and working-class kids in the adjoining neighbourhood, who once hung me and a friend in a tree by our hands for a couple of hours. Or it might be the dreaded Frankie Anderson flopping his dick in your face in the locker room for amusement. Or my own neighbourhood's Grey Boyd simply beating somebody bloody senseless—even to the point of hospitalisation, in a couple of cases—out of pure boredom some afternoon on the way home ... I must admit that I took delight in hearing that Boyd is now serving 25 years in the state pen for some crime or other, doubtlessly violent.

Compared to many in the neighbourhood, though, I was lucky to escape much of the adolescent violence. I found refuge in the school and the city libraries. None of the Highland Gang would ever be caught in a library, so I was left in peace to read *Boy's Life Magazine*, the history of the Shenandoah Valley, Pericles' orations, Jack London, *Fur, Fish and Game* magazine, countless books on painting and great painters, Civil War diaries, *American Heritage*

Magazine, and old hardbound editions of *Lord of the Flies*, Richard Wright's *Native Son*, Dickens, Genet, Sartre, and Rimbaud—all in a marvellously undirected pursuit of the mind. I came to lust after the world that rolled away endlessly from the Shenandoah Valley. There was a world out there of grim or glorious cities, exotic ideas and peoples, and onrushing progress. With the impending entry of mankind into outer space, it was as if I could feel like the churning dynamo of my own century. It made me optimistic. It seemed to be a great time to be alive, a fortunate time to be born—as long as I stayed inside the library walls.

HOT DAMN, TIME FOR ANOTHER EDUCATIONAL FILM! Another chance to get out of regular class for about 45 minutes. One good thing about town life was that the school system showed lots of so-called educational films. All through the 1950s and 1960s, American public schooling was packed with propaganda films. They didn't die out until the 1980s, when they became too laughable for even the worst educators to stomach. More than 3,000 were made and shown in American classrooms.

There was *Shy Guy*, extolling the message that fitting in with society's most urban conventions was the key to social happiness. In *Shy Guy*, a new kid in school, named Phil, is lonely because the other kids avoid him. Dad teaches Phil to study the most popular boys and girls, and to buy the same clothing that the other guys buy, and basically to kiss arse all the way in order to achieve social success. Girls had their own versions of these 'conformity films', according to Megan Stemm-Wade in *The American Dream in Postwar Classroom Films*. One was *Habit Patterns,* starring an obviously lower-class girl named Barbara. She learns to improve her chances by buying the same clothing as her more affluent classmates and learning to talk like a 'middle-aged art patron': 'I've bought tickets to the entire concert series' ... 'I just love the museum, they have a wonderful costume exhibit.' Barbara resolves to changes her habit patterns. The narrator lauds her decision, but cautions her to stay the course, because 'you know how quickly you can be left out of the crowd'. Be left out of what crowd? Recently, I saw old group photos of those sixth- and seventh-grade classes. Fifty years later, I can see that perhaps six of those kids managed to live the mannered middle-class consumer lifestyle portrayed in the conformity films.

Corporations such as Coca-Cola, General Motors, and Kimberly-Clark sponsored many of these films, selling their food products through dating and dinner-etiquette versions, and their cars through driving instructions (the Ford Galaxie and Fairlane seem to have been favourites) with what then passed for subtlety.

But the most club-fisted of all had to be the capitalist 'concept films'. The American Petroleum Institute's *Destination Earth* exalted petroleum as the key to civilisation through the free-market system, and taught youth that buying a car was the way to battle communist despotism. In *Destination Earth,* a Martian is sent to Earth in order to discover the secret to America's greatness. His research shows that petroleum products and the free market are what makes America the greatest civilisation on the planet, and the reason why America has not succumbed to communism. Overcome with gratitude and excitement, the Martian not only carries the message back to his planet, but also destroys the totalitarian 'Masters of Mars', bringing democracy to his own planet.

There was no way I could buy the right sweaters like the lonely Phil in *Shy Guy* did ... or ever hear any of our family's dinner conversation resemble the white middle-class model in the films ('Fä-<u>th</u>ər, would you please pass me a baked pə tāt'ō?'). But, even though I had not the slightest interest in cars or driving (I didn't get a driver's licence until I was 36), I was damned well against a Martian-style communist dictatorship right here on Planet Earth!

My friend Beaky felt the same, but posed the question, 'Zactly how do you know a communist when you see one?'

We both agreed that Marvin, the only effeminate male member of the sixth grade (who came out as gay thirty years later, after getting about as far from our burg by land as is possible—San Jose, California), was probably a communist.

At that young age, we felt no need to worry about those filthy communist nations across the waters. We had atomic bombs. And, by feeling such confidence, we proved ourselves to be America's first thoroughly government-brainwashed generation. Eventually, I read Nevil Shute's *On the Beach*, and lost confidence in nuclear weapons; in doing so, I was joining the previous generation, though I didn't know it.

Horrified by Hiroshima and Nakasaki, a majority of our parents and grandparents had felt that America should give up its nuclear weapons after the war. Even Pap figured that, 'Now the atomic bomb has done its job, they need to put it where nobody can get their hands on it anymore.' In 1946, some 54 per cent of Americans thought that the United Nations should control all the world's major weapons, especially nuclear weapons, including those of the US. And a staggering 40 per cent endorsed some form of one-world government, according to Gallup polls of the period. That same year, fourteen states adopted the Constitution for the Federation of the World, as an expression of their belief in 'One World or None', and 'Peace in the World—or the World in Pieces'.

With much assistance from the military-industrial corporate complex, Americans eventually overcame their unreasonable fear of being vapourised or turned into staggering, cancer-ridden mutants. The Pentagon, Truman and, later, Eisenhower, spent many millions to reverse America's strong distaste for anything nuclear. Government advisers stressed that the key was to influence the next generation, the post-war babies—us. Thousands of programs in the public schools were funded to grab youthful minds. 'Friendly Atom' school programs and science clubs focusing on atomic energy sprang up in nearly every school in America.

Participants in the Friendly Atom programs consisted mainly of brainier, more upscale kids, the college-bound ones who'd be future technological and engineering majors in universities. Certainly not Beaky, who called it a good day in school if he didn't get sent to detention; nor me, who harboured a secret fear of maths that took decades to overcome. The Friendly Atom program was social-class selective in choosing its friends. We understood that.

'Atoms in the Schools' worked. We learned to accept the atom so well that we are now deep into our fifth nuclear war without flinching. Or even noticing. However, I suspect Beaky flinches now at least a little, given that he has a grandson on his third 'rotation' in Iraq. Indeed, the last five US conflicts have been nuclear through their use of depleted uranium. Ever innovative, the military's happy solution to the problem of what to do with our nuclear waste turned out to be the production of millions of little radioactive weapons—the depleted-uranium, armour-piercing shells and other ordnances that have made stretches of Afghanistan, Iraq, and Yugoslavia horror zones of cancer and birth defects (over 1,000 tons were expended in the first month of the Iraq War alone, mostly in cities). Most Americans still do not know this; and those who do, could not care less.

But almost no Americans know that, for a few years at least, we were a nation that believed a peaceful world was possible through co-operation and humility, and were willing to prove it through disarming our own nation of all major weapons.

CHAPTER EIGHT

A Culture of Shame

Equality is simultaneously the greatest accomplishment and worst failure of America. It is the place where idealism and reality come to blows in American culture.
— Stanley Aronowitz

A fine old shotgun is an elegant thing—a thing that moves effortlessly up to the shoulder, so gracefully balanced on the left hand at the forestock, so symmetrical in its distribution of wood and steel that if floats skyward into the autumn sunlight as if naturally seeking the game at hand. It's one of those things that America once made well as a matter of course—one of those functional things in this world that employs the mind, body, and craftsmanship to create a momentary act of grace, a dance with the self, brief and elegant. I feel the same way about old handmade guitars. Such old guns and old guitars create a fourth dimension unto themselves, an American Zen, assuming that the man employing these things is up to their engagement.

The Harrington & Richardson double-barrel that Pap

bought in 1946 was such a gun, and by the winter of 1959 it had been passed on to my daddy in the knowledge that, like the two ancient 18th-century duelling pistols that Pap kept in a cedar chest at the foot of his bed, it would be handed down for generations—with me being the next in line—along with the hunting stories accompanying it in the mountain bardic tradition. December is a great hunting month in West Virginia, with the season open on all sorts of deer, small game, and birds in their prime. Couple that with the fact that Christmas also occurs in December, and you cannot imagine a more exciting month for a 12-year-old Appalachian boy. We always went Over Home on Christmas Day, both for the huge dinner celebration and the hunting.

In December 1959, we were living in Winchester in one of the many rented houses we'd occupy. This particular winter, Daddy was recovering from a heart attack. Unable to 'drive truck' anymore, he'd managed to find a job at a garage that, besides doing mechanical work on vehicles, involved running its car wash (although rushing, stooping, and stretching around a car or truck with a washing mitt, sometimes in the dead of winter, certainly must have been more strenuous than sitting in the cab of a big rig). He was tired and drawn, and there was a feeling in the air that we would be moving again when the rent came due. The garage job barely bought groceries and kept the lights on. As for medical bills, they piled up as he made weekly payments on them, on the terms of 'whatever you can afford each week'. Though there was often no interest on medical bills back then, 'whatever you can pay' carried the assumption that you had something left over after food, rent, and utilities to pay with.

Still, it was the Christmas season. And that meant going Over Home and cutting a 'nigger pine' Christmas tree, tying it onto the car, and bringing it home. 'Ain't no Christmas tree prettier than a West Virginia nigger pine,' the old man would declare every single year. Nigger pine is the colloquial name for Scrub Pine (*Pinus virginianus*), a spare, scraggly-looking thing, especially when used as a Christmas tree. Like those of us who remember it as the yellow-needled Christmas tree of our youth, it manages to grow, even in the poorest of conditions. Along with the wild red cedar, the lowly nigger pine was the Christmas tree of the hill-and-mountain country. Each wild red cedar was said to hold the spirit of a vanished American Indian standing in silence to watch the white man. I still cannot pass these lone cedars in the high, dead hillside grass of winter without imagining an Indian wrapped in a blanket with his arms crossed, a silent sentinel of the ages. But it is the lowly nigger pine that most often elicits memories of childhood in my father's generation of hill people. And in me, too. The gaping stretches between the straggly branches were filled in with strings of bubble lights—tubular tree-lights filled with brightly lit bubbling liquid—and glittering strands of metallic icicles. Ugly as they were in retrospect, the remembrance of them still summons the spirits of the season.

Also summonsed was the short, mild argument between my mother and father about the proper application of the pieces of tinsel. My father held that standing back and tossing them on gave a more natural look; my mother was for placing them individually for a better aesthetic. So he did half of a thirty-cent box of tinsel his way, and she did the remaining half her way. The three of us kids split a box and were left frozen in indecision as to which way to put them on, as both parents watched to see which way we were going to choose—the stand-back-and-let-her-rip method, or artful placement. But you knew Christmas Eve was here for sure when you heard the testimonial to the beauties of the humble nigger pine and the snippy exchange about tinsel application.

'I'm Robert the Robot, the mechanical man, guide me and steer me wherever you can.' The scratchy, tinny voice of the ten-inch-high toy robot repeated the sentence continuously as it blinked its red plastic eyes and rolled around on tiny-wheeled feet under the Christmas tree. A long, thin wire connected Robert to the battery-powered control box in my hands. Being 1959, it was the beginning of the 'Space Age'. All things alien, electro-mechanical, and futuristic, even those as boxy and clunky as Robert the Robot, symbolised a marvellous, unlimited, technological future America: rockets, robots, jet-like fins on earthbound automobiles …

More than I had ever wanted anything in my life, I'd wanted Robert the Robot. Now I actually had him. Which was astounding because, first of all, in our house there was no 'What do you want Santa to bring you for Xmas?' We got whatever the hell Santa decided to bring, and we knew it. And his tastes seemed to lean toward cheap little stamped-metal cars and especially bags of plastic 'cowboys and Indians', with those strange bowed legs that allowed them to be placed onto the horses. If you were really lucky you got a few cavalrymen in the deal, or a couple of brown plastic palisades of a log fort. But in testimony to a gun-loving tradition, you also *always* got a cap pistol, however small and cheap, and a box of paper caps so you could smoke up the house with burning sulphur, while shooting it out from behind the couch or under the kitchen table for the rest of the day. Girls got teensy plastic plates and cups, and the like. Their equivalent of the cap pistol was a small tin stove with painted-on burners. Moreover, we were being trained to participate in the two most important mountain-folk survival skills—cookin' and shootin'.

By midday Christmas that year, our extended family was Over Home. And as the men assembled on the porch to go hunting, just like on any other Christmas, I saw that my father was carrying a shotgun borrowed from an uncle. Nobody had to tell me what had happened. I just knew: he'd sold the Harrington & Richardson to buy the toys we'd received. A sick feeling came over me. For maybe the first time, I realised the trade-off that was going on between town life and the old life. I did not realise it fully, but I understood that my father, too, felt the pressure to provide something resembling the new 'have-everything society', or at least some small part of it for his kids.

It was complex. On the one hand, when everyone did the 'What didja get for Christmas?' routine upon our returning to school, I wouldn't be embarrassed in answering, for the first time since we'd moved to town. Early on, I'd learned to be embarrassed about nearly any material comparison with town families, and had learned to avoid most of them simply by staying within my own social class, which I was slowly figuring out. But when teachers asked students to stand up and tell their classmates what they'd got for Christmas, it was unavoidable. So usually I lied, and that had been working just fine. I'd seen fresh-from-the-country kids like myself do the same thing. But this time was different. In a rare instance of getting a material thing I wanted, I could feel that it was at the cost of sacrificing part of my family heritage. Over a lifetime in America, I would come to learn that in gaining material things and advantages, I would always be sacrificing, or at the very least hiding, my roots and my people's way of life. And I would continue to do so for another forty years before I broke through American materialism's shame barrier. Come to think of it, 'broke through' is not really the right term. So let me rephrase it, and say that it took until I finally got so exhausted and felt so hollowed out by this kind of relentless experience that I just gave it up. There was no act of moral courage involved—just fatigue. Shame is exhausting.

SINCE THEN, I'VE HAD PLENTY OF TIME TO THINK about the American culture of shame, and down here in my basement I am yet offered another opportunity. Under the yellow glare of a bare bulb with the automatic washer rattling through its spin cycle, I am looking at a rusty old corn-cutter fashioned from a Confederate sword. Alongside it on the concrete floor lies a picture of Jesus painted on an inch-thick slice of a pine log. More than twenty years ago, I gathered up these artefacts from both sides of my family: photos, old letters, war medals, tools used by ancestors ... Pap's pocket knives and dollar watches, the afore-mentioned piece of 'log slice art' that once hung in my grandparents' living room, a bell scraper used to remove hair from scalded hog carcasses, Bibles, my mother's journals and diaries ... Civilian Conservation Corps Camp memorabilia, papers of indenture, ancestral revolutionary war documents and Civil War letters ... and two gaudy, fringed silk-pillow covers sent home by uncles from Okinawa and Hawaii during the war in the Pacific. And photo albums: I created one for each person's life, dead or still living. Ultimately, I bought an antique trunk, put everything in it—artefacts and photo albums—and said to myself, 'Aha! An heirloom trove for future generations.'

That trunk remains unopened in the basement, except when I perform my yearly mould checks on its contents, enduring both the insult of the busted lawn chair under which it rests and the family's general lack of interest. Through no fault or failing of their own, neither my son at Berkeley law school nor my daughter at Cornell University—both of whom were raised in the western US—find any personal connection with the trunk's contents, the people's stories it contains, or the relics of the place that their old man and nine generations before him grew up in.

Blame it on geography. These days, most Americans rather accidentally grow up in one location or another, in what author James Howard Kunstler called the 'geography of nowhere'. It is unidentifiable by any uniqueness or specifics other than slight differences in very broad attributes, such as the age or size of a suburb, and the number of its malls, plus practical considerations such as commuting distances to work, school quality, and property tax rates. These bland statistics, along with marketing attributes such as 'economic vitality', proximity to nightlife or outdoor recreation and cultural pursuits (most Chamber of Commerce marketing materials include the number of nearby mall Cineplexes as 'cultural assets') comprise 'the desirable life'. Overlay all this with a digital and technological commercial for Americanness, and you get what passes for a sense of place—that is, the United States of Consumer Commerce—the flashy, slick, and disposable society of immediacy. Thus, it seems perfectly reasonable that one old man's trunk of memories is a younger one's crate of junk. Especially in an age when few young folks can afford the kind of living space to accommodate said crate. I know of a young couple in Manhattan living in an apartment so small that they have to go sit on the fire escape when the cat takes a shit in the litterbox located under the kitchen table.

But when it comes to the old trunk, there is also an unspoken shame attending the cultural roots represented by the trunk's contents, located as they are in the South, and saturated as they are with white Christian fundamentalist culture. Southern or not, Christian or not, this culture of the commonplace is to be found in every state in America's non-urban and suburban stretches. Few care to claim the artefacts of hog scraping, Bible pounding, semi-literacy, and heartbreaking toil as their heritage. As I said, I spent much of my life denying them during my own on-again-off-again tenure in the suburban middle class—which, in part at least, must account for my children's aversion. Even allowing for my own failure in connecting my children with their roots, no doubt their lack of connectivity stems from the types of shame we learn by living in America.

The world of which I write is neither glossy nor entertaining compared to Wii or Second Life, except in the ways it can be made the butt of media humour. Lacking outer sophistication, its denizens snort and fart, drink, pray, and play the lottery, and it is streaked with as much sadness as beauty. Even its human beauty is of the wrong sort, and its inhabitants speak with the wrong accent in a dead language—the language of the profoundly ordinary, the commonality of place or preferences that are generations old. The first of these—commonness—is extraordinarily boring to modern, hyper-real digitised sensibilities. The second—connectivity over generations through abidance in shared, commonplace activities of sustenance—is utterly alien to most Americans. Fixing a vehicle together with your buddies, or attending a church where the preacher is a fellow you knew in grade school, or having an after-dinner smoke together at the kitchen table in your parent's house while you swap hunting stories with your dad, just as he did with his ... in a country whose entire public culture is media kitsch, these sorts of connectivity are bad taste, proof of being white trash or close to it. So here I sit, an old white guy in kinship with a trunkful of white-underclass heirlooms.

But at least my kinfolk and I are certifiable white underclass of the purest grade. I looked it up on the Internet, by golly, and was verified in pedigree by Professor Kim Pearson. A Princeton graduate and teacher at the College of New Jersey, she is teaching ADHD students how to make video games (and you thought video games were already hyper) in a project underwritten by Bill Gates. According to Peterson's online faculty page defining white trash, 'Males are perceived to be white trash if interested in stereotypically "manly or macho" things, such as sports, tattoos, body piercing … especially hunting and motor sports, guns, tobacco smoked and chewed, alcohol, mostly beer and sex.'

I can get behind most of that, except for the chewing of tobacco—a filthy practice if ever there was one. I'm a Camel smoker, myself. You can keep the body piercing, too. Having been stabbed with a kebab skewer once by a coke whore in Denver, I've not been keen on body piercings of any kind ever since. Be that as it may, piercing and tattoos are apparently a matter of class taste. For instance, we have a redheaded gal here in town named Rita whose nipples have been transformed into strawberries by the tattooist's deft art. This qualifies as white trash, as low art, despite rave reviews from guys at the Twilight Zone Bar and Café—including her husband. On the other hand, the Asian spiritual tattoos of San Francisco's white culturati don't seem to count as trashy. I met a guy with what was apparently Mount Fuji on his back and two dragons on his arse, one per cheek, who was considered the embodiment of urban modernity. They say he had a piercing below his belt buckle that I don't even want to know about.

And finally, there's this one from Pearson: 'Females are perceived to be either very submissive or aggressive in their social behaviour.' That covers a helluva lot of women in this country, whether they are rattling their jewellery at the Met, or sucking down a Coors Light in the front booth of Buddy's Beer Barn. It's not an either/or proposition.

I've had women at parties kiss me on the cheek one minute and threaten to cut my whang off an hour later. Kimbo, we gotta talk about these definitions of yours.

Meanwhile, I think I'll grab these two fringed silk pillow-covers, one emblazoned with 'Mother, Queen of My Heart' and the other with two big-titted hula girls, and put them on my living-room sofa.

OK, Bageant, have your fun at Ms Pearson's expense. But, remember, she has a steady job. You don't.

Good point. The whole white-underclass thing centres on jobs, doesn't it? And to have an underclass you must have a middle class, right? So exactly who's in the underclass?

Being middle class has nothing much to do with how much money you make. Pimps make a bundle; they aren't middle class. So do narcotics dealers; they aren't considered middle class, either — unless they're sales representatives for pharmaceutical giants. For all practical purposes and to most Americans, regardless of race, the term 'middle class' means one thing: 'white'. More specifically, the agreed standard for appearance and behaviour is white: the ideal type is a male who's got a white spouse, white kids, and wouldn't be caught dead in a titty bar. And, most important of all, he's got a steady, white-collar job. Or, in some cases, a blue-collar job that pays more than most white-collar jobs.

Another way we define inhabitants of the underclass is as 'losers'. They are people who cannot talk, think, or act like middle-class professional and managerial workers; people who cannot even be posers. From reading research papers, I see that social scientists dislike plural nouns, and consequently shun the word 'losers'. So they call this the 'educational underclass'. Either way, it comes down to folks too woolly for office society. Nobody denies that the losers all deserve to have jobs. Just keep them away from the water cooler.

Yes, from the ages of eight to eighty, whether crippled, blind, or crazy, Americans do agree that every man or woman of reproductive age in America should have a full-time job. Except those women who manage to snag a wealthy man — they are exempt. So are the middle-class commissariat's own beer-guzzling spawn, the ones keeping the pizza joints and the all-night video arcades thriving in college towns across our republic. Middle-class college kids don't have to work. Not unless they flunk out.

When it comes to the underclass, there is no arguing that some people are members because they are so damned uneducated they cannot count their toes or read well enough to fill out a job application. Scientifically, this is called 'nobody's fault but their own'. Others are quite smart enough, but just don't care to do the smiling, grammatically correct, customer-service-zombie thing. They prefer swinging a bigger hammer than that — doing real work, like America used to do. And doing it without kissing arse, which is why they are called the 'permanently jobless'. As sociologist Christopher Jencks pointed out, 'There is no absolute standard dictating what people need to know in order to get along in society. There is, however, an absolute rule that you get along better if you know what the elite knows than if you do not.'

Feel free to call all of this anecdotal evidence — you won't be the first. I was on a National Public Radio show in

2008 with a couple of political consultants; demographers, as I remember. One, a woman, was obviously part of the Democratic political syndicate. The other was a soldier in the Republican political mob. The Democratic expert said dismissively of my remarks, 'Well! *Some* people here seem to believe anecdotal evidence is relevant.' Meaning me. I held my tongue. But what I wanted to say was this (lordee me, I feel a rant coming on!):

Sister, most of us live anecdotal lives in an anecdotal world. We survive by our wits and observations: some are casual; others, vital to our survival. That, plus daily experience, be it good, bad, or as ugly as the arse-end of a razorback hog. What we see happening to us and others around us is what we know as life, the on-the-ground stuff we must deal with or be dealt out of the game. There's no time for rigorous scientific analysis. Nor need. We can see the guy next door who's drinking himself to death because, 'I never did have a good job, just heavy labour, but now I'm all busted up, got no insurance and no job, and it looks like I'll never have another one, and I've got four more years to go before Social Security.' He doesn't need scientific proof. He doesn't need another job, either. He needs a cold beer, a soft armchair, some Tylenol PM, and a modest guarantee of security for the rest of his life. Freedom from fear, toil, and unnecessary pain.

And furthermore, sister, we cannot see much evidence that other, more elite people's scientific analysis of our lives has ever benefited us much. When you're screwed, you know it. You don't need scientific verification.

I wanted to say all that on the radio, but I didn't. The little white-guy mojo voice in my head told me not to.

So I just laughed good-naturedly. Like any other good American.

May God forgive me.

THERE PROBABLY SHOULD BE A LAW AGAINST rednecks drinking bourbon, because so many of us get argumentative on the stuff at the very least, and downright pugnacious at worst. Like Herman Melville's description of sea-going men, we enjoy 'the prospect of an exhilarating disturbance'. But since we invented bourbon, and since prohibition did nothing but put us in the moonshine business, there's little hope. Yes, I know this is a stereotype. Big deal. We Americans are all guilty of secret assumptions, which are nothing more than stereotypes, no matter how politically correct we appear outwardly. Especially about inner-city blacks and white-trash Americans. And besides, for all practical purposes, some of them are true. You don't meet many Muslim pig farmers, and you don't meet many blacks who yodel.

So when I found myself in a Hollywood, California bar behind eight shots of bourbon (which is admittedly exactly one shot too many), with two young media types, one Jewish and the other a Connecticut resident of white Anglo-Saxon Protestant descent, I couldn't resist. They were lamenting their tribulations in their attempts to meet 'the right kind of partner' in that city of 10 million. Which I assume, in their cases, meant the right liberal woman, but the WASP guy looked like he could have been talking about a male. I dunno. Even drunk, there's stuff I don't ask.

Instead, I asked, 'So would you marry somebody from a trailer court in West Virginia?'

After some hemming and hawing—'too many cultural differences', 'lack of mutual interests', etc.—it was clear that the answer was no.

'So, if she were really fun and really, really good looking, would you screw someone from a trailer court in 'bama?' (It's yammer like this that keeps me from ever making it as a serious literary type.)

'Probably,' they agreed.

Evidently, screwing is outside the box of cultural differences, although I've always found that it requires at least some 'mutual interest'.

Now if I had asked them, they would have told me in the high dudgeon of political correctness that they do not believe in stereotypes. No thinking person does. Right? This, despite the fact that thinking, liberal strongholds such as New York recently went through a 'white-trash chic' fashion trend, based mostly upon pop-media depictions of lower-working-class Americans.

When you look at depictions of poor and working-class rural whites, which are generated by the middle and upper middle class (since the working class, by definition, actually works, and does not write TV shows, popular literature, or manage the media), you can see the psychic conflict in the American mindscape. On the one hand, you get the working-class rural and small-town white as the perpetrator of all of white society's crimes, lynchings, the working-class soldiers' crimes at Abu Ghraib (as if the military gives you a choice in any matter whatsoever), racial hatred, and gun-owning people prone to violence.

These depictions allow urban middle- and upper-class Americans to vicariously enjoy the violence, lewdness, and rule-breaking of the white trailer-trash stereotype, and at the same time to feel superior and guiltless about such things as racism (despite the fact that the country was built on slavery, either directly, as in the south, or indirectly in the northern textile mills that purchased slave-picked cotton, and despite the fact that the middle and upper classes still benefit to this very day from the foundational wealth that such oppression created). Openly reviling 'trailer trash' or redneck culture—and it is a legitimate American culture of its own—also serves as an offset to their own inner classism.

On the other hand, they get nostalgic, idealised depictions of good and pure country folk in a simpler life or time, in order to reassure themselves that there is some essential aspect of white people, an unarguable goodness and purity, an agrarian nobleness. Of course, they would never do a lick of such work themselves, but it's nice to know that some white people may still be capable of it. And so the white sweating classes provide dramatisations of guilt, and good and evil, for the educated, empowered class.

Lest the noble, bawdy bumpkins themselves forget their roles in the national drama, they are tele-prompted, as it were, by tabloid TV: by *The Jerry Springer Show*'s hair-pulling fights between married working-class women and their husband's young blonde piece of sexual side-action, or by regular segments on the *Maury* show that answer such questions as, 'Guess who the real daddy of this white-trash child is?' The implication, of course, is that the mother is a slut, causing every male viewer to secretly assess her physical assets. ('Nope, too fat for me,' we silently think. 'If she'd lay off the cream-filled Ho-Hos and beer, though, she wouldn't be all that bad.') Then Maury Povich leers into the camera: 'Stay tuned! We'll be right back after the commercial, with the DNA results!' Povich says the same thing every damned week, and nobody finds it even a little strange, much less ludicrous.

For the middle and upper classes, the great soup of working-class imagery represents what they fear falling into: social instability and loss of status. While the middle class fears such loss, the true elites could not give a damn. As Gore Vidal has pointed out in one of his essays, the CEOs of the major networks admit that they do not watch television at all — just the ratings.

I don't know if working-class whites have always been scapegoats of the educated classes, but they certainly have been so all of my lifetime. For the past forty years, the tool most often used to mock or denigrate my people has been political correctness. And the cornerstone of political correctness is race. White, rural, working-class people — especially the Southern working class and 'white trash' — are supposed to be the bedrock of racism. Being stereotyped as such has definite rural connotations, such as white southern farmers in Ku Klux Klan robes. Yet the Klan of the Reconstruction era was founded and led by upper-class whites, who invented and supervised the violence and terror inflicted upon blacks to protect the status quo. And they depended upon the uneducated whites (to whom they purposefully denied education through their refusal to fund public education in the south — partly because they did not want to pay the taxes, and partly to keep labour cheap by pitting blacks against whites for work). But, as the years went by, it became imprudent for upper-class people to head up the local Klan that protected their financial and political interests (is there a difference?). So, decades later, by which time the machine they had designed and set in motion was still lynching and burning, the elites had quietly receded back into their social positions and educations: their hands were clean.

According to popular history, it was white working-class racists who killed those little black girls in the 1963 Birmingham, Alabama church bombing. But the truth is that most lower-class whites did not behave especially cruelly toward blacks. That they did so is a class myth. Utter bullshit. Their innate cruelty was no more or less than that of their descendants, or Hispanic or black Americans who now perpetrate atrocities on Muslims in Iraq and Afghanistan at the bidding of another generation of elites and their institutions. It was the Supreme Court elites who upheld *Plessy v. Ferguson* in 1896, and thus the practice of segregation.

It was legislative elites who created Jim Crow—under which, incidentally, poor whites were also purposefully prohibited from voting, through property-owning requirements and poll taxes. My own father would not have been allowed to vote in Virginia until 1966, when the Supreme Court struck down Virginia's poll taxes and property requirements for voting (*Harper v. Virginia Board of Elections*). There was and still is a tremendous fear that poor and working-class Americans might one day come to understand where their political interests reside.

Personally, I think the elites worry too much about that. We dumb working folk were clubbed into submission long ago, and now require only proper medication for our high levels of cholesterol, enough alcohol to keep the sludge moving through our arteries, and a 24/7 mind-numbing spectacle of titties, tabloid TV, and terrorist dramas. Throw in a couple of new flavours of XXL edible thongs, and you've got a nation of drowsing hippos who will never notice that our country has been looted, or even that we have become homeless ourselves. We can always hijack someone else's cable TV and lug it into the cardboard box we call home. And, besides, there's always bourbon.

CHAPTER NINE

Lunchpails and Laptops

On a clear spring day, before the intervening trees flushed out in leaves, I could see the slate rooftop of Doctor Milton Racey's house from my tenement's upstairs-bedroom window. Unbelievable as it seems, there was a time when doctors and attorneys did not necessarily wall themselves off from the front yards and Saturday-night domestic scraps of the sweating classes. And so, in 1959, the home of the doctor who had delivered me in 1946 was in visible sight. By all accounts he was one of the most prosperous MDs in town, despite having been paid variously in potatoes, yard work, plucked chickens, slivers of land, and other such things over his long career. Doc Racey's fee for dragging my screaming arse into the light had been an exorbitant $100—and for a Caesarian birth at that—because the US army was writing the cheque. The good doctor, in any case, lived close enough that my old man could walk a five-dollar payment over to his house on payday, and Doc Racey would likewise walk over to our house when we came down with the croup or pink eye.

As a kid, knowing that such an educated, prosperous man lived so near to our shabby apartment was somehow comforting. I found the sight of his roof, and the occasional sound of classical music drifting from his weathered brick house in the dusk, quietly heartening. It was a sort of reminder of something that even a poor boy might possibly aspire to, given an education. And so I would open a library book, and, in a very studied pose, sit on my ratty bed and read, one ear cocked to the faint strains of an *étude* or *adagio cantabile* drifting from Doc Racey's — without the slightest damned notion of either — and fantasise about becoming a man of art and letters. An educated man like Doc Racey.

Not that the working folks we knew generally aspired to an education — especially a higher education. They didn't, and I didn't. (My man-of-letters day-dream was not an aspiration, but a passing fantasy, like being a knight or a cowboy.) Such things as going to university are not contemplated when you go all the way through the public school system without ever hearing it suggested or mentioned even once. Beyond that, we vaguely understood that college was prohibitively expensive, out of reach for our kind. This is not to say that we didn't have a few Horatio Algers among us. And I am sure that the town's class-denying local feudal families and their arse-kissing minions will point them out in *The Winchester Star*'s letters to the editor after this book's publication.

Families like mine and those of my friends were still connected to the pre-war working-class tradition and its assumptions. And one assumption was that we could always make some sort of a living — pay the bills, at least—without being very educated, or even very bright, for that matter. All you had to do was show up faithfully and work very hard, and your future security was assured. If you needed proof of that, you could read it nearly every day in *The Winchester Star*, whose owner, Senator Harry Flood Byrd, authored the worst of American anti-union legislation—still in effect today—not to mention a Virginia poll tax, and a voter-literacy test for blacks and poor whites who were known to be 'uppity' that was sometimes written in Chinese. 'There's always plenty of work for any man who is not lazy,' attested people such as the noble senator.

Our assumption about jobs was reinforced by the booming war years, when people like my mother, who'd been bereft of even a high school education, had worked in defence-plant offices at the age of fifteen. A high school education seemed more than adequate to us, considering the jobs available in east coast agricultural and manufacturing-based towns like Winchester. As my cousin Ronnie later speculated, when we both found ourselves married as teenagers with a child apiece, 'We can always work the docks [load and unload trucks and railcars] if we can't find anything else.' Forklifts hadn't come along yet, and a slew of Americans worked at lifting and moving things everywhere. I would come to unload many a truck and boxcar in my early twenties, and Ronnie ended up driving a forklift for much of his working life. Overall, making a working-man's living seemed to require little education. Even during the 1960s and early 1970s, I had a few janitorial and construction bosses who could not read or write. Common working-class life took a strong back, not brains. 'Back work' and rote production work, and hard work of all kinds, were just part of plain American life in a plain American town. Nor was anyone ashamed of working as a janitor or a loader of trucks and railcars for a living. The main thing was to work as hard as possible. That's what made a man a real man.

Looking back, the only compliment my father ever paid me came after I'd dug a fifty-foot-long, three-foot-deep ditch with a pick and shovel. He said 'Boy, you are a good worker.' As a pre-teen and teenager I'd won a youth talent medal from an artist guild for a nature painting, and had won many other drawing and painting awards, using homemade materials scrounged from house paint cans, canvasses cut from discarded truck tarps, and the like. Yet the one and only acknowledgement of pride in his son was for my digging of a ditch. And it made me burst with pride when he said it. I didn't know fathers ever complimented their kids for anything—I'd never seen it done. Now, I understand that it was the only kind of compliment he knew how to give. Moreover, it was probably a blessing, because I've never been unemployed a day of my life that I did not want to be.

Over my lifetime, I've seen personal dignity in plain, honest labour sucked right out of the workplace through job fears, miserable non-union wages, and worker anonymity. As times changed—in school, church, and on the job—we started hearing about 'the work ethic' and the social respectability that accompanies it. In place of the old inner dignity that came with the willingness to labour hard and sincerely, we were issued artificial job titles as status markers. Everybody was suddenly an engineer: garbage men became sanitary engineers; and janitors became building engineers. Salesmen became account representatives, and the bill collector became a customer representative. My old man worked at a gas station that had three employees, one for each shift. All of them pumped gas, fixed flat tyres, and did at least some car repairs. They were all paid the same money by the old drunk who owned the place and spent his time swilling the profits at the American legion beer hall. But my dad was the 'service manager'. During summers, I'd help my old man 'bust down truck tyres' from their rims at the gas station, working under a sign that read 'Tyre Technician on Duty'. As a teenager, I thought the title was cool, and said so. 'Words is cheap,' Dad answered. 'No matter what you call it, you can't get ahead bustin' tyres for $45 a week.'

We did, however, know a few families of veterans like my father who were getting ahead—some by getting a union job with good wages in the naval shipyard down in Norfolk and, in a couple of rare instances, by getting a college education on the GI Bill. But the odds of veterans using the much-touted GI Bill of Rights for college were not good for most working-class veterans. Which meant most veterans. Twenty-five per cent of World War II inductees were found to be illiterate at a time when the standard for literacy set by the US Census was completion of a fourth-grade education. No wonder my old man made staff sergeant so fast—with a sixth-grade education, he must have looked like a genius. Of the 16 million Americans who served in World War II, 2.2 million attended college on the bill. So, yes, the much-vaunted GI Bill did produce the first college graduates in many American families, especially African–American families. Others attended vocational schools, too.

The writers of our social history and media—which in this country are the same thing—haven't let us forget about it since. When any modest and just move toward social progress is made in America, even if it is fifty years behind the rest of the industrialised world, there is a tendency to ballyhoo it for the next hundred years as a triumph for all of mankind, steadily adding layers of mythology with time.

My alarm clock-radio awakened me this morning with a promotion for a National Public Radio special broadcast about 'How the GI Bill helped build the most powerful economy on earth.' Which is either a coincidence, or the thing that initiated these remarks about the bill. Either way, such a summary still comes down to state propaganda.

Everything in America, especially education, must be reckoned by its quantified value to the economy of the state. Learning for learning's sake is considered more or less laughable by ordinary Americans. All learning is now subject to corporate state amortisation. Thus as America now closes the books on two million veterans of World War II now dead or retired, it finds them to have been black ink on the ledger book.

But the other side of the ledger is this: far more of those people were victims of America's post-war class undertow. And their descendant generations are still feeding from the bottom of the employment pool, competing with foreign immigrant workers for the last available jobs in America (all three of them). Recently I was informed by a local businessman that, 'They're not economic victims—they're a bunch of losers!'

Maybe so, but not as he meant. That rural generation, equipped more often than not with less than a high school education, strong backs, and the ability to endure the toil accompanying farm life, were losers in a new race they weren't equipped for. They lost in the competition for the perceived conveniences of industrial, urban society. Most of these conveniences turned out to be the chief contributors to our continuing energy-sucking ecological and economic disaster, but that's another story.

MEANWHILE, AS WE OF THE HEARTLAND'S DESTINED-to-sweat class (along with no few millions of labourers in the big cities) were straining the limits of our educations to use the new-fangled *TV Guide*, the smarter bugs were swarming elsewhere to build colonies of their own. The cognitive elite, as we'd call them today, were aggregating in universities, scientific laboratories, publishing, and financial institutions. They were bright folks who understandably enjoyed each other's company much more than beer drinking and arm-wrestling contests with the rest of us out in the lonelier reaches of the nation. Predictably enough, they married their own kind—the better-educated sort with a sense of dental hygiene and a reasonably attractive number of teeth—and raised similarly bright children in neighbourhoods of like couples. From that point, all it took was social, political, and professional networking and a diligent-enough sex life for them to eventually become a class apart.

Minority that they were and still are, they considered themselves the majority. When they looked around their communities, they saw themselves. They saw people who had read a good book recently, people who understood the ramifications of compound interest, or office politics, and the pitfalls of consuming cheese fondue too close to bedtime. Not a bus driver or carpet layer or food-service worker was in sight. Nary a Hank Williams record played in the distance. America, to them, was Scarsdale or Brookline or, in the case of Winchester, the Washington and Stewart Street neighbourhoods, or a variation thereof, where everyone's job consisted of fiddling around with whatever type of paperwork their degrees designated, in as self-serious and well dressed a manner as possible.

To us these were not real jobs, mind you, not the kind that made you sweat bullets, but rather the fun kind we saw on television: the ones with pretty, wise-cracking secretaries who seemed to regulate office traffic in riotously enjoyable workplaces. The kind of workplace that Dick Van Dyke had on TV. They sure looked like they were getting smarter. Richer, too. I remember my family's amazement when Van Dyke's wife, Laura, bought a $30 outfit: 'A clothes horse is what that woman is!' declared my old man. But I'm sure he thought to himself: 'Nice legs, though.' These 'middle class' people on television, who invariably lived Up North somewhere, played tennis and golf and ate things like chicken a la king, whatever that was ... well, they were definitely 'holding the good end of the stick', as they say.

Here at the other end of the stick, in places such as Winchester, Virginia and the Stockyards neighbourhood of Cleveland, and working-class environs large and small, the opposite seemed to be happening. Somehow, we were becoming dumber and more given to consumer spectacle. Arm wrestling, and the even that good old staple 'The Saturday Night Fights', could no longer hold our increasingly debased attention spans. Television doubtless played a part. But somewhere along the way, speed and stupidity were added to the mix, begetting NASCAR. No culture in which NASCAR flourishes can possibly last another decade. But then, I've been thinking that for thirty years.

As I said earlier, there were exceptions within our class. A few blue-collar people in town managed to get degrees, even advanced degrees. Whereupon they fled town screaming, 'Thank God almighty, free at last!' Although a few did return to Winchester to take up the whip of the management class at local banks and factories, most fled to more upscale realms, where presumably they mowed their lawns in Madras shorts and anticipated their 6.00 p.m. highballs. The rest of us stayed here, or moved to places similar to Winchester chasing employment, and continued to breed our own sturdy-if-dull stock in an atmosphere where the values of hard physical work prevailed, mainly because we were destined to hump the heavy stuff for the rest of our lives anyway. If you must sweat like a mule to earn your beer, you might as well call it a value. Of course, we had the work ethic and our new job-titles to comfort us. I once was promoted from 'brick hog' (which involved crawling into a kiln cooled down to 150 degrees while wearing a 75-pound asbestos suit, to pick up bricks spilled from a kiln railcar) to 'surface applicator'. Which meant that I coloured one side of bricks with a chunk of white chalk all day in the blazing Virginia sun. Once or twice I passed out, but at least I was not passing out inside a furnace. The brickyard's manager, an otherwise kind Jewish fellow and a third-generation college graduate from New England, looked down on all this from his air-conditioned office.

It is most politically incorrect in America to suggest that we are not born equally endowed. Yet I cannot help but contemplate what effect, if any, the flight of several generations of the brightest kids from heartland labouring America has had on the working-class gene pool. Or, for that matter, the consequences of the selection process that goes all the way back to the 18th century, when our mountain people were selected by the English landed gentry to fell trees, plough, and take Indian scalps along their frontier holdings. (It was whites who invented the practice of scalping Indians, in order to show proof of having killed an Indian, to collect the bounty price on dead native Americans.)

As any dog breeder can tell you, slow wit can be bred in as easily as bred out. This may even help explain the popularity of such things among my class as snowmobiles, Garth Brooks, hot chicken wings, and deep-fried pickles. Or the inexplicable willingness of people to wear foam-rubber cheese wedges on their heads and display threatening tribal sports slogans on their exposed beer bellies in freezing weather at football games.

Whatever the case, today we are unarguably looking at a porcine white underclass—one far, far larger than is acknowledged by our media, which are obsessed with the Latino and black portion of the American underclass, mainly because colour coding the class struggle enables even the ditziest airhead anchorperson to connect the dots. And, let's face it, street-gang killings make for better TV ratings than, say, watching Cousin Ronnie out there on the back porch cooking weenies on his electric bug zapper for his family's dining amusement. For those interested, cooking time is measured in seconds, and *never* try a whole chicken breast. Still, as my sainted father used to say, 'Ignernt is ignernt. Some people just never amount to nothin', and he's one of 'em!'

Most of the white underclass may not be chortling in the glow of a bug zapper, but enough ignernce prevails to sustain the heartland's delirious happiness with all things Wal-Mart — assuming we ever see enough money again to go shopping. Don't be fooled by their Discount Dockers and the polo shirts ($14.50 and $8.00 respectively at Wally's). The guy wearing them probably owns a bug zapper.

A white underclass has always existed in the US, but who would have guessed that it would become the biggest class? Whether in Australia, Austria, or France, capitalism has always required some sort of an underclass. We Yanks are just better at doing it to death. But regardless of media-manufactured hallucinations, in this country only one class is paying half a week's wages or more for a single doctor visit (more than a week's wages if medical testing is involved) to a member of an upper class.

But, like I said, the smart bugs flyeth from the wretched nest. American universities have always cherry-picked the brightest of the bright from our burgs and crossroad towns, our cheesy working-class housing developments, to run up their college application scores and, in the new American financial order, to indenture them into decades of student-loan debt slavery. I write this while sitting in the apartment of my son, Patrick, who is at Berkeley law school in California. He is doing his summer internship with a corporate law firm—earning $3,000 a week, fer chrissake! Even he calls it 'obscene compensation'. Pat will owe over $100,000 in student loans, plus interest, the day he leaves Berkeley. That pretty much ensures he will be forced to stay within the ranks of the Empire's legal commissariat if he is ever to pay off the student loan. I kid him that he now has an official licence to steal money from the slobbering masses. He promises not to steal more than he can spend. Pat's a brilliant young man, modest, thrifty, and kind. I'm happy for and proud of him. But still, it's debt-enforced class flight. It leaves the slower bugs to simmer in their own little genetic pond. Kind of like the Uighurs hedged in by China's dominant Hans, who can't get a date outside their own neighbourhood for ten generations. (There goes the Uighur readership market. My apologies to my publishers.)

The potential genetic implications of class-flight-as-selection are something that Americans, especially political and social progressives, refuse to even consider—though I cannot imagine why, given their enjoyment of their own moral and intellectual superiority. But when it comes to the possibility of people, especially black and brown people, being born dumb, their minds snap shut. Being born dumb is a special category reserved mostly for white American Southerners, who unfortunately make every effort to prove them right for the sheer orneriness of it. For sure, this is a squeamish topic. But I'll tell you this: if you ever have the misfortune of being in Wellford, South Carolina for its annual hubcap hurling and bobbing-for-pigs'-feet contests, you would not be so quick to dispute my point here.

Once we subscribe to the idea that all people are not born geniuses — which is easy enough for those of us living out here, where people eat deep-fried Twinkies — corrective remedies are in order: spend billions on affirmative action and more computers in the classroom. Make everybody a smart bug. But, sadly enough, evolution is indeed real, and the specimens of the smart-bug colony have developed special antennae for the presence of money. So affirmative action quickly slips into a subsidy for already-well-heeled people of colour. I know two black attorneys who've sent their kids to college on affirmative-action programs. Go figure. But let me go on record here as not being against affirmative action, despite the fact that it has blessed us with the likes of Condy 'The Smiling Stiletto' Rice and Supreme Court Justice Clarence 'Panty Ripper' Thomas — thus proving that some people probably shouldn't be educated, no matter what colour they are.

As for the computers and technology in the white-underbelly classrooms, they have not panned out as expected, either. The cognitive elites — who themselves have no problem at all in setting up a spreadsheet or a digital video-conferencing program — believe that ever-more computerisation of the classroom will somehow lead to underclass kids preferring Immanuel Kant to cruising the mall and smoking dope. And, indeed, the computers are more efficient for the kids. A laptop on every desk enables them to cut and paste bootleg homework assignments faster, so they can get to the mall sooner. At best, and probably by design, it prepares them for a life of data entry in the global economy's digital electronic plantations — assuming they can rustle up the plane fare in these economic times to India, where such jobs are now located.

The bottom line, however, is that they can't read. Feel free to blame anyone you choose, except the free-market system's extreme preference for dim-witted consumers and workers. You can blast the public-school teachers, who actually don't have much say in any of this, but at least they are close to the crime and easy to hit.

Ultimately, these kids will join the millions of adults who cannot read. And they cannot read because:

1 They do not have the necessary basic skills, and don't give a rat's arse about getting them;
2 Reading is not arresting enough to compete with the electronic stimulation in which their society is immersed;
3 They cannot envisage any possible advantage in reading, because the advantages stem from extended personal involvement, which they have never experienced, are conditioned away from, and is understandably beyond their comprehension; and
4 Their peers do not read as a serious matter, thereby socially reinforcing their early conclusion that it's

obviously not worth the time and effort. On Planet White Underclass, that's a reasonable assumption. On the other hand, playing digital war games trains you for exciting employment in Iraq and Afghanistan—and probably Iran, too, sooner or later. Career planning takes many forms.

Nevertheless, members of the educated American overclass, liberal and conservative, insist that we are all equally capable of learning new ways of doing things. 'All are created equal', runs the mantra. Every last one of us knows that's not true. But it's vital that everyone keep up the pretence that Cousin Ronnie's flabby 200-pound 16-year-old, who recently speculated on 'how they manage to grow spaghetti so straight', has an equal chance in society with the kid in private school purposefully taking his SATs three times in order to get the highest score possible. Equal or not, somebody has to muck out the Imperial stables and fight the corpocracy's wars. It won't be that kid lugging his Toshiba laptop around.

Some part of our national denial is not pretence. It is the ignorance of ghettoised, educated elites. Ensconced out there in suburban cupcake land, or perhaps Manhattan, they seldom if ever encounter this class that they inwardly loathe but claim to care about. Someone needs to tell them that loathing is not only legal, but that it's OK with the loathed. We don't much like them, either. It's the pretence that galls us, the ignernt. Which is one reason that so many of us mutt people see the highly educated as arrogant phonies. This is by no means entirely true, but we like stereotypes as much as the next fellow does.

We ain't all equal, and a hundred more years of affirmative action will continue to liberate only the brightest among us, who will then promptly move into the American overclass, to join the unacknowledged loathing. If they are lucky, that is — the number of slots shrinks daily.

The most leather-balled conservatives, on the other hand, entertain no illusions about computers in the schools, or about anything else. Instead, they stick by the notion of American free-market capitalism as the road to personal and national success. We have over two hundred years of evidence strongly suggesting that America's favourite theological premise, Adam Smith's 'unseen hand', is a sorry thing indeed for any sane person to risk his arse on, given its endorsement by the smuggest, the greediest, and richest among us. Most working folks would simply prefer an even start — a fair break for everyone, without depending on unseen-hand theology crafted by a man who avowed that the self-interested pursuit of money somehow made men more altruistic. Despite modern apologists' assertions to the contrary, Smith also believed that the unseen hand was that of God, 'whose wisdom works itself through competition for wealth', and that 'providence rightly divided the earth among a few lordly masters'. He disliked government, except when it was clubbing down 'the vice ridden and slothful poor'. Property is government, he said, and, 'Till there be property there can be no government, the very end of which is to secure wealth, and to defend the rich from the poor', thereby defining the armature of American conservatism a full 89 years before the Republican Party was even born. Even allowing for the times, the guy was a bloodless prick.

By now you must have asked, 'How can the largest class be an underclass?' Simple. The few can indeed screw the many. (Shock and horror! Who would have guessed?) Screw 'em right into the dirt under the very nose of Lady Liberty. Amid the current financial carnage, she still lifts her lamp beside McDonald's' golden arches, beckoning ever-cheaper labour, Arab oil despots, and Chinese loan sharks willing to help revive the same global American Ponzi scheme that burned the world's arse from Taipei to Timbuktu. Again, it's the pretence, the utter refusal to call a spade a spade, that allows the overclass to hide its advantage. It allows the bright, cognitive elites to stand on the throats of an unacknowledged, uneducated majority while setting up a college fund for their little Cameron. It pays them good money to go off to the office and write the deep psychographic marketing campaigns that make Cousin Ronnie and his wife Tracy believe they need to buy a Dell computer on a fried-out credit card for the educational benefit of their kids, despite evidence to the contrary. It pays the financial managers of the extractive economic schemes that have bled tens of millions of Ronnies to death by a thousand tiny cuts hidden in their utility bills; or pits my relatives and class against Malaysian villagers living on 1100 calories a day, just so my people can keep their jobs soldering worthless gewgaws on an assembly line … until they are sent off to Iraq or East Fuckistan (after all, they're just crackers and Midwestern corn-feds who like shooting) to defend the managers' investments in IBM or ConAgra.

It isn't numbers that define an underclass. It's which end of the screwjob you live and die on. And it's not just about money: some of the working class, such as mountaintop-removal coal miners, earn surprisingly good wages. It's about inherited advantage, and never having to dodge IEDs in the Middle East, but writing the worthless insurance policies for those who do.

You'd think the widening affluence gap would inflame the underclass, wouldn't you? Nope—not if both classes refuse to acknowledge it. Especially the underclass. (Which way would you like your screwjob today, Ronnie—doggie style or missionary?) Instead, the national mythology holds that we are a 'nation of rugged individualism', the implication being that there are no classes, no masses, just 300 million rugged, freedom-loving Daniel Boone/ Marlboro Man types in charge of their own destinies. OK then: there ain't no underclass—just 200 million rugged individuals being pissed down on by a small class of people up on the forty-fifth floor.

On those very rare occasions when class is acknowledged by working-class Americans, they express the simplistic consumer-state-induced view that class is entirely to do with money, and say they are all 'middle class' in a country that is pretty much divided into only two classes: the super rich, and themselves—the middle class. The middle of what, they have no idea.

Regardless of our national class hallucinations, only one class is counting on social security for its entire retirement income—at least 67 per cent of Americans, and rising, by last count.

In 2008, the top 1 per cent of Americans earned as much

as the bottom 45 per cent. Tired of hearing that one yet? We might allow that this derives from a concentration of abilities due to the aggregation of the brights. But they've aggregated into a clear-cut, self-serving elite who make the rules, and author their own bailouts. No arguing they're bright, they're tight, and they're out-of-sight American products of freedom and democracy. It's the 'freedom and democracy' part that stinks up the joint … as if things were not already rancid enough.

Lest I sound unduly mean-spirited here, I must give the American overclass its due. We may not get a kiss when they rape us, but we seem to have the undying affection of the perps. Liberal or conservative, the overclass professes belief in and affection for 'the people'. Then they do everything humanly possible to ensure that their families will never be exposed to them. Not that they know any of the underclass personally, but they know they don't want to be around them, and definitely don't want them anywhere near their kids. Yet, about the worst that could actually happen should we all be forced to live in the same condominium is that all parties would be mutually bored to death.

Affection aside, the screwjobs continue to escalate. Now, you'd think that the screwees, especially in this age of information availability, would rebel. After all, illiterate Indians in Chiapas are doing it and getting results—finally. It comes down to the way that the myth of a classless America is cultivated by the cognitive elites who run the media, information, entertainment, and education industries. It comes down to understanding that, in our system, there are insiders and outsiders.

Millions of outsiders labour to create value, and a select few appropriate the wealth of hundreds of thousands of the outsiders for themselves. Take healthcare, for example. Were underclass awareness of health and healthcare cultivated, every doctor in America would be strung up by the nuts. Spell out how banks actually make their money (besides receiving bailouts), and no banker in America would dare leave his home.

So what is to be done to establish at least some semblance of an equitable society in which all or most members operate on a reasonably common plane, rather than having to compete by claw and tooth? One in which mutual human respect dominates because long-denied classism is exposed and then, over time, dissolved?

Thinking people know the answer to that one: education. Create an environment in which the working poor can come to learn to think for themselves. But that would cost more than ten Iraq wars. And now that we're completely bust and in hock for generations, it's not very likely, is it? What needs to be done would have to be initiated before first grade for every child, and continue over generations — things like universal healthcare and purposeful husbandry of security and love in the homes where children are raised. And they could only flourish in the home if Mum and Dad were not clawing their lives away in the Darwinian Survival Working-Class Reality Show. Nobody has the arse to demand an American makeover that will cost, at the very minimum, maybe ten trillion dollars over at least two or three generations. And besides, the money is no longer there, and it never will be again. When empires die, they die broke.

Whatever the case, somebody has to keep on paying lest, God forbid, the managing class is forced to drink boxed wine. And it's gonna be Cousin Ronnie. And eventually Cousin Ronnie's fat son. No wonder we get school bullying, in which Cousin Ronnie's boy smacks the snot out of 'the rich kid' at the mall. Somewhere down inside he grasps the truth.

Not long ago, I watched an upscale mum and her two kids get out of the family Nissan Maxima at the Smithsonian Naturalist Center near Washington, DC. As the big, tinted plate-glass front door flashed in the sun and then swallowed them into its serene realm of mysterious bones and flies sleeping off eternity in amber, I noticed that both kids were armed with notebooks and digital cameras for their 'unique hands-on museum experience'. I couldn't help but think of Ronnie's kid and his straight-spaghetti theory of botany. It's a laughable thing. Even Ronnie laughed at it. But it was the kind of laugh meant to hide family shame.

Acknowledged or not, it is also our national shame, this denial of the existence of a massive, permanent underclass in America. In doing so, we deny the one truth held in common by every enlightened civilisation: we are our brother's keepers.

I recently walked by that old house where I once peered out at Doctor Racey's rooftop and once briefly imagined becoming something better than what was offered by the life I saw around me. Now part of an upscale historic district, the once-rundown old brick tenement I lived in has been restored and turned into a single family dwelling by an affluent young couple—expats from the soulless grind of government jobs in Washington, DC. The same has happened to Doc Racey's home, now occupied by a very attractive, single, middle-aged woman named Annie, who lives on a trust fund, plus rents from several other houses she owns in that block. On occasion, I've had drinks downtown with Annie—way too many, in most cases. Maybe the truth is as she explained it to me one evening: 'The key to saving these neighbourhoods is replacing them with a better class of people.' I replied that she was an example of everything wrong with America, and I meant it. (Nonetheless, I thought to myself, given the chance, I'd screw her. Ole Johnson ain't got no conscience.)

Changing the subject, she asked, 'Did you see in the paper that Old Toliver died?'

'No. Really? He must have been a hundred years old.'

'He was in somewhere in his eighties,' she said. 'I can't remember exactly.'

'I shink we need 'nother round to cel'brate the memory of old Toliver,' I suggested.

'One of us doesn't need another round of anything, except maybe coffee.' Annie stood up, smoothed her dress a bit, and said goodbye, leaving me to reflect upon Toliver in the company of a lonely olive at the bottom of the glass.

CHAPTER TEN

The Oligarch's Complaint

I was about fourteen when I first sat with old black Toliver at a card table under a tulip tree, looking down across the expansive lawn that looked over the town. We ate toasted peanut butter-jelly-and-bacon sandwiches that Lula the house cook had carried out to us. With his black bow-tie and bald, brown pate, with wisps of close-cropped hair at the sides, Toliver was a dead ringer for the black butler on the Uncle Ben's rice box. Somewhere in his mid-forties, he was a valet—or gentleman's gentleman, as they were then called—a manservant who laid out well-to-do white men's attire each morning, and saw to it that his boss never had to do such things as draw his own bath, or light his own cigarette if other people happened to be observing.

The boss himself, the man whose lawn I was there to mow, was Harry Flood Byrd, one of the 'landed gentry', a US senator and a FFV (First Families of Virginia) member whose original ancestor, the son of a London goldsmith, had arrived in 1652. That ancestor amassed an empire of plantations across the state, upon which many of his descendants still live in Georgian mansions. Today they no longer derive wealth from the land, and mostly use their estates for fox-hunting events and to breed jumping horses. True American oligarchs, with an eye for money and over three hundred years' worth of inside connections and political power, they came to own banks and other financial institutions. Today, their income is mostly derived from the healthcare industry. But back when Toliver and I sat there eating peanut butter and bacon, the now-deceased Flood Byrd still derived much of his income from his apple plantations.

I was there to mow the man's lawn—an all-day job that paid five bucks—not to speculate on the aristocracy of my town; although, given the Georgian mansion and splendour of the location, it was hard not to. Toliver was reading the local newspaper, which Senator Byrd owned (along with several others around the state). Byrd sat about fifty feet away, talking boozily to a local judge over 'fortified iced tea' and pound cake at a linen-covered, wrought-iron table on his high-pillared portico. Both he and his wife were notorious alcoholics, though she stayed pretty much indoors, leaving the house only to be chauffeured to 'must attend' political events in Washington and Richmond. I'm telling you, folks, life among old-line Virginia families often seems like a scene from *Gone with the Wind*.

Between bites of cake, Flood Byrd was bitching about his white orchard-workers. Like other big growers, he had recently begun to 'import' cheap Bahamian pickers—which he mispronounced as 'Bohemians'—to replace the rural white pickers who used to camp in his orchards during picking season. But pruning, spraying, and maintaining the orchards and equipment throughout the rest of the year required experienced local employees. Mostly white and rural.

'I don't know which is the biggest pain in the arse,' the orchard king declared, 'hiring the dumb hillbilly sons-a-bitches, or owning niggers outright like they used to do. The hillbillies are a world of trouble, always pissed off about something, or so hung over they can't see straight. Always wanting an advance on their paycheque, which they damned sure drink up.'

Old Toliver raised an eyebrow, and said to his other servant, Lula, 'Someday these people's ways are going to come back to bite them in the arse.' (Apparently nothing is that hungry—Byrd's family is ten-fold richer now.)

Toliver's remark shocked me. In fact, so young and stupid and socially indoctrinated was I at the time that I was sympathetic to the apple baron's position. A man of property and community standing should not have to put up with such stuff! Outsiders doubtlessly find it difficult to understand our peasant-like respect for our social 'betters' (though most Americans practise the same in the form of celebrity awe), and how it is inculcated in us from birth. We are born in hospitals named for them; we attend public schools named for them; we read the newspapers they own and which publicise their goodness, mercy, and worthiness; we drive highways named for them; we borrow money from the banks they own; and we see them on floats or in open-topped limos at our parades and festivals …

But a few moments after the orchard baron said what he said about his white workers, I began to feel shame. Many of my relatives were or had been uneducated white orchard workers. All of my daddy's people — Pap, Maw, Daddy, Uncle Nelson, and Uncle Toad — at some time or other had camped in this rich man's orchards in the autumn to pick fruit for a few cents a bushel. By the time I was a teenager, it was up to 17 cents a bushel, before the orchardists found cheaper labour from the Bahamas. These days they use Jamaicans.

From the orchard baron's standpoint, I'm sure that poor white employees were indeed a world of trouble for upstanding capitalists like himself. So many of us still are — with our rebel flag tattoos, drinking ourselves to death, kicking the shit out of each other in bars … angry, ignorant, uneducated animals in a Darwinian labour economy's fight for survival.

So there was tall, black Toliver, and short, black Lula — both 'house niggers' — and me, a skinny white-cracker kid, on the lawn of a Southern mansion. Here was an iconic image of race and class in the South, if ever there was one — one that makes Northern Americans feel historically smug, and visually reinforces the national assertion that race has always been the primary historical and cultural problem of the American South. Which is pure bullshit.

It's always been about one thing down here, just like everywhere else in America: cheap labour. Free slave-labour may connect Southern history, but cheap labour connects all of American history. True, preserving free slave-labour was the reason that southern congressman Preston Brooks clubbed the living snot out of Massachusetts anti-slavery senator Charles Sumner right there on the Senate chamber floor in 1856. But the main theme has always been about powerful men and, more recently, faceless, bloodless corporations—more powerful than any oligarch of earlier times—aggregating wealth from human toil. That's why there were hundreds of thousands of white indentured servants in America before the slave economy rose to the level it did. And that's why the US has such strong union-busting laws as the Taft–Hartley Act and the misleadingly named The Right to Work Act, pushed through by right-wing corporatists, which floods union shops with scab labour until the unions are so weakened that they cannot negotiate.

In some respects, oligarchs such as Flood Byrd—or, more accurately, his sons—have it better than their progenitors did before the Civil War, when about half their wealth consisted of human bondage. Slaves were expensive: a couple of thousand dollars each (around one hundred thousand dollars in today's money). They needed lots of them to work their large tracts—dozens in some cases, hundreds in others—and were directly responsible for the feeding, upkeep, health, and productivity of their investment.

By contrast, today's workers are a dime a dozen. You can dump them at will if they get sick, or if business is slow. Or just because you don't like their looks. And you can be assured that plenty more will line up for work when you again need workers to fulfil your newest state-highway building contract or to drive your fleet of trucks. Aside from the government and what few union shops are left in America, employers can blow workers right out of the water at will.

Sometimes, though, through anger and class self-hate, we blow ourselves right out of the water, even when things are going fairly well. I saw this a while back when a kind-hearted, idealistic friend of mine, John D—, a small-time masonry contractor and by no means an oligarch, had to fire a trusted employee who got strung out on Oxycontin ('hillbilly heroin'). Oxy made the employee a hazard and a liability to both John and his clients as he dozed and stumbled around on the scaffolding. One incident of personal injury, one lawsuit, and John stood to lose his small farmstead, his business, everything. He felt awful about having to fire the guy, and still does. To John, who was raised in a suburban middle-class family in Maryland, his ex-employee's behaviour was inexplicable. After a decade of dependability, why such a crash?

Personally, I've seen it happen so often that it seems normal. It is a generational trauma caused by the ancestral workforce experience of exploited and oppressed labour. Blacks have suffered the same generational trauma. The aloneness of the struggle is so deeply internalised that you cannot beat it in one generation or by getting one good break in your working life. A working man or woman is more than the sum of his or her own individual experience; they are part and parcel of a chain of historical experiences. Perhaps you, dear reader, have belonged to a union, in a nation that allows dignity to exist in work. But if your experience has always been under the boot, as a cheap, purposefully uneducated throwaway body, there can be no dignity at all in your labour. A man knows that inside, and the frustration grows like an ulcer upon a man's soul—a little each day for a lifetime. And a man drinks and busts up a few things now and them. Or he just stays in bed some morning, and never shows up again. Or he tries some oxy. Or maybe he joins a Holy Roller church to gain the cold comfort of the preacher's message that Jesus loves even an utterly impotent piece of shit like him.

Yes, you poor, dumb son-of-a-bitch, Jesus loves you. But the elites need you. They need you to pay for their lawn parties and trips to Europe, and to ensure the financial security of their pampered whelps for generations to come. As for the 'American corporations', they don't even need you anymore. They've got the labouring throngs of China's Mandarin capitalism (where civil rights are not an issue); and they've got Vietnamese and Indonesian factories, and Haitian factories, and those places in Bangladesh where caged workers can be had for $11 to $42 a month, and the floor boss takes home a different teenage girl every night.

And now, under Obama, the financial elites have captured one-sixth of the American economy under the ruse of the new 'healthcare reform' legislation. Only in labyrinthine American capitalist politics could such a Trojan horse be conceived. The healthcare reform bill was never about health care or reform, and most certainly never about direct, free, and on-demand medical care for all. It was about *insurance* for all. As a result, the government now requires 35 million mostly poor and working-class uninsured Americans to buy private health insurance. This will guarantee at least $70 billion in new annual revenue for the insurance industry—probably more. Another 11 million among the uninsured will get limited government help under the plan. Of course, the insurance corporations made a few small concessions: they may no longer kick you off their plans if you get an expensive illness, and they cannot refuse you if you have a pre-existing condition. On the other hand, they were granted the right to increase insurance rates up to 25 per cent immediately, if they choose to do so—this, in the wake of four years of double-digit annual increases. Doubtlessly, Maw would be without healthcare were she alive today—unable to afford either insulin or health insurance to pay for it. She'd be worse off, really. Under our new healthcare reform bill, she would be required to buy private health insurance. For a 63-year-old diabetic, that is about $1,500 monthly. If she were poor enough, the government would kick in perhaps $400 of that premium.

The corporations that sell the insulin are better off today. In exchange for supporting Obama's plan, the president promised the drug industry that any health legislation under his administration would ban the government from negotiating lower drug prices. However, in an interesting piece of logic, the government may use its $98 billion purchasing power to negotiate *higher* drug prices, if deemed necessary for the smooth operation of its programs. As a result, health insurance stocks immediately rose, and the share prices of pharmacy-benefit managers hit all-time highs. The news media called it 'historic legislation on the order of Franklin Roosevelt's New Deal'.

So, get used to it, my redneck brethren. Your heart may belong to Jesus, but your arse belongs to the same people it always has. So keep on living from payday to payday and sending your kids to shitty schools until they reach the legal dropout age. Which we both know you will, because it's been seen to that you'll never know anything better.

I have laboured all over this country of mine—on hog farms, in brick kilns, iron foundries, and car washes, doing hot-tar roofing, and collecting garbage, you name it—and I can tell you straight up and without hesitation that the combination of our poorly educated workforce and ruthless demagogic oligarchy are not a nationwide problem: they are a national tragedy. It's one that's getting worse and is not likely ever to be fixed. The Empire is collapsing inward upon its working base. The oligarchs and financial elites have skipped town with the national treasury; many have multiple homes in other countries. The inherent natural resources upon which America was initially built by labouring men and women have been squandered. Sure, there will be a few brief respites and meaningless economic recoveries along the way. But there's gonna be a lot more meth labs, or some future equivalent, and more unseen domestic abuse in the ever-poorer working-class households, even as the few aware individuals in the underclass struggle to piece together an equitable worker society that was never a fair go from the outset.

Declining as the Empire may be, and despite the fact that we can never, nor should ever, again enjoy the wasteful materialism it once provided—the earth being a finite resource—we may possibly yet enjoy dignity. If we do, it will only have come through unity and solidarity. Because dignity must be social reality before it can be a personal one. A secretly self-nursed sense of personal dignity in the face of insult and oppression makes for good movies, but in the real world it is like a diamond set in lead. The non-manifested dignity of a man in jail or an elderly woman eating cat food may be spiritually noble, but it also means that the bastards have won. Not until dignity is right there in the open, for all the world to see, are other men inspired to it as a universal cause. As a human right.

Meanwhile, you there! Yes, you, my oxy-addicted nephew, my drunken, redneck backhoe-operator cousin, you, the unemployed Holy Roller ... Be assured that you will be allowed to work again. And again. For that is your sole purpose in the system, your lone value to it, as a replaceable moving part made of flesh. Just remember never to utter these two words: 'union' and 'solidarity'. Otherwise you are a free man in a free country. You will be free to accept another job if and when it is decided you are again needed by the oligarchs, or perhaps a presidential 'make work' program to give the appearance of change afoot.

LEST I PAINT TOO BLEAK A PICTURE OF A LATE-1950S redneck working-class childhood, let me say here that a boy's life had its exciting distractions. Chief among them were explosives: M-80s, cherry bombs, and the like. This was an exclusively male pursuit, as I've never met a girl who liked to blow things up. The biggest problem then, as now, was where to get the ash cans and cherry bombs, given that they were illegal — the chief difference being that today you'd be charged with terrorism for possession of either. So when we moved to Winchester and I could hear the detonations around town, I considered at least one aspect of town life, the anti-personnel aspect, to be a vast improvement over the farm or any of the other places along the road we'd lived. But where to get the goods? This problem was solved when I got an after-school job helping at a boarding house, one of the nameless type which abounded in those days, marked by a large, painted sign that simply read: ROOMS. Enter Cecil Boyce, fresh out of jail. Cecil was a 24/7 dealer in high-grade illegal fireworks to young boys (and not a few grown men), bootleg pints of Old Crow whiskey on Sundays, and French Ticklers—whatever they were.

Back on the street again, Cecil Boyce couldn't afford house rent, not even on Pluck's Alley (the worst street in town until it finally burned down). So I met the erstwhile jailbird while he was availing himself of the comforts of ROOMS. The owner, chain-smoking fiftyish Ardella Bright, heard Cecil long before she ever saw him.

'Jeezits Kee Riest, this place would gag a buzzard! Somebody ought to open some windows,' the owner of a nasal voice demanded from down in the boarding-house hallway. The voice had a point. The air at Ardella's stayed punky from feet, stale towels, Airwick, griddle grease, hair tonic, and hickory smoke leaking from the wood cookstove over which Ardella laboured.

'Well, nobody dragged your tail in here,' Ardella shot back at the voice as she headed for the hallway with much officious wiping of hands on her apron. There in the hallway stood about the cheesiest-looking character ever to come through the boarding-house door, which is saying a lot. Packed like a sausage into a woolly green suit, this obese personage sported a purple dime-store turban and a three-day growth of beard. Cecil had arrived, fresh from the Virginia State Work Camp #6—the state pea farm—decked out in what he judged to be a rather exotic outfit. Ardella's instincts told her that Cecil wasn't playing with a full deck, period. They were right. And for about the first time ever, she had reservations about taking some potential boarder's money.

'That's a pea farm gitup, if ever I saw one,' she said.

'Nice, ain't it!' he replied, clearly pleased with himself. 'They give me my pick of the suits for doin' such a good job in the sweet corn. This and $44 in cold cash.'

'You sure they turned you loose, proper? I mean, with papers and all?'

'Yessum. I offered to stick around and help get the rest of the corn in, but the warden said ...'

'Forget it,' Ardella cut him short, having already decided she could handle this half-wit. 'It'll be twelve dollars for the first week's roomin'. Eighteen if you figger on eatin' here, too.' Cecil counted out eighteen dollars and forked it over. Ardella bent down and stuffed the bills into her stockings, which were rolled down around two mountain-skinny legs with that lacework varicose legacy of hard-working women everywhere. She came from across the West Virginia line, too, sometime during the mid-1950s. Leading Cecil up the stairs to his room, she paused to ask: 'Don't that woolly outfit itch you some?'

'Sure do, ma'am. Sure do.'

Cecil's stints on the pea farm totalled four, averaging slightly less than a year each, and roughly a year apart. They were never for anything serious, mostly just the illicit ordnance of boyhood. Invariably, some kid would end up blowing a thumb loose with one of Cecil's ashcans, or set one off in school, get caught, squeal—and off Cecil would go to the pea farm again.

'Damn it, Cecil,' the judge once observed. 'You're just dumb enough to be pitiful and just smart enough to be a dangerous pain in the arse.' Adults who knew him generally agreed. But in our lives he was a rather exotic, mob-like figure, given his fireworks connections.

Ten minutes after Ardella handed me my weekly five dollars, I was up in Cecil's room copping the goods. An hour later, my old man had them in his possession. 'You're gonna blow your damned hand off with them things,' he yelled, red-faced, as he snatched away the sacred ordnance. Yet it wouldn't be twenty-four hours before Daddy and his buddy Elwood would be down by the river setting them for their own enjoyment. About the best I can say for my dad is that he *tried* to be a good example when it came to dangerous explosives. But he was still a male and ... well ... frankly, I wouldn't much trust any American male who failed to inherit the cherry-bomb gene.

By the time I'd turned eleven, my bomb-making gene was in full expression: I made a bazooka from a six-foot piece of drainpipe. Powered by a long strip of tyre inner tubing at one end, it could easily send a cherry bomb a distance of 65 metres. And that's exactly what it did on the first test firing ... up, up, and arching over the high stone wall that separated our kid-hardened dirt yard from the lush, green lawn of the historic Old Presbyterian Church. Rather unfortunately, 65 metres away on the other side of that stone wall, a church picnic was going full blast, as it were—if elderly Presbyterians can be said to do anything full blast. The sizzling, short-fused cherry bombola landed smack in the middle of a potato-salad bowl at the centre of those good people's soiree, with the deep-throated *krump!* of a mortar shell. Need I describe the ire of thirty potato-salad-embellished Presbyterians?

'Miss Mary' Markle, the red-faced spinster caretaker of the historic church where, according to the bronze plaque, John Singleton Mosby (The Grey Ghost) had often hidden his horses during the Civil War, knew precisely where to come looking for the perps. After all, there had been a previous incident wherein six panes of irreplaceable 200-year-old glass were shot out of the parsonage with a Daisy BB gun, the good old lever-action kind that held a whole tube of BBs. No one squealed, thus several of us got our arses whipped so that the offender could not be missed. Lobbing explosives at decent, God-fearing Presbyterians was a moral felony, as childhood offences went. Today it is the stuff of juvenile incarceration.

ADOLESCENCE BEING WHAT IT IS, OUR LIVES WERE a strange mixture of innocence, confusion, and growing sensibilities about status awareness, all wrapped in extreme self-consciousness. Many of us carried an unarticulated anger over our social position in life by the time we got to high school. Because we'd had it hammered into us that America is a classless society, we were not allowed to express aloud what that position obviously was. We had no word for our position, but for damned sure it was near or at the bottom. The most alienated of us cruised around in old cars with army-blanket seat covers, clutching tyre irons and looking for fights. Monday mornings in school centred on recounting the weekend's fights and car wrecks. Class time was spent secretly reading paperbacks such as *Run, Chico, Run* and *The Big Rumble* by the prolific Wenzell Brown—trashy pulp novels aimed at teen hipsters. Violent as it sounds, this came under the heading of stress relief. It had its comic moments at times. Once, when we read about New York Puerto Rican gang members 'smoking tea' to 'get high', we rolled and smoked half-a-dozen Lipton tea bags. Sicker than dogs, we never did get what all the fuss was about.

Mercifully, when we turned eighteen there were better things to do than smoke tea bags. At that age, you could legally drink at the roadside joint or the downtown tavern. With their mournful steel-guitar music bleeding onto the streets, and sideburned daddyos seducing the sweet young honky-tonk roses with flat beers and hillbilly hipster gab, these beer joints were temples of our culture. They exemplified a main-drag Saturday-night America that I still long for. There are still a few around, but they have moved across the West Virginia line ... closer to that mountainous bastion of the marginal whites. Dirt-eating poor as much of that state may be, never let it be said that marginalised whites don't still have a natural home 'across the cold Jordan'. It's called West Virginia.

But, for the time being, I was just another sawn-off, horny adolescent stuck in the 'bad neighbourhood'—the one where people had a shower after work, not in the morning before heading off to work. Truthfully speaking, America's class line begins in the shower.

Our bad neighbourhood was, and still is, wedged between the old railroad station and the town's two Civil War cemeteries — one for the Yankee invaders, and one for our own 'hallowed Confederate dead'.

At that time, I was buddies with — if you could give my idolatry such a mild label — James and Rick Kilby, two older high school boys who lived next door in a sagging clapboard tenement. They were true teenage hillbilly hipsters who dressed like James Dean, played guitar, and turned me on to Carl Perkins, Jerry Lee Lewis, and Little Richard. They had a tomboyish sister, Karol, who kept her haircut short, and could handle any horse that was ever born. This was because their old man, Tom Kilby, kept a couple of not-so-good small-time racehorses at a rundown rented place out in the country. The horses had cost him a small trucking company and lots of trouble with the Internal Revenue Service. But, at the age of fourteen, I couldn't imagine anything more worldly or absolutely hip than hanging out with such an exotic family, and especially with Jim and Rick, who were respectively two and three years older than me. I was prepared do anything to be allowed to hang out there. Jim rode as an exercise boy at the nearby Charlestown race track, and I spent scores of hours polishing his jockey boots and saddle — anything that would let me be around these two older guys while they played every Sun record that Sam Phillips ever stamped his big rooster upon. The fact that neither had a girlfriend never got in the way of me wanting to hear them voice their expertise on the subjects of women and courtship.

Today, that old neighbourhood looks much the same,

as if it were painted by Edward Hopper and then bleakly populated with work-crippled old men, hard-faced, hard-working single mums, and clusters of bored, overweight teenagers—the only new addition being a sprinkling of crack vials scattered around for local colour. You can see some of its families going through the same struggle for modest respectability as in 1961 when it was the poorest edge of white Winchester, though it's now mostly black: tinfoil-wrapped flower pots on crumbling porches, and lawn edges cut crisply in the earth along sidewalks, as if the red clay pounded by the feet of neighbourhood kids were going to produce enough grass to threaten the walkways.

Often, while passing through that neighbourhood, a crazy pain from the past jumps me from behind—the stabbing kind that only lasts a second, but makes you flinch as you remember some stupid moment of adolescence. I have often wondered if everyone has them; I suppose they do. Around the corner from the Kilbys' old place and a block up Piccadilly Street still stands the house where, for the first time, I asked a girl for a date.

Her name was Patti Hensley, and everyone at school knew that Patti was going to be an airline stewardess (this was back before they became 'flight attendants') because (a) she said so; and (b) she was excruciatingly beautiful—which was, as far as any of us knew, the main requirement for the job, judging from airline advertising, in which airline stewardess all looked like Sandra Dee. And, as if we needed any further evidence, Patti was already dating high school boys when she was in the eighth grade, proof that she had the required sophistication to become

230

a globe-trotting bunny of the skies like those we'd seen in *Playboy Magazine*. For all I know, Patti thought of it the same way at the time.

Despite her beauty, Patti Hensley was unarguably as sincere an individual as anyone could ever imagine. Accepted in the best cliques of girls, and invited to every exclusive teen party by the boys of every old name or wealthy family in town because of her looks, she nevertheless kept her sincerity intact. If she was guilty of any sin, it was vanity. Patti never had a hair out of place, and obviously spent thousands of hours grooming herself. Certainly we weren't complaining about the result.

Patti may have lived in the same neighbourhood as us, but she lived slightly beyond the shadow of the dingy round-the-clock clattering textile mill. And she lived in a whitewashed stucco house—not one of the usual stark, crumbling frame houses with the front and back porches boxed in and converted into draughty bedrooms. Hers was crisp and white, with a wraparound porch pleasantly strewn with wicker furniture and shaded by climbing wisteria that seemed like an extension of the deep-green lawn and shrubs in front. Her father, a foreman at the mill, could be seen on Saturdays, through the wisteria, smoking and reading. Given the ridiculous class-awareness of native Virginians, compounded by the agonising self-consciousness of being a teenager, one block and a coat of whitewash was the difference between Grosse Point and Hell's Kitchen.

How I ever got the idea of asking her for a date is beyond me, all these years later—Patti with her penny loafers, pleated skirts, and circle pin; me still in cheap flannel shirts and boxy jeans from Sears, like the smaller boys over at the elementary school. A fool could spot the chasm between us. I seem to have done it partly as a courageous shot in the dark, and partly because I had absolutely no idea how the world of dating worked.

So I spent the first half of a July Saturday getting ready, dressing as coolly as a guy could in cheap, woven brown-nylon shoes with crepe soles—blackened with liquid stove-polish for the occasion because, as everybody knew, cool guys did not wear brown shoes. Taking small steps so as not to dent the crease in my stiffly starched and ironed blue workpants, and sporting a fifty-cent haircut from the drunkest barber in town, Dody Cribbs, I stepped out of our house. The day was hotter than two rats humping in a wool sock, but I didn't care. The act of spiffing up had put me in a buoyant mood. I thought of how Patti's neck must smell as I knocked on her door. I was sure that even on the worst date you must get close enough to at least smell a female. I'd settle for that. I'd grovel for that.

But, when Patti Hensley's screen door opened and I saw her soft silhouette loom before me as the polished hardwood floors swept away behind her, panic struck. My head began to roar with the thundering of love's poisoned hooves about to trample my naive hopes. It dawned on me that I had never spoken to this girl in my life and that we only knew each other's names because we were in the same grade.

'Well, hello, Joey!' she said, with that warm, buttery smile of hers, a hint of slight confusion flashing only briefly across her face. 'Would you like to sit down on the porch for a moment? Or come in?'

'Ah, no … I was just wondering if you'd want to go to the dance at the Fire Hall tomorrow.' Subtle, right? Completely out of it. Yet here she was, inviting a grubby little pud who'd appeared on the front porch into her house.

'Oh, I'm sorry, but I don't think that would work out.' *Work out? What did that mean, for God's sake?* My mind jammed, and I could hear the teeth being stripped off its every gear.

'Okay … well … I was just in the neighbourhood (*like I didn't live in the friggin' neighbourhood!*), an' I thought I'd ask.' It surely must be flattering to a girl to be asked out just because a guy walks by and thinks, 'Huh? Oh, a female lives there—guess I'll just walk up and ask her for a date.' Brilliant, Bageant. Brilliant.

'Sure you won't sit down for a minute?'

'No, I gotta go now.'

I practically leapt from the porch to the street. On the way home, I looked down to see my blackened shoes starting to melt in the heat, producing tiny rivulets of stove polish. Worse yet, the blazing sidewalk had melted the surface of my crepe soles, leaving faint, sticky footprints on the glossy, enamelled porch.

My next mistake was telling James and Rick about having asked Patti for a date. Jim howled, 'Every guy in the school wants to date Patti Hensley.' The oldest of the two brothers, Jim was tall and thin, with the kind of scooped-back dark hair that made him spend hours admiring his profile in the mirror. And though they spared me the misery of teasing, they gave each other looks of utter bafflement that I could be so stupid. Surely they had quite a laugh over it later. For years afterward, day in and day out, I ducked Patti in the hallways at school, avoiding her attention in every way possible. Oh, crazy regret.

From there on, things went from bad to worse. Crushed between the rising tide of adolescent hormones and the now clearer picture of class structure in our burg, I started noticing that other guys in our neighbourhood seldom had actual dates, and that their girlfriends smoked and had the same ratty look as ourselves.

After the Patti incident, I would not ask another girl out for a long time. Clearly, the girls I admired—the brainy ones with the crisp Villager blouses and polished, saddle-leather penny loafers, the artistic ones and the graceful ones, whose lithe bodies seemed to float over my wet dreams like angels—could never be allowed to see where I lived or to know anything about my home, with its rust-mottled coal stove in the living room, our crappy, green couch, and our empty refrigerator. On a couple of occasions when a girl was interested enough to say, 'Let's walk home by your house', I'd lie that I had to go to the library. By now, I understood why it was that we all knew what the more upscale kids' fathers did for a living—doctors, plant managers, attorneys, small-business owners, and the like. They didn't know what our fathers did for a living; but then, too, they didn't give a shit. The underclass culture of shame is as one-sided as hell.

When I did get it up to go on another date, it was with Karol Kilby, Jim and Rick's sister. It was a drive-in double date with Jim, who'd finally managed to break into the dating game himself. The movie was Elvis Presley's

Girls, Girls, Girls!, in which Elvis plays an improbable, hip-swivelling, peasant Hawaiian fisherman—hounded, of course, by sexy young girls. Over the course of the evening, Karol and I wrestled around in the back seat, got in a dozen-or-so awful kisses, and I managed to feel her tits and play stinkfinger, despite the encumbrance of her tight jeans and heavy black-leather belt. She seemed feverish to participate. Too feverish, in fact. The whole event left me feeling weird, but at last I knew what a woman smelled like.

Years later, I would learn that she was a lesbian (the heavy leather belt, close-cropped hair in a bouffant era, and the denim shirt should have been a damned clue). But neither of us knew that at the time. It must have been miserable for Karol, suffering such sweaty groping during a confusing, painful attempt at imitating a sexuality that denied every molecule and sensibility in her poor young soul. Today she lives in a trailer with a long-time partner, and cleans houses while both of them wait for the mercy of social security. To Karol, I say: I am sorry. We gave it one helluva shot, trying to be 'normal teenagers' by the ridiculous, soul-strangling definition of the times.

DESPITE MY MISERABLE HIGH SCHOOL EXPERIENCE, and despite the fact that I'd been a drop-out, I was up for it when my class's thirty-fifth Hadley High School reunion rolled around. I felt comfortable, excited enough to even shell out a couple of hundred bucks for printing the little updated yearbooks, the obligatory 'Where are they now?' handout. After all, I'd had a pretty exciting career by local standards, had met all sorts of famous people, and had travelled the world more than I'd ever really wanted to. I'd never been to a school reunion; but, from the other side of fifty, they start to take on new significance—particularly if you've been away for years and are the normal sort of person who wonders what time and its river has done or not done to us all. Beyond that, I felt attracted by the idea of being around a few people whose very presence verified that I was once young and devoid of modern life's fatigue and cynicism.

The reunion was held in the main room of a colonial-era inn, a heavily timbered and dark catacomb of rooms highlighted with oil paintings of fox hunts, red-linen-topped tables, and antique silver. There was the usual sprinkling of shrivelled old teachers, escorted by greying former star pupils from the right parts of town—men and women who'd become college professors, lawyers, or teachers, or had simply made a lot of money in real estate. Watching each person or couple enter, I experienced that slow, warm recognition of faces once known, some now discernible only by their eyes.

In towns like Winchester, class-reunion attendees are always the same sort: movers and shakers of those high school days, people who had near-perfect high school experiences and stayed in their hometowns living middle-class lives of unadventurous continuity, taking turns organising high school reunions. Which guaranteed that not one person would be there who I could say had been a friend of mine in high school. Certainly not Jim, who had died in a motorcycle accident; nor Rick, now retired from the Virginia State Highway Department, work crippled, and a born-again Christian who wouldn't go anyplace where alcohol was served. A little disappointed, I was still excited to see these changed yet deeply familiar faces go by in the cottony world that martinis and dim lights create. Too many martinis, really, so I must have been uncomfortable at some level.

I wasn't looking for Patti Hensley, and hadn't thought of her in years when she introduced herself to someone standing near me at the bar. Despite what I might have expected, I had no embarrassing memory of that day on Piccadilly Street. Nor did I feel any of the usual writer's interest to hear about what had become of her life. Because there she stood, in a designer's black cocktail dress, with that thin, deathly look of someone being treated for cancer or AIDS. For once in my life, I did not want to know the story. Why spoil a good evening by asking a question that everyone else there probably already knew the answer to?

Accompanying her was a heavy, well-groomed man with a silver moustache who was, as I gathered from their conversation, her husband—a retired airline pilot. Patti's caught me staring at her. But, like most extremely attractive women, accustomed to a lifetime of men staring at her, she took it to be the plain ogling of a fool, not recognising me in the slightest.

All I could think of was what good fortune can sometimes come from lugging around forty unwanted pounds, and turning up with thinning hair and in a good suit.

CHAPTER ELEVEN

Draw Me!

For months, I'd carried the 'Draw Me!' matchbook cover in my pocket—the one with the profile of a pretty, dark-haired young woman with heart-shaped lips and long lashes, her hair pulled back under a small, polka-dotted scarf to better reveal her perfect neck. When one cover wore out or went through the washing machine, I'd replace it with another. The Draw Me! correspondence art-school advertisement on the matchbook represented my imagined future as a commercial artist. And when fear for my future crept in, I'd tell myself that, one way or another, I'd become an artist. I seldom truly believed it, but it gave me something to cling to.

You remember me from grade school. There's always a kid in any school class who can draw very well. They were born with special hand-eye coordination, and always scored in the 99th percentile in spatial relationships on the aptitude tests. I was that kid. Throughout my younger life, I could—and still can, even today—draw well. In fact, given a couple of days to get the hand and eyes working together again, and an easy, unlaboured stroke loosened up, I could probably do a more than passable portrait of you.

So imagine my enchantment with the Draw Me! matchbook cover queries: 'Would you like to earn up to $100 a week as a commercial artist?' Or, 'What would you give to be able to draw professionally?' The unwavering answer was: my left nut. Or maybe a leg. Or both, if necessary.

These commercial-art correspondence courses, the ads for which could be found in most pulp magazines, flourished in America up until about 1980. There was Art Instruction, Inc. out of Minneapolis, the Famous Artist School in Westport, Connecticut ... Hard as it is to believe today, the various Draw Me! correspondence schools were quite legitimate, and most of their graduates went on to jobs in some form of commercial art. Staff at these schools boasted nationally successful artists, including Norman Rockwell, Charles Schultz, Matlock Price, and Albert Dorne. It was a different era indeed.

Over time, I worked up enough nerve to take the Draw Me! test, copying the head of a cute girl off the matchbook cover. I'd copied it a thousand times, but this time secretly mailed it in, hoping to get some idea if I was any good or not. The answer arrived two weeks later: I was too damned good for my own good. The test caused a correspondence-school salesman to come knocking at our door one evening. Not unannounced, mind you, because the school had sent a letter ahead of him. Somehow, unimaginably, I'd not noticed.

And now, the correspondence-school salesman is sitting by the stove in our slightly sooty living room. A beefy, good-looking man in a burgundy regimental tie, dark-blue suit, and glistening black shoes, he speaks to me and my father with an educated Connecticut accent. With nothing of the salesman's air, he is clearly sincere. 'The first course is one year long; four years all together to get a certificate,' he says, 'or shorter if you work very hard at it. But it can be as long as you like, if you need more time. Personal mentorship is provided with each lesson until completion.' *Mentorship? Remember to look that word up tomorrow in a school dictionary.*

Daddy is looking nervous. I'm about ready to puke, both from fear and excitement.

Salesman to Daddy: 'The young man is, without a doubt, extremely gifted.'

The young man blushes.

Daddy: 'Joey's always been able to draw. Even when he was four he drew pictures on everything in the house—envelopes, and blank pages in books ...'

Salesman: 'Look, we give out thousands of dollars in scholarships every year. And we've decided to write off two-thirds of the cost as a scholarship grant.'

The young man in question: 'Daddy, I'll pay half of it. I'll take on another newspaper route.'

Daddy: 'It's still just too expensive; there's no way we can afford one-third of $335.'

At this point, I realise that the salesman has never mentioned the actual cost, nor has he handed us any literature showing the cost. Yet Daddy knew what it was. Like a sledgehammer, it hits me: my father had intercepted and done away with the letter of response. No wonder I didn't get the Draw Me! test results. At any point in the previous week he could have jumped me, told me never to send off for things like that again. I would have quite expected that, under the circumstances and from past experience.

Daddy looks uncomfortable, embarrassed at not being able to afford the course, despite the reduced rate. In fact, all three of us look embarrassed and awkward. The salesman must feel like shit, sitting in a barren room and suggesting that this family, one that obviously has a hard go of things, contemplate spending over one hundred dollars.

Salesman (getting up to leave): 'If I didn't have a family of my own I'd buy the course for young Joseph myself. I really would.'

Daddy: 'Yeah, we all got family needs to think of first.'

The salesman says his goodbyes and heads for his car. Daddy looks at me. A complex expression comes over his face — one I cannot read — before it melts into stoicism. In that brief moment, though, I understand that he feels pain. That he feels terrible for his inability to encourage me in the thing I definitely have a talent for and care most about, even if he does not much care about or even understand it at all. (Such mutual incomprehension plagued us all of his life.) Daddy walks upstairs without a word.

Never again did we speak of the matter. For years afterwards, I secretly wondered how differently my life might have turned out if I'd had that one opportunity — a simple mail-order course — as an affirmation of what small aspiration I could muster in the face of what I knew lay ahead. I already knew that the future promised to be a struggle, probably of the most anonymous and grinding kind—the struggle to get by. Still, though, Daddy felt bad about it. And that was something: it resembled empathy for my loss, and unspoken affection for me. I felt as bad for Daddy as he felt for me. Resentment on my part was out of the question. I wasn't going to be an artist after all. *OK, then,* I thought, *there's always some way to make a living. Nobody starves in this country.*

'ANY GUY WHO CAN CUT HAIR WILL NEVER STARVE,' Dody Cribbs, the alcoholic barber, said as he dusted my neck with the fluffy talc brush.

'He'll sure as heck always have enough money to drink himself to death,' quipped one of the men waiting for his turn in the chair.

'That's alright,' Cribbs shot back good-naturedly, 'as long as he closes his shop before he opens the bottle.'

Everybody laughed. Including my father, who never drank. I could see this was the humour of grown men, so I smiled as if I understood the full implications of the joke, never once wondering why Mr Cribbs wore such heavy 'smellum goods' and constantly chewed peppermint gum. Boys did not interject during the conversations of grown men in those days, and probably shouldn't now. But I got up nerve enough to try.

'Uh, how'd you learn to cut hair, Mr Cribbs?' I asked.

'I went to barber college over in Pennsylvania after the war. Then I was an apprentice, then a journeyman barber, and then I got my licence.'

Having few mental associations with the word 'college', other than images of sweaters and green campuses in some faraway place, like in the movies, I was left to ponder just what a barber college must look like. Long shafts of light illuminated dust motes of talc in the air as I imagined men in white coats, with their nails trimmed to surgical precision on their scrubbed hands, majestically teaching the tonsorial arts to eager young men — men about to embark on a solid and respected trade, trimming hair from the necks of the priest and the plumber, the card scoundrel and the clergyman alike, while hot towels, scissors, and nose clippers, straight razors, and all the gleaming accoutrements of one of the world's oldest trades stood waiting in their steamers or narrow beakers of alcohol, ready to be applied in the mysteries and arts of the barber.

As it happens, 'art and mysteries' was the term used in the 1768 paper of indenture for my ancestor John William Bageant, in which John William, aged twelve, was indentured to Mesheck Sexton to learn the craft of the cordwainer (a leathersmith, a maker of gloves, shoes, and saddles). In the indenture — which was a term for any kind of signed legal document — Sexton promised to give John William 'such meat, bread and drink as is befitting an apprentice', to teach him 'to read and cipher to the power of ten', and to supply him with 'the tools of the cordwainer's art upon completion of this indenture'. In return, the 12-year-old Winchester orphan John William promised not to frequent 'race courses or gaming houses, and never to reveal the art and mysteries of the cordwainer, or any other secrets of his master's art'.

Having any kind of trade in colonial America was elevated above ordinary rote-toil at a time when the most common working category was 'labourer'. A tradesman generally worked indoors, out of the weather—which was an esteemed situation—and possessed a valued skill. Things had not much changed in Winchester by the middle of the twentieth century. We thought of having a trade in about the same terms.

Nowadays, I walk by the location of John William's workshop every time I go down Winchester's main street. The site where he cobbled shoes is across the street from a shoe store that sells only sweatshop-labour imports and outright slave-labour-made shoes from Asia and sub-Saharan Africa. Not that there is much of an alternative. For all practical purposes, there are no other affordable shoes available for most people. Certainly none made as in old John William's day, by a member of one's own community or anyone you might ever meet. Compared to the cold, monetised anonymity of our scientifically stimulated and managed consumption, you'd almost have to grant that there was indeed mystery and art in the cordwainer's craft—if for no other reason than that those things do exist in the well-engaged, skilled, and disciplined hand. Could you make a pair of shoes? Or satisfactorily cut twenty men's hair in a day? Me neither.

At that moment, though, with my neck bent down as Mr Cribbs dusted hair from my shirt collar, all I could see was his highly polished cap-toed cordovan shoes. If barbering enabled a fellow to wear such shoes, it had to be a pretty good trade; I would have been proud to end up as a barber. Descending from the high, green-leather-upholstered chair, I straightened my shirt with manly aplomb.

'Here, boy,' Mr Cribbs said, proffering a closed hand. 'Here's your ear back.' The men guffawed at the mouldy old barbershop joke. I blushed at being the centre of attention of these men, none of whom wore cordovan shoes, but all of whom diligently polished or cleaned their own common leather ones, as self-respecting men were expected to do. For these tradesmen—nearly all of whom were raised on farms—shoes, regardless of type, were material possessions to be kept maintained and, if you were going downtown or any public place, to be brushed and polished.

The logical thing for new arrivals from the farm was to 'take up a trade' if possible. Many of my father's friends and gas-station customers were the town's tradesmen—electricians, carpenters, concrete-foundation men, brick and stone masons, welders and fabricators, just as he himself was an automotive mechanic. They crawled under people's houses chasing wiring and vent pipes; they leaned over fenders deep into motor vehicles; they climbed electrical poles; they shaved alloyed metals down to a one-thousandth-of-an-inch accuracy on bed mills in machine shops. Confidence comes from competency and, like any good tradesman today, they had it.

The tradesman's is the easy, unpretentious confidence that comes with knowing how the world operates. Strong and blunt, the tradesman's confidence (the ease of 'self-agency', as writer Michael D. Crawford insightfully calls it in *Shop Class as Soulcraft*) is today seen as crude by college-educated people, as a definite sign of lower-class social status. Yet the expertise of tradesmen is the reason we are entitled to expect any appliance to work when we hit the switch, because they wired it the right way, and why we never think about how the water gets from the reservoir to our showerhead. They create and maintain most of the important hidden functional aspects of the material world that we take for granted. From the steam lines at the power plants that drive your Mac, to the plumbing that drives your morning turd away from sight, tradesmen create and keep humming both the exotic and mundane mechanisms of daily life.

From the tiniest to the largest of devices, tradesmen and craftsmen built most of the Western world until Taylorism came into full bloom. Taylorism refers to the 'rational efficiency movement' of the early twentieth century; in particular, Frederick Winslow Taylor's 'scientific division of craft'. Taylor broke down craftwork into dozens of individual, simple, repetitive motions to be done by a series of workers along a production line. Today we assume that this is the only way to create or assemble things. But when Henry Ford launched his automobile company, each wheel, for instance, was made by a single craftsman who assessed its relationship to the whole machine and to what fellow craftsmen were creating; and parts were uniform, but with great attention paid to the quality of materials and workmanship. A tradesman viewed efficiency as efficacy. He considered himself efficient if he produced things that lasted and functioned for many years.

For Taylor, however, efficiency had only one dimension: company profitability, and to Taylor that meant utilising unskilled workers; they were much cheaper than tradesmen, even if he had to hire twice as many. To eliminate the tradesmen's knowledge of the entire product, he emphasised that knowledge of the whole system had to be contained within management; it was never to be shared with workers, so that they could never demand higher wages in accordance with higher skill-levels. The 'Taylor system of efficiency' gained momentum, destroying every craft in its path—especially those related to fabrication. Combined with corporate capitalism's appetite for cheap labour, unchecked Taylorism eventually girded the globe with sweatshops that, in turn, buried America under piles of techno junk and textiles, and made 'recreational shopping' one of the nation's top pastimes. Those consumers may have been stumbling instead of running down the store aisles of late, but recreational shopping is still a major driver of the US economy. Americans are still doing their bit to save the country, even if they hit the mall with only ten bucks to spend.

And why not? We're talking about *brand-new stuff* here, folks—like the 'improved iPhone and its must-haves for shoot-everything-that-moves apps for gamers' (from an actual ad). The survival of American-style corporate capitalism depends on the public perception of such unending 'newness' and 'improved must-haves' to sustain abnormal market growth. To that end, it has buried us not only in junk, but also in junk efficiency, in the encrustation of ordinary goods with electronics—things designed to delight consumers by their novelty.

Toward the end of his working life, my father was very frustrated by the 'electronic crap plastered into every corner of a car'. Now ubiquitous, it is crap that cannot be fixed; it can only be replaced by the dealer with a new piece of the same junk. All this, as the old man put it, just so 'some lard-arse doesn't have to crank his own window down, or wants to hear his car talk to him about its battery. When you take it apart, you see it's not only junk, but there's nothing to it. Just a couple of wires and some cheap little plastic switches. But the guy gets to see his window go down because he pushed a button. People are like little kids that way. They'll pay money to believe they have a talking car, yet never change the oil.'

My father never lived to see the ridiculous levels all this would reach, or the learned helplessness that would be inculcated in Americans through consumerism. But he did have satisfying work, even if there was far too much of it to sustain his health. As a dedicated mechanical tradesman, his job required knowledge of the whole, and thinking and doing simultaneously, which is the very definition of satisfying work. Thinking alone does not lead to the satisfaction of understanding, and doing any work mindlessly and isolated from the whole of things drains even the best men of spirit. The problem-solving monkey must engage the world with both mind and body to feel the spark of his best nature.

Anyway, a week or so after my haircut, Mr Cribbs came by the garage to pick up his car, a 1955 Chrysler with a flathead straight-six engine, as I remember—a damned-good car if taken care of. Mr Cribbs certainly could never be accused of that. As a result, there came a point when every time he started it up, the car would 'shake like a dog shitting peach-pits', in his own words. 'Like the engine mounts is loose. I swear I believe that's what happening—loose engine mounts.' Anyone familiar with cars knows this is extremely unlikely in any fairly new vehicle.

When he returned for his car, my father told him, 'Didn't need nothing but a good full tune-up, plugs, points, everything, so it would run smooth again. You're good to go.'

Dody Cribbs was grateful and much relieved it had been that simple. And that he could avoid having to go to the dealer, and instead could go to a tradesman—someone he knew well—to get help. Even back then, no one but the rich were dumb enough to trust the motor dealerships' repair services. Plainly, Mr Cribbs was delighted to pay the tab. Both men were smiling. Both got something more out of it than the money paid or the work performed, which was no great mechanical-repair feat by any means. I've never experienced any work—and I include writing—that is as fulfilling as making the people you know and see and talk to regularly feel that they're 'good to go'.

'Do you know how good your daddy is, boy?' Cribbs said, exhaling a hint of whiskey.

Mr Cribbs was tipsy, as usual. But it was still true.

In that simple moment of an ordinary thing having been well done, I was very proud to be the son of a man who, for $45 a week, helped keep the world tuned up and reliable … by looking out for people who, for one reason or another, didn't always look out for themselves, so they needed to place their trust in others.

Funny how such a small moment, such a mundane thing as an engine tune-up, can stick in a fellow's mind for fifty years.

STILL, THOUGH, MY FATHER WAS WORKING SIX ten-hour days a week—for, as I said, about forty-five bucks—and he was always tired and irritable. More than irritable, he was volatile. Any little infraction could set him off: he would start beating us with his wide belt, and when he got started he couldn't stop. This wasn't because he was a sadist, but because of the pent-up rage that comes with the culture of shame.

On the one hand, he had the self-agency that comes with competent workmanship, but only so long as he remained at work—and there was certainly no choice in that. No workee, no eatee. So it was sixty hours, sometimes more, for forty-five bucks, take it or leave it. Those were the terms of the business-owning class, even the smallest businesses among them. Especially the smallest. They wrung their employees hardest of all to gain momentum in their upward mobility—the more they squeezed their employees, the better they lived. Even today, lauded though they are as the backbone of the nation's enterprises, heartland America's small-business owners are among the most ruthless in exploiting workers.

At the same time, life at home was daily testimony to my father's inadequacies at dealing with town life. One day, I came into the house to find him sitting at the kitchen table, head bowed, a heavy hand to his forehead so as to hide his face. He was looking down at a yellow slip of paper on the kitchen table. Though he pretended otherwise, he was crying. I had sense enough not to ask why. Grown-up problems were grown-ups' business, and kids had no place in them. However, he revealed the source of his anguish.

'Just about the time we get a little bit caught up on the bills, Gladys has another nervous breakdown, and there goes everything all over again.'

He was not so much telling me as talking to himself. Some of both, I guess. The yellow slip was a medical bill for $700. So my mother was not down at the Charlottesville university hospital for another operation on her back, after all.

At the same time, my father was buying a small bit of heating oil each week in the hope of accumulating enough to get us through the coming winter. When he wasn't home, I used to go out and drop the measuring stick into the oil tank to judge his progress. Staying warm was everyone's concern. He couldn't buy enough to warrant a delivery, so he'd bring home five gallons at a time from the dealer. The tank held 200 gallons.

Daddy couldn't buy his required work-uniforms new, so he was always wearing someone else's cast-offs. He was lucky to buy the oval work-shirt patches that said 'Joe'. And when he couldn't, there was just that darker, unfaded oval over the right breast pocket, where someone else's name had been—perhaps a 'Marv' or an 'Earle'. As I've said, he couldn't even afford to buy his kid cheap mail-order drawing lessons when the kid was willing to pay half the cost.

But this was Sunday, and soon he would be leaving to make the 224-mile round trip to Charlottesville to visit Mama. So the best thing for me to do was keep my mouth shut, start getting a meal together for my younger brother and sister, and wait for him to leave. There was no sense in talking, no sense in taking the risk of setting him off with my 'constant yapping', as he'd say when he was stressed like this. No sense in risking a beating for my most recent infraction—and God knows there were many on my part, just lying out there like a minefield waiting to be recalled.

Years later, Jim and Rick told me they used to stand outside the house and wince in horror at the sound of our screaming: 'Please, Daddy, stop! Please!' If I were a child today, bearing some of the broad, red welts I carried to school—the kind with the little red dots of blood dried on the pores—I'd probably be in foster care. Teachers in those days, however, overlooked such things and, besides, foster care was mainly reserved for orphans.

Strangely, I never hated him for it, and came to think it was the natural order of family life. Pap had probably beaten him, too, at times, though surely not as often. The beatings went on until I got to be about sixteen and reached the stage where I was capable of fighting back There was a commonly acknowledged fact in that culture, one which still exists in many corners of the white underclass: you are finally a man when you can whip your old man's arse. We came close to that—we had a couple of rough scuffles. We never quite reached the punch-out point, but only because I went into the US Navy. There was no way that a sixteen-year-old could have whipped a 35-year-old working man. I'm glad I wasn't around long enough to go through what would have undoubtedly happened.

Between mental breakdowns and back operations, my mother worked at least forty hours a week in local textile mills and clothing factories. Most of it was at piecework rates, wherein the production line was alternately sped up and slowed down. It was sped up to make quotas, and slowed down to prevent having to pay the piecework rate when workers started earning too much for management's tastes. A couple of the plants had unions, but they were mostly fake 'house unions' that rubber-stamped the companies' practices, thereby instilling a distrust of unions in the local workers. It was a brilliant tactic on the companies' part (so successful that companies in Virginia still do it).

Slowly, town life and the inability to gain economic traction was taking a toll on everyone. Mother was the first to break down, first in her body, with numerous operations on her back and legs, or 'female surgery,' and then in her mind, with those semi-secret mental hospitalisations. 'Your mother has to go in the hospital again,' Daddy would announce. My younger brother and sister assumed it was yet another back surgery.

But, after the crying incident, I knew it was for what were then called nervous breakdowns. Over time, they progressed—if that's the right word for such a thing — from crying jags to catatonic depressions and suicide attempts.

If the institutionalisation was not expected to be for too long—say, a couple of weeks—I would become the primary care-giver for my younger brother and sister. This wasn't a particularly new role for me, as my parents worked opposite hours; for years, they were seldom together during waking hours. If the hospital stay turned out to be a prolonged one, we kids would be farmed out to relatives.

Work for money, and money for work: life demanded

that everyone, even kids, worked every non-school minute of the day. I sold newspapers on the street corner, earning fifty cents a day, which I turned over to my father to buy coal, food, or whatever was needed. The wealth economy was so hard on my parents and people like them that, by the time they were forty, they were already praying for old age and its small Social Security cheques. I've done it myself, and millions of Americans still do. At least it's steady.

Life for the working poor was essentially tough; I'm sure that the work was more physically brutal back then. By the age of seventeen I'd loaded boxcars of bricks by hand, using tongs holding six bricks each—66 pounds per lift of back and arm. (I have two fused vertebrae to show for it.) I've hauled 70-pound bundles of asphalt shingles up a two-storey ladder all day in 95-degree heat. I've had my feet scalded by molten iron in a foundry that allowed fifteen minutes for lunch as the sole break in an eight-hour shift. And I'm here to tell you that there ain't a goddamned good thing about such wage labour, except the paycheque at the end of the week.

Youth was a hurried, frustrated, ball-busting affair. But adulthood's relentless struggle to stay afloat left you looking back at youth fondly. You hear a lot of work-crippled old guys, men who went to work at the age of fourteen, fondly recall 'back when I was a kid'. The truth is, they never really had a chance to be kids.

While life on the wrong side of the tracks was far tougher than on the manicured side—the side where the kids did not have to sell newspapers on street corners to get school-lunch money and help buy the coal, or have to 'bust crates' (hand-load trucks) on weekends, like those other now-old men who did the same—nowadays I prefer to recall the little that was good. Like the country song says, 'As long as old men sit and talk about the weather; as long as old women sit and talk about old men.' I prefer to recall the cherry bombs of summer, the swimming holes, and the cute arses of the once-young girls.

CHAPTER TWELVE

The Sediment of Memory

Not only can poverty not be bought, but the very memories
of its psychological pain, losses, and defeated dreams can
shape-shift, reinvent themselves, and come prancing back
in new raiment to rule over a past that never was. In 1987,
I was sitting with my father in his small modular home
just outside town watching the Minnesota Twins beat the
St Louis Cardinals. Weak as he was, very sick with the
heart trouble, hypertension, and diabetes that would soon
kill him, I could see through the side window that he had
nevertheless planted yet another big garden.

'Living out here sure beats living in town, doesn't it?'
I remarked, trying to make conversation — something we
could almost never do comfortably as adults.

'Yep, it's better, alright.'

'I hated our life in town after we moved to Winchester,'
I said. 'It was miserable.'

'Miserable? What are you talking about? They were the
best years of our lives.'

To my mind, the prime years of his life, the years

between the farm and the heart attacks that finally enabled him—through modest disability cheques—to sit here in his pyjamas and enjoy the World Series, were stressful and miserable for all of us most of the time. I don't have to do any research to remember his stress and rage, and the uncontrollable beatings he gave his children. Nor the volatility and tension.

'Them was the good years,' he said. 'We had everything we needed. We was happy back then.'

I was stunned in disbelief. All the times he'd been screwed on car loans and mortgages, cheated at jobs, the 173,000 hours of his life he'd worked at below-minimum-wage salaries, the loss of his small trucking company, the fact that only one of his three children ever graduated from high school, that two of his three children had fathered or birthed babies out of wedlock, the emotional collapse of his wife, the piles of medical bills that smothered him most of his working life, the moving from one rental to another every time the rent went up as little as five bucks, the fact that he had never had a vacation in his life, and that he had to suffer massive heart attacks to finally get some leisure time …

'Them were good years,' he reiterated. 'This country has been good to us.'

'Good to us? You sound like a refugee from some Balkan communist country. This is your country; it's *supposed* to be good to you, not do it as a favour!'

All around the room were symbols of Christianity and patriotism, but mostly Christianity, as if to reinforce the idea.

'We've had a good life,' he concluded.

'What was so good about those days? How were things better off after you left the place down home? In the years after the war?' I asked.

'We always had everything we needed when you were growing up. Everybody made better money after the war. People got ahead if they were willing to work. People had more fun—more of everything. Our Lord provides for his sheep.'

'Aw, fer God's sake!' I said.

'*You,*' he snapped, 'are one of those people who always look for the worst in everything! Take the Lord's name in vain again, and I'll throw you out of this house!'

My mother, who had microwaved some green beans and frozen-fish sticks, broke the tension by announcing that lunch was ready. There was the obligatory table grace: 'Dear Heavenly Father, we thank you for the food that is about to nourish and bless our bodies ...' During grace, I first started to realise how malleable memory is, and how powerful the things that reshape it can be. His generation's memory, as well as my own, had been seeded by the national post-war mythology. We had been brought up on all the old war movies, television shows, and commercials for Americanism that were—and still are—passed off as news. Not to mention the unquestioning acceptance that was fostered, even demanded, by the ultra-patriotic American fundamentalist churches. Though I did not know it at the time, that conversation was the beginning of this book. Short scraps of memoir began to accumulate on floppy discs and note pads, some of which you read in the preceding pages, with me never having any thoughts of publishing them. Frozen in the years they were written,

I like to think that they are closer to the bone than if I set out to write them down today. However, I also like to think that some of my old suits in the closet still fit me; yet I dare not try them on.

But you can try on other people's suits, and you can check other people's memories and memoirs. So I did. Some of this book relies upon the unflinching journals that my mother kept over the decades. Her in-the-moment observations were brutally honest. She can remember minute details from seventy years ago — the smell of a room, or what someone wore. With this in mind, I asked her about the decade or so following the war.

'Yes!' she exclaimed. 'Them was the best days of our lives, wasn't they!' For all the anxiety, grief, and hardship, she too was remembering those times as the days of rainbow pie.

Surely it would be easy enough, not to mention more convenient, to dismiss my parents' rewrite of their painful lives as the merely compensatory mechanisms of two elderly rednecks I've dearly loved, and sometimes feared, and sometimes feared becoming. But the fact is that America is simply not good at remembering. We're so bad at it, in fact, that we've been called the Republic of Amnesia. Anything and everything is readily forgotten in our complete involvement in the present and in our expectations of the next momentary gratification or new titillation. Even our wars evaporate almost before they are over. Popular interest in the Iraq War died about midway through it. The average American no longer bothers with the news noise about it.

As for past wars, you will have to search hard to

find anyone, outside of those who participated, who remembers our 1980s Persian Gulf war. Or the invasion of Panama (1989), or Grenada (1983), or Somalia (1990s), or Operation Desert Shield (1990–91). Other than a handful of news and political junkies, most Americans recall nothing of these wars and conflicts. They have but a vague remembrance of the names, and even then only because of having heard them on television at the time: 'Aw, yeah, Somalia. Didn't they have missiles or something? I forget.' This, from a 42-year-old businessman who was 26 at the time.

Couple the national amnesia with our dysfunctional public educational system and our engorgement on cheap spectacle, and you get a citizenry whose level of world and social comprehension is somewhere between a garden toad's and a bonobo chimp's. Even less than the chimp's, if we are to believe the Nature Channel.

THE MASS MANIPULATION OF OUR NATIONAL MEMORY through media has been made easy by the nature of memory itself. All memory—yours, mine, and everyone else's—is easily contaminated by the slightest outside suggestion. For that reason, virtually no one remembers anything as it actually was. From the moment it is formed, memory begins to decay, and the mind immediately begins blending fact with fiction as a normal function. This was demonstrated by University of Washington Professor Elizabeth Loftus in her famous 'Lost in the Mall' experiments. Her work began during the rage in America for 'recovered memory' during the 1990s, when everyone from Miss America to Roseanne Barr suddenly remembered having been victims of incest. In the process of proving that it is possible to distort another person's memory, and that all of memory is distorted naturally as we age, Loftus ended up proving that entirely false memories can easily be planted. In fact, she demonstrated that false recollections are often unintentionally planted by therapists seeking to excavate repressed memories of trauma, with both therapist and client 'discovering' false traumatic memories.

'But nobody forgets *real* trauma,' Loftus says. 'No Holocaust survivor ever forgot he was in a concentration camp, and no plane-crash survivor ever forgot the experience.'

In her now-famous 'Lost in the Mall' experiments, Loftus gave her subjects a memory book containing four short events from their childhoods. Three of these events were true, and were put together with the secret assistance of family members. A fourth incident about being lost in a shopping mall was inserted. Loftus had her suspicions confirmed that suggestion could plant the seed of memory: her subjects 'remembered' being lost in the mall as children. But more surprising was that the subjects confabulated minute details of their fictional childhood experience, what toys they were looking at, what thoughts went through their heads ... As time went by, the details of their fictions grew. The 'memory' became an unshakeable reality for them.

Is it any wonder, then, that the national memory of the post-war era is all bright new bungalows with shiny new Kelvinator fridges and dancing the Bunny Hop on polished floors? Our national false memory of that era is compounded by the fact that it is one or two generations removed from the event. Half a century of purposeful social, government, and business suggestion, and the sediment of subsequent experience, has accumulated in the depths of the mind where the bones of actual events slowly deteriorate.

There, in the unconscious, we sleep upon the psyche's oceanic floor, together like some vast bed of kelp, each wavering strand an individual American, swaying in the currents of national suggestion. In the form of a giant Portuguese man-of-war, our government hovers, rippling above us, showering freshly produced national memory spores on the fertile bed of our forgetfulness. Schools of undulating corporate jellyfish pass over, sowing the brands of products and services … followed by the octopi called media and marketing, issuing milky clouds of sperm to fertilise the seeds with the animating plasma of The Great Dream, which is to say any dream whatsoever — dreams of speed, regained youth, lips like cherries in the snow, improved sex, immortality through celebrity or wealth, success in all things, yes, yes, yes, all things and more.

Being made up of human psyches, nations are collectively even more susceptible to the seeding of memory, owing to the human desire to conform to group reality and to reach consensus. The planted seed becomes socially viral. When purposefully conducted by experts at a government level, it is called propaganda. More insidious, though, is the seeding of American capitalism's memes through media imagery — television in particular. Since World War II, they have told us who we are, by telling us who those around us allegedly are and/or once were, how they lived, and how they supposedly thought and acted, and for what reasons.

Post-war American television moved quickly from wrestling and re-runs of old westerns, through variety shows, to behaviour-modelling shows such as *Leave it to Beaver*, with Ward Cleaver wisely smoking his pipe as he sat on the couch next to his wife, June, advising Beaver and Wally on America's moral cornerstones. What Ward did for a living was never quite clear and did not matter because he modelled a manufactured ideal of productive and upright American home life. He had a home office of some sort, where he balanced his chequebook and mildly disciplined the boys for various moral transgressions in a weekly national electronic parable. Later in the series, as the post-war migration peaked, he started commuting into 'The City', briefcase in hand, in various new cars—alternating between Ford and GM, as an equal-opportunity promotion for both automotive giants—to work for a 'major trust corporation'. Along the way, the world globe in their living room was replaced by a television set.

My apologies for citing the much-overused *Leave it to Beaver* series, but it left a strong mark on the post-war generation, both kids and adults. Honest to God, I can show you old boyhood friends who grew up in the same crummy blocks I did, including one whose father was a semi-employed alcoholic and a philanderer, who remembers his boyhood as classic *Leave it to Beaver* stuff. I don't doubt that he believes it's true.

The accumulation of sedimentary national 'story truths'

in our collective memories through suggestion—purposeful or otherwise—is unavoidable. No event is fixed in the moment as it actually was. There are no flies in amber. Today the sedimentation is squared by an onslaught of textual and digital retelling and redefinition. The events of even one month ago are morphed. No fact can stand against this relentless onrush of atomised information, which becomes plastic and malleable in its sheer volume. Americans will never again be able to recall any national happening as it really was, assuming they ever did; the most that they will know will be shaped and presented by our information gatekeepers, television networks, or Internet portals.

We now remember and understand our selves, our culture, and our nation in the ways that best serve our wealth-based corporate economy. Corporations own all the media, and employ TV and cinema writers to do our national dreaming for us. The dream they produce solely relates to wealth, and why we are particularly entitled to it as Americans, with no reference to its historical human costs (such as slavery), or to its continuing costs (such as the fate of our sons and daughters, or of Iraqi and Afghan children), or to the money spent on two wars that could have lifted millions of Americans out of poverty. For most of the previous century, historical memory has been shaped to serve the ends of empire.

Technology enabled us to create a more uniform national field of consciousness than was ever possible, and thus a homogenised national storyline. Although challenged by immigrants and various ethnic groups, those groups do not own significant media. Outsider groups

264

write history books read mainly by their own kind. And even those recountings suffer from their own particular memory sedimentation. These underclass-challenger versions, usually ethnic or racial, seldom include the fact that they share their underclass status with a legion of whites several times their own combined number. Beyond that, the challenger versions of national memory include the same seeded basis as the accepted version, such as that all white Anglo–Americans have steadily gained in quality of life throughout our history, as they marched arm in arm toward the American Dream of affluence, sharing equally in it.

That makes it doubtful that there will ever be an authentic new American Dream to replace the original one — which, whatever it may or may not have been, was pathetically reduced to one of maximum material wealth and ownership of goods and commodities, and the 'freedom' to pursue those things until you dropped dead. No wonder that, despite our material accoutrements of wealth, we have come to experience the quiet nightmare of national and personal inauthenticity and cognitive dissonance. And the question nags on: If we are so rich, why do I feel so insecure? If we are so united in our goodness and purpose, why am I so lonely? I know I live in the best of all possible worlds, in a benevolent and plentiful democratic nation. The History Channel and PBS wouldn't lie.

THE EMPIRE'S PONZI SCHEME HAS LEFT OUR economy toasted. The financial elites have absconded with the family silver and everything else that was not nailed down. We have tent cities of homeless citizens. According to the CIA's *World Factbook*, in 2009 the nation ranked 46th in international infant-mortality rates (beneath countries such as Portugal, Greece, and Cuba), and is slowly sinking. Over 40 million working-class people suffer food scarcity or actual hunger. And yet what do the Empire's media pundits point to? They have set up a hue and cry about the decline of 'the American middle class' and its 'investments', as if the class they describe ever existed in the terms they describe, much less as a majority. Even more ridiculously, tens of millions of generationally trapped white-underclass people howl indignantly from the basement of society as if the loss were their own—so strong is the national indoctrination of a classless society.

They are trapped for the same reason that the post-war white rural migrants were. Our system builds traps to snare cheap labour. Furthermore, if they ever do manage to make it up the labour ladder a rung or two, or even to the middle rungs, they almost never stay there permanently. At some point, they find themselves booted back down, where they usually stay for the rest of their lives. The boot up their arses is called 'recession'.

Periodic recessions guarantee a permanent cheap labour supply by restocking its ranks through the layoffs. The definition of recession depends upon what class you are in. If you are on Wall Street or the typical economist, recession is the market's way of adjusting labour costs. If you are a plant owner or a typical Republican business owner, recession is good old Adam Smith's unseen hand rightfully jamming it to those unwashed, unworthy, and ungrateful bastards on the expense side of the ledger. And if you are a regular working mook, some Charley with only a high school education, you believe recession is one of those unavoidable acts of fate or God that just comes along—one of those things you just accept and suffer because, let's face it, nobody gives God any grief.

When a recession strikes, Charley has to run up the plastic until it smokes. He has no safety margin, no buffer, because his previous scant savings are looking back at him from behind his daughter's eye operation. He assumes that, sooner or later, he'll catch another job like the one he lost, if he humps enough job apps to enough personnel offices. He'll get back on his feet, and maybe even ahead of where he was.

But research shows that Charlie ain't got a snowball's chance on a barbecue grill. He's now a permanent member of the underclass. According to Columbia University researchers tracking previous recessions through government employment records, workers laid off during a recession seldom achieve their former level of wages. Five years after a recession layoff, the wages of those booted from their jobs remain 30 per cent below those who kept their jobs. Twenty years later, they are still earning 20 per cent less than those not laid off. The laid-off workers only have a one-in-four chance of ever regaining their former wage level during their entire lifetimes, and a one-in-ten chance of exceeding their former income. 'It's permanent and it's substantial,' says Till von Wachter, an economist and co-author of Columbia's research study.

And as if this were not enough to guarantee a never-ending supply of desperate working-class job-seekers, each recession saws off a chunk of the middle-management class, casting it into the ranks of the working class. If they are lucky enough to find a lower-paying job there, like busting cartons on the night shift at Wal-Mart, they never make it back up the wage ladder either. Meanwhile, these fallen mid-managers are replaced by some eager and cheaper employee he or she used to manage. Counter-intuitively, these days, recession spells outsized rewards for those on the top rung. Chainsawing those workers' jobs saves costs. Blowing a fellow executive out of the saddle and off the payroll does, too. Business goes to hell, layoffs sweep the country like a grassfire, and yet bonuses swell into the millions individually and into the billions company-wide for those execs who survive the corporate career plots and intrigues. There is cold comfort in seeing that some of the big dogs go down, too.

Von Wachter points out that these high earners suffer a higher percentage of lifetime income loss than the rank-and-file workers. If factory workers lose 30 per cent, fired investment bankers probably lose 40 per cent. Oh, bring me my crying towel, Bubba! Some bastard who's made upwards of $800,000 a year for the past decade-and-a-half has lost his job. Nothing to do but flee to his Tuscan villa and sulk.

There is no adequate accounting by middle-class bureaucrats and academics of the scale of the white underclass. Considering that they cannot even agree on what constitutes an underclass, I rather doubt their ability to count heads anyway. But if there exists a proper accounting of America's foundational white peasant class, I'd like to see it. I'd even beg for it. Until then, I'll stick with what I know.

On any given day in America's heartland towns and cities and suburbs, I can find innumerable Americans whose class experience has been the same as mine. They are without a doubt an underclass measured by the standards of the developed world: they are ignorant; under-educated; given to unhealthy vices such as smoking and alcohol; underpaid; semi-literate; misinformed; given to crude entertainments, sports, and a love of spectacle (particularly violent spectacle); disposable as a labour force; quick to violent solutions; easily misled; simple-minded in world view; superstitious; and poor in parenting and social skills.

I still hold the quaint notion that seeing is believing. And what I have seen over time accounts for many things that educated middle-class Americans find unfathomable. Such as the millions of the white working class who turn to Christian fundamentalism for an explanation and definition of virtually everything. Or the millions more still clinging to the warlike, Jacksonian worldview of manifest destiny at gunpoint. While educated, thinking Americans discarded the notion of manifest destiny long ago, it serves the interest of Empire that the peasantry adhere to that expansionist and profitable doctrine.

Illiterate? In poor health? Underpaid, disposable, superstitious, and exploited?

Big deal. That would describe much of the planet. The difference is American class-denial. The usurious middle-class loan shark in India is just that—a licensed crook. He knows it. And he knows he is a member of a mid-level economic class that is permitted to screw the peasants.

The peasants understand that, too, even if there is little they can do about it.

In the United States, the middle class is built upon the same extraction of the fruits of production of those below them as in India, but is perpetuated through denial of that truth, which runs counter to the nation's egalitarian mythology. The salaries and retirement funds of the middle class have always grown at the expense of the many millions more denied a fair wage or basic human entitlements. The middle-class advantage has been maintained through hundreds upon hundreds of downhill legislative screwjobs serving middle-class interests, such as tax laws, labour laws, college deferments to keep their children out of places like Vietnam, regressive sales taxes, 'sin taxes' on predominantly underclass pursuits such as smoking and lotteries, making mortgage interest tax-deductible for middle-class home owners, 401(k)s ...

The minority of Americans who lived the American middle-class dream enjoyed a damned-good ride on the backs of the underclass for five decades after the war. But somebody left the American Dream in the toaster too long. Assuming that the Dream ever existed (the very term smells of PR hype), it's now burnt to a crisp. But while it is forbidden to say so publicly (which in itself makes one wonder), the End of the Dream is all that literate, informed people talk about privately these days, when they are sure that no children or foreign press are listening.

Even many immigrants aren't buying it these days. Whole neighbourhoods of affluent East Indians and especially Chinese are moving back to their native countries, now that they can afford an American houseboy there. Older naturalised citizens, formerly immigrants to America, tell me that it's not the same country they came to a few decades ago, and that the heart has gone out of the dream. Many new immigrants say they feel cheated.

Others claim that enonomic opportunity still exists for them because they still know what Americans have forgotten: how to pull together in a labour-based miniature economy called the family. 'Americans,' an East Indian motel owner tells me, 'spend all their money, never save a penny for their children's educations, then kick their kids out of the house or send them to college at age eighteen, bestowing their children with massive debt. Immigrant families expect the entire family, including the children, to work hard in the family business every spare moment. Then the business succeeds and pays for the children's college educations. The children become wealthier than their parents, and inherit the motel or whatever other business later in life. That is the key. That is the surest way—remembering how those before you succeeded.'

REMEMBERING HOW THOSE WHO CAME BEFORE US succeeded: that's a pretty good description of how Maw and Pap did it in a time before the national amnesia developed into a national case of Alzheimer's. And apparently we have to import such skills these days.

On a gravel road a half-mile off the main highway, not far over the Morgan County line, is a tiny frame cottage. Light blue with a neat, brown-shingle roof, the cottage sits squarely in the middle of an edge-to-edge garden of tomatoes, peppers, lettuce, pole beans, corn, cabbage, pumpkins, and squash. This is the home of Acilano and Maria Cordero, legal-as-hell immigrants from Mexico, and their four children. The Corderos are part of the under-underclass—the Empire's nannies, cooks, gardeners, and builders—of which the most affluent Americans sometimes import whole families. Far from complaining, Acilano makes the most of what must be called poverty, since in the final tally he works for less than the minimum wage (but gets almost free use of the cottage). Employed by a gentleman hobby farmer, a US government official in Washington, DC, Acilano cares for the great man's tax-write-off cattle. He also raises hay, builds stone walls and fences, and does masonry, carpentry, and restoration work on the owner's six-bedroom colonial-era house at the back end of the 200-plus acre estate.

Self-taught, Acilano speaks and reads English fairly well. He is an avid fan of *Popular Science*, and follows the news on both Hispanic and US TV channels. When they are not busy on the estate, the Corderos work their own garden crops, each member doing some part of the planting, tending, and harvesting—every bit of it by hand, as their own fathers and mothers did. Like America's rural working-folks of a couple of generations ago, Acilano is capable of doing just about any practical thing that needs doing, and Maria is the same. Pap would have admired their skills. Sometimes I think that Mexican immigrants are about the only competent people in the US. You name it, one among them can do it. With some help from the estate owner, America now has two more competent citizens.

On this particular Saturday, a late-summer dusk has come, and the sky is almost as red as when Nelson and I saw—or imagined we saw—a panther in the sycamore tree. Acilano is turning under this summer's spent pea vines for mulch, and Maria has canned, dried, or frozen enough food to fill the bellies of every member of her family well into next summer. Watching them work is to see the soul of husbandry everywhere. The metallic slish and clink of the hoe in dry earth evokes images for me of Pap and Uncle Toad, of their lives that turned with the seasons until their own seasons were over. I am suddenly choked up inside, and wonder, *Can I possibly have let myself get so far from the earth and its matrix of soil, chlorophyll, and blood as to tear up upon encountering it again?*

Acilano's boss has driven back to his home in the great churning capital of an unrestful nation in a fearful season—a complex place where temples of finance have collapsed, trade and commerce are withering, and the oracles have pronounced an age of peak everything, possibly even the end of our petroleum-based civilisation. All this and more is being debated in halls of the marble city while Acilano and Maria hoe wilted pea vines into the soil for mulch.

Maria's father and mother were Braceros, skilled agricultural workers from Coahuila, Mexico. They thinned beets and harvested peas in California, and Maria says that on some nights the family would sit on the bales of pea vines and watch the distant arc of light over another great city, San Diego. The city and the pea vine.

Now if you go looking for the origins of both Acilano's pea vines and the city as we know it today—as a

273

concentrated centre of commerce and wealth, religion, art, and ideas—you will find them both in the same spot in Turkey. Civilisation's first real city, Catal Huyuk, or what's left of it, rests in the middle of a field of peas. Catal Huyuk was the taproot of all of Western civilisation and of all trade and philosophy, long before the Fertile Crescent bloomed. Multiracial and cosmopolitan, this city-state teemed with commerce, luxury, and wealth as it was then known; and, though it held but 6,000 residents, it was the greatest Neolithic city on earth.

In order to defend its wealth, Catal Huyuk was walled. Just outside those walls lived a Neolithic peasant society of ploughmen—sowers of wheat and barley and peas who, it is thought, seldom entered the city except for making certain religious observances. Catal Huyuk slowly rose, thrived, and fell while this humblest class of men, tillers like Acilano and Maria, watched. The nature of farming is to observe things that happen slowly: the growth of plants, the seasons. Catal Huyuk expired, and the tillers continued their planting and their watching, year in and year out, for the next 7,700 years. They still watch, guiding their ploughs around the mound of rubble that was Catal Huyuk. There can be no question as to which will endure longest—Washington, DC or the humble pea vine and its people.

They have bones of clay and blood of the earth's rains, and make to rise up the goodness of creation. The green carpet upon which their infants are born shall become their blanket in death, and it shall remain theirs alone forever.

CHAPTER THIRTEEN

Over Home is Over With

We've strayed quite far from this book's beginnings along Shanghai Road. But such roads run through the man born there, as much as through the landscape. And for all the byways a man travels forever after, through the cities and the towns, that same old road will lead him home again.

By 1960, Over Home was over with as a family lifestyle. Year after year of relentless pressure from an escalating transactional-wealth society had eradicated the ancient farm life, though we had still managed to return weekly to participate in our traditional activities: hog butchering, apple-butter making, and hunting. Especially hunting. But there was far less time for clan-sustaining activities, which had been slowly dying out for lack of available family members to help. Everybody was trapped in jobs. Except Nelson. He was unemployable, although he did mow the Greenwood Church cemetery, and gathered wild walnuts and shelled them for sale to neighbours, mostly for tobacco money. Without family labour, Maw and Pap had to buy what they once made for themselves.

Along with thousands of other small farmers at the time, Maw and Pap went into the egg-production business to earn some cash. Pap and Nelson built a small 'brooder house' in which the chicks were raised up to pullets under warm lights, and then transferred to the big plain-board chicken house that would hold a couple of hundred laying hens producing 200-plus eggs a day. With their strong orange yolks and deep flavour, you never saw better eggs. Fed laying mash and oyster shells for eggshell strength, they roamed freely during the afternoons, scratching and clucking their way across the surrounding hayfields. We would call them free-range chickens today. At dusk, they came home to roost in the safety of henhouse for the night, and the last task of each evening was to close the henhouse doors.

The egg business had become a national trend with small farmers. After a couple of years, with so many farmers producing eggs, the price fell—but not so low that there was no margin to be worked with, if there was no heavy debt load. For a while, eggs were sold to the emerging large grocery chains that were beginning to reach the smaller towns and regional rural markets, wiping out the crossroads stores. Soon, though, giant mechanised corporate egg-production operations sprang up, some with 20,000 chickens or more (which would not be considered especially large today), along with an agri-biz shipping and hauling industry to supply the chain-store distribution centres. Grocery chains came to dominate the market because of their sheer scale.

It did not take long for agri-biz to figure out that it was better to let individual farmers own all the taxes, debt, and risk. Big Ag poultry wholesalers began financing small farmers to set up poultry and egg 'factory farms' in what amounted to a franchise. The farmer was obligated to pay off the loan for the buildings and equipment (with his land being held as collateral, of course), and to buy feed, equipment, and antibiotics, etc. from the agri-biz franchiser—who, as the sole buyer, set its own price for eggs and poultry. Big Ag had captured and consolidated poultry and egg production through the orchestration of financing and the farmers' labour. In the process, Big Ag had brought back the illegal practice of sharecropping, the wretched capturing and holding of a farm family's labour in debt bondage. On paper, it was just another business deal between two consenting parties. Vertical integration had won.

The work on one of these factory farms was (and still is) gruelling and stressful as hell. Sixty or seventy hours a week was not at all uncommon as the farmer raced both the calendar and the clock, pushing the birds' productive capability to the absolute limits before they burned out. In between, the farmer had to fix the cheap aluminium feeder-belts that wore out quickly from round-the-clock use before they were even paid off, and the pumps and watering equipment, and fulfil the labour-intensive but ineffective poultry waste-disposal requirements.

But even before agri-biz conquered farming, back when the egg-market glut first appeared, small producers like Pap were left with two choices. They could either buy and erect the metal buildings, mechanised feeder belts, feed storage-hoppers, and watering and waste-removal equipment, and purchase their feed and mash by the truckload, and double their labour input—or fold.

Wisely, as it turned out, Pap decided to fold in time. Soon, agri-biz would push through laws such as the Egg Products Act that would eliminate small farmers in the regulatory equivalent of a death of a thousand tiny, and sometimes not so tiny, cuts. Among the dozens of provisions was that all eggs sold commercially had to be candled—held up to a strong light to check for any abnormalities. No problem there; farmers had been doing that for time immemorial. But standards were then set for the specifications of lighting devices, which came down to expensive and industrially made lights—designed by university agriculture departments, naturally. A strong light bulb was no longer good enough. Nor were normal chickens. More productive but expensive and, in some cases, more disease-prone, breeds were pushed by university ag departments in conjunction with the US Department of Agriculture and agri-businesses. The White Leghorn kicked out more eggs per lifetime than any other breed—before, that is, its flock died of coccidosis or blue comb. So antibiotics had to be added to the feedstock. The White Leghorn breed duly replaced hearty, traditional pioneer breeds, such as Rhode Island Reds, Barred Rock, Plymouth Rock.

Then, using America's agricultural and land-grant universities for credibility and research (which it heavily funded toward its own ends), agri-biz interests amended and added to the Egg Products Act specifications that only an academic pinhead could come up with: there was the 'depth of air cell' within the egg, there was 'yolk definition' and 'exterior egg shape' … Later, through the USDA and other agencies, came packaging-material requirements and, of course, inspection fees to fund their enforcement.

At first, Pap was eager to comply. But, after a while, he decided, 'Chickens has been making eggs for a right long time. And people has been eating eggs for just as long. Seems to me we already had everything pretty much worked out between us and chickens before the Department of Agriculture decided that both us and the chickens wasn't doing it right.'

American capitalism demands unnatural, superheated growth merely to survive, much less to grow. To stand still means death, and even that requires a vast money-producing and -extracting apparatus, many incremental fees and costs, and innumerable tasks and functionaries, however unnecessary, all along the way. Each one draws from the individual act of production of a genuine, measurable product — even one so natural, mundane, and venerable as eggs. Things eventually reached the point in the egg industry where there were thirteen middlemen between the farmer who gathered the eggs and the consumer, each exacting a price, most of which was subtracted from the farmer's margin so that the public would not see the true costs of such an elaborate, needless system of wealth extraction by the owning and financial class and its institutions.

Millions of small farmers tried to soldier on, to go along with this new kind of expansionist, credit-based farming. In the end, they were left with big feed bills, no market, and eating chicken for a long time to come as they folded — screwed without even getting a goodbye kiss. A generation of small farmers, through debt and regulation, financed a formative transitional stage in the rise and dominance of the super-capitalist agri-food industry and Wall Street.

So Pap had folded the show before it folded him. That ended the only attempt at commercial farming at Over Home. Soon, though, would come the end of everything, and it would arrive with a telephone call.

IT WAS NEVER A GOOD THING IF YOUR PHONE RANG late at night on a country party line. In all likelihood, on the other end of the line was Thanatos or any of his gruesome attendants—fire, pestilence, a summons to the hospital death bed of an elder, or word of a terrible car wreck involving some young neighbour or relative. That winter night in 1962, when the party line lit up, the grim message was from Irra, the God of fire. The homeplace had burned to the ground.

In less than an hour, a late-night chimney fire had reduced the entire house to a bed of coals filling the cellar. By grace, everyone had escaped, though barely. Maw, Pap, and Nelson stood in the snow and bitter cold, wrapped in the quilts they'd grabbed during their terrifying dash from the burning house. Maw had also grabbed an iron skillet and her music box, which played Stephen Foster's 'Beautiful Dreamer', and which contained a lock of Cousin Teesie's hair. Nelson had grabbed several of the family hunting guns from the rack in his bedroom. Ironically, as the fire consumed all they had ever known or owned, they were forced to stand close enough to its heat to keep from freezing. They turned sideways so they would not have to look at the horror.

But even amid the grief, there is also an amazement that attends such house fires, a chilling astonishment that so much can be reduced to so little. Everything in that huge old place was reduced to a layer of coals and ashes that did not even completely fill up the cellar, marked only by an occasional glob of melted metal that had once been a section of tin roofing. A lone, blackened iron bedstead was jammed at a crazy angle into the ashes, as if it had been hurled to earth from a malevolent heaven. It seemed unbelievable that the smouldering, grey ash so resembling Pompeii's had once been a glorious cellar of fruit and vegetable bins, and dozens upon dozens of canned jars of peaches and green beans, pork and beets, applesauce and abundance. Somewhere down there were the molten remains of a set of heirloom duelling pistols that came over from England with John William Bageant in 1745, alongside the shoe lasts used by his son, the Revolutionary War soldier–cobbler. And the less venerable stuff of life: dentures, old pictures of ancestors whose exact names nobody was ever certain of, a couple of secretly stashed girly mags (I know because I put them there), Christmas ornaments, and love letters … Somewhere down in there lay the history of our world, all reduced through the mundane physics of flame to the same fine ash that one discards from a woodstove.

By dawn, only the stone chimney stood, a monument to utter loss, with three figures shivering in its shadow: a skinny, stubborn old man; an ageing man-child who'd scarcely ever been off the place; and a sick, diabetic woman, old beyond her years. A neighbour, later recalling the fire, said, 'When I saw your grandmother's face, I knew she wouldn't last long after that fire.' When the sun was fully above the horizon, Pap said, 'I'll get a cable from the barn to pull that chimney down, before it falls over and kills somebody.'

He was still the same man who'd been married in his work clothes 46 years before; still the same man whose horses stood hitched and ready during his wedding. Pulling down the chimney was 'the next thing that needed doing'.

By the time he had the cable cinched around the chimney, there were plenty of neighbours to help pull it down—thanks to the party-line telephone grapevine, an emergency system of neighbours the likes of which we cannot imagine today. From up on Sleepy Creek Mountain, while taking a late-night piss, Joly Vernon had seen the flames two miles below. From then on, the party line was wide open for hours as word was passed around and supplies were gathered. Given the road conditions, up-hill neighbours risked becoming trapped in their own wrecks as they eased downhill in their vehicles, half-driving, half-sliding forward. Others walked across the snow-covered fields in the direction of Over Home, carrying things that would be needed immediately: shoes, more blankets, overcoats, coffee …

A week after the fire, Maw, Pap, and Nelson moved into the chicken 'brooder house', a heated hatchery shed they had built during the ill-fated commercial egg-production venture. Neighbours and family had immediately come together to insulate the building and add two small bedrooms, a kitchen, and a bathroom, and had furnished it throughout, right down to the hand towels. These were goods from their own homes, not stores, filling the pantry with home-canned fruits, vegetables, meats, cleaning supplies. For each neighbour, it was a sacrifice of some sort, large or small, because of their closer-to-the-quick lifestyle than we live today. But they saw to it that homelessness and hunger were impossible in their community.

After the fire, the physical heart of the clan, the sense of its place in the world, the one rooted in centuries and land, was gone. What remained of the ancient style of family connectivity had gone up in smoke. Now scattered and working across several counties in low-wage jobs, there was no central place on the earth for these people of the earth. Family members continued to return, even to the chicken-house home, for emotional and familial succour. But the connective tissue of shared work for shared sustenance had disintegrated in the face of the monetary-wealth-based economy. Only the clan patriarch and matriarch remained, but Maw died of her diabetes not long after the fire. She was sixty-three. (My father also died a diabetic at the age of sixty-three. I am diabetic, and this week I turned sixty-three.) As per her wish, they played 'Beautiful Dreamer' at her funeral.

One member, however, did not change much: Nelson. When Maw died, Nelson grieved wildly and openly for a day, then went to his chicken-house bedroom and rearranged the furniture. And that was it. He came back, lit his pipe, and sat down to wait for her funeral to begin up the road at Greenwood Church.

Nearly a decade later, Pap died of cancer, tied down to his hospital bed, vomiting up chunks of his lungs and calling out for Maw. The Morgan County Hospital was a small one. Most of its employees had lived in the county all their lives, and everyone, especially nurses and doctors, knew everyone else. The bedside nurse holding Pap's hand when he died was his daughter-in-law, Cousin Clayton's wife. When he expired, she said, 'We've lost the last of the old oaks.' Everyone knew what she meant. When you are born in and spend your life close to the natural world and its animating forces, an oak tree is more than just a metaphor.

That only left old Nelson in the chicken house. He cut firewood and lived in the old ways by himself, canning and cooking and doing the same things as when Over Home was full of family. Even into the 1970s, he was still smoothing axe and hammer handles with glass shards, just as his colonial ancestors had done. He kept on planting the huge vegetable garden each spring with Uncle Toad. Like salmon swim upstream, like old elephants return each year to drink from the savannah-land springs where they were born, these Bageants needed to plant as an act of renewal. The first thing my father did after the heart attacks forced him into retirement was to plant a huge garden. Each spring, Uncle Toad returned to the farm and, bending toward the red earth alongside Nelson, he planted. All his life, Toad had planted in that same garden with his brothers, with one interruption caused by the war. When he returned from the fighting in the Pacific, he resumed planting there each spring. After his wife Midge died, he still returned and planted. Toad continued to do so until the day he died. To Pap, Daddy, Uncle Toad, Nelson — to all of them — it was The Path. Right action. Call it The Tao of dirt. Call it Bones of Clay.

BY THE 1970S, A NEW GENERATION HAD TAKEN OVER business life, such as it was, in Morgan County. The sons and daughters of the local business class had come into their own. One arrived at Nelson's little place on what was left of Over Home, encouraging him to sign a phoney debt my grandfather had allegedly incurred, so a debt lien could be placed on the farm. The lien would be collected from the estate after Nelson, who was obviously getting on in years, had died.

Pap had been a tightwad. He had hated debt, and was not likely to have left a debt unpaid. But some of the newest mercantile generation weren't near the men their daddies were—not that some of their daddies and granddaddies were all that honest to begin with. The younger ones seemed to herald the new cunning of a more monetised America.

We rednecks expect a certain amount of cunning from the business class, even those plying their businesses out here in the sticks. But preying upon a man like Uncle Nelson? Well, tough old bear that he was, Nelson turned out not to be easy prey. It's pretty hard to tell an illiterate deaf man why he should sign his name on a legal document, when it's something he has no concept of to begin with. After a couple of visits, Nelson started greeting the scammers at the door by waving an iron-stove poker at them. They quit showing up. Nelson kept right on growing pole beans and tomatoes through his summers, and carrying in firewood in the winters, until a stroke sent him into a local nursing home at the edge of secluded woods about fifteen miles from the farm.

That's where he was when I visited him during the

last week of the twentieth century as America plunged once again into the orgiastic Christmas consumer rite of unneeded sweaters, never-to-be-used convection ovens, and hangovers.

But that morning in Morgan County, West Virginia was a bright, cold one, with snow and real cardinals on the green-black pine boughs, as a bent, old Nelson hoisted an American flag up the pole just as he did every day. He stood there watching it snap at the sky. He never learned to read and, being deaf, had never heard a patriotic word uttered. But he'd watched John Wayne in *The Sands of Iwo Jima* with my father, and had ultimately seen my father go to his own rest in a veteran's flag-draped casket. Nelson knew exactly how to fold and unfurl the colours.

These things went right over the heads of the care-centre staff. Kind as they were, many of them children of neighbours from the old days, they nevertheless treated him as if he were a child. At 83, a man, even one with a low IQ, is not a child. 'We let him raise the flag,' smiled one 'nurse'. She could never know that, in the larger scheme of things, no one ever 'let' Nelson do anything. The psychologist who dropped by the place twice annually once told me that Nelson's feelings were 'close to the surface'. This was not exactly news: his feelings were written all over his face throughout his entire life. He cried freely, but seldom out of sadness. When I last visited him, he came limping across the nursing-home lawn, his broad, hillbilly face streaming with tears of simple joy. My knees nearly buckled under the sheer weight of his love.

Nelson never knew about such things as the Middle East crisis; he never knew of the Columbine massacre dominating the news that year, or of career battles such as I have fought in my day. He knew that when spring came, he would plant a garden in the back of the nursing home with special permission. And he knew that, like plants, we all rise up to life, and that our season passes eventually—just as Maw's had, just as Pap's had, just as all his brothers and sisters had, my father being the last before Nelson.

AS MY FATHER LAY DYING AT THE WINCHESTER Medical Center, my mother wrote in one of her tattered life journals, as if she knew her children would one day read them:

> Some days I don't know if I can stand going to the hospital to see your daddy. I'm there twenty-four hours at a stretch, yet he seems so lonely and just stares and says nothing. I keep having this terrible nightmare: I am walking in this beautiful meadow with a baby in my arms. In the distance I can see a speck of a person coming. As it gets closer I can see that it is a man in a uniform, and finally that it is a soldier and he is as young as when I first met him. The closer we get the more he ages. Then he comes faster and faster and as we come together his face is a skull and he is biting my face, eyes to eyes and nose to nose and I am screaming.

After Daddy died, my mother moved into a cottage in the backyard of my home, which was in Oregon at the time, during one of several geographic pauses in the course of my following a job, as my predecessors had done. And from my own journal of that time, written on a hard drive, comes this:

The mornings are always foggy, and the yellow lights of that tiny house look as if they are fighting for survival through the mist. Her silhouette totters as she apparently dances to some strange rite with that 'spider stick' of hers. She is poking at spider webs both real and imaginary, an activity that consumes much of her time. She's quite crazy. Not dangerously crazy, or the kind of crazy that might cause her to hurt herself—merely the kind of crazy not too difficult to live with, providing you don't care what the neighbours think. She has grown huge from inactivity and vanilla wafers and litre jugs of Pepsi. When Daddy died, a horrible experience for all concerned, she pretty much caved in for good.

Right now, Gladys is crashing toward my back door on that scooter of hers, one of those three-wheeled jobs used by paraplegics and old people. With a milk crate bungeed onto the back to haul cargo from the Goodwill store, an orange flag sticking five feet in the air, plus an umbrella lashed on the handlebars, it's a sorry sight. Today she sports a wet cowboy hat and several layers of clothing, and is smoking a cigarette. So sour is the smell of cigarette smoke in her clothing and hair that people stand back a few feet.

'Joey,' she is calling, 'I got something I wanna show you,' as she lumbers off her scooter and huffs her way into my house, plopping down today's newspaper and waving a magnifying glass over a picture of the White House.

'See all them men in lifeboats in the dots there? An' see that devil's face?'

'Frankly, I don't.'

'Sure you do,' she snaps angrily.

After a couple of minutes I concede, but she's not happy with that. She has inward doubts about it, too, and is secretly angry with herself. Her face is wrinkled like a walnut kernel, and when I look into her eyes each wrinkle becomes a ditch containing all of our mutual ghosts — Daddy, Ony Mae, Maw, Pap ... They're all there, and I can never look at them for very long.

On the wall above her happens to be a large framed photo of her as a young woman. She is wearing my dad's army fatigues and hat, with her hand on her hip standing jauntily in the snow. She was absolutely beautiful in 1947.

'Damn it, Joey, I know you can see them lifeboats! Are you trying to tell me I'm crazy?' She lurches back to her scooter and goes home — all of 60 feet away.

That love can come packaged in physical revulsion makes for some conflicted feelings. Lord, please take me quickly when it's my time.

CHAPTER FOURTEEN

A Long-Promised Road

There is a road unto which I will deliver you, up and out of Egypt, away from the Pharaoh's land, and you shall be tested by your journey on that road.

— From an early Methodist sermon

After Nelson entered the nursing home, Ony and Belmont's son, Clayton, moved into the chicken house for a few years with his wife and kids. And when Nelson, the last direct heir, died, the farm was sold off, except for seven acres and the chicken house, which Clayton chose to accept in lieu of cash payment. The other ten heirs, including me, preferred the money, because everyone was in debt.

The rest of the farm was purchased by a would-be developer just prior to the sub-prime mortgage bust. Slowly returning to brush and early forest, like much of the rest of Morgan County, it awaits an 'economic recovery', some new bubble to come along. For now, though, Morgan County's abandoned fields remain open and neglected. Orchards and fields beg to be valued and made productive again. But the only value acknowledged by the American wealth-economy is debt. And debt is something that this county, which once thrived on thrift, has plenty of these days.

Clayton built his modular home higher up the hill, above the site of the old home place, thanks to having one of the scarcest things in America: a union job, as a telephone lineman with Verizon.

Last week, Clayton and I sat on his deck celebrating his 58th birthday. Most of a lineman's work is performed from a bucket-lift truck these days. But, at 58, Clayton can, and still does occasionally, strap on a set of climbing spikes and go up a 40-foot telephone pole to wrestle a dead transformer. He weighs 230 pounds, the same as me, but the pounds sure ain't in the same places.

Country music spills from the open doors of a beefed-up pick-up truck parked on the lawn. 'Take this job and shove it, I don't work here any moooore,' sings Johnny Paycheck to the bleeding-to-death strains of a steel guitar. Three tables piled with food stretch before us—real country cooking from the older wives, and not-so-good quick-fix processed stuff from the younger, third-generation women. A fiftyish couple dances cheek to cheek.

Eating fried chicken, drinking beer, and smoking, Clayton and I sit in folding lawn chairs, watching his grandchildren raise a ruckus on the giant inflatable water slide he has brought in for the occasion.

'Clay, did you ever think we'd be the old-timers up here on the home place?' I asked.

'Who's old? Me and my two boys can outwork any five men around. My boys can work.' I thought of the only compliment my father ever paid me, the only compliment he knew how to give: I was a good worker.

From where we sit, we can both see the old garden spot beyond the water slide. Evidently we are seeing the same ghosts. Clayton says, 'You know, after I moved back onto this place, on the first warm day in May the phone would ring, and there would be Uncle Toad on the other end: "We'll get the peas planted tomorrow morning, boy."' *They have bones of clay* ... We laughed in remembrance. That's what I mean about abidance in place. You remember its dead even as you take joy in its laughing children, because you've experienced that place long enough to know you belong to it. Almost telepathically, Clayton said, 'Nobody is ever gonna take this place from me. Ever.'

The truth is that these few acres will never truly be his—partly because the earth cannot be owned, only occupied and either cared for or neglected or abused; and partly because nobody ever owns anything in America's debt-as-wealth economy. Clayton borrowed money against the property to build his modular home; meanwhile, his labour is at the pleasure of the distant lords of a giant telecommunications corporation.

Clayton's home ('Fort Clayton', as we sometimes call it) is part of the county's patchwork of heavily mortgaged property. Each parcel is occupied by a dwelling, with its own septic system, well, powerlines, and driveway, carved out of farmland and mortgaged to the hilt. In the wealth economy, all things are only worth the amount of money that can be borrowed against them—the amount of indebtedness that their 'owners' can carry for corporate financial entities. The dwellers are occupants, almost never outright owners. The earth they stand on is the property of the lien-holding bank, while the occupants seldom if ever pay off their thirty-year mortgages in their lifetimes — they effectively rent the right to occupy the property, then pass that right on to the next 'owner'.

Clayton will never live to see the day when the place is paid off. Something will come along — a monstrous medical bill, a funeral — that will cause him to take out a new loan against the place. I know that; Clayton knows that; every working-class American knows that deep inside. But, honest as Clayton and I are with each other, as men of the old school with too much personal pride to discuss our fears, doubts, and debts, we'll never discuss such things. And, besides that, I'm certainly not going to piss on Clayton's parade, on today of all days.

Except for Clayton's house and the chicken house, the outbuildings and accoutrements of Over Home are gone, mouldering in the earth like the people who worked away their lives here. The nansy patch, the hundred-year-old Pippin apple tree, the pear and peach orchards, the concord grape arbour, the smokehouse, corn crib, woodshed, springhouse, barn ... gone. Of the many floral plantings, snowball bushes, lilacs, and others, only Pap's two rose bushes remain, carefully nurtured in his honour, and in Maw's, on an acre of smooth, green grass. Even with so much missing, the 'placeness' of it remains for those of us who grew up there. Somehow, in our mind's eye, the poppies still nod through the heat.

Clayton's four-year-old granddaughter is water slide soaked, rolling and laughing across that lawn, under which all time and things are geological, and the courses of future rivers are being plotted. One day, no doubt, she will be plunged beneath her own river of family blood and memory, guilt and glory, because she is still of this place and its people. And, because of that, in all likelihood she will one day plant a garden. But, for now, she is innocent. In fact, innocence is too trite a word for her joy.

AFTER HE'D BUILT HIS PRESENT HOUSE, CLAYTON and his sons used the chicken house as a deer-hunting cabin. Somehow it was fitting that it be a place where the menfolk could butcher deer on the screened-in porch by lamplight, and sit around the woodstove retelling the ancient family fables of the many hunts that took place on this land.

No more, though. Now, one of his sons, Clay Junior, a construction labourer, lives in the chicken house with his wife Krassie and their three children, after having lost their own home in the national mortgage rip-off. Among America's disposable millions with disposable jobs and disposable lives, and among the grandchildren of those 22 million displaced rural folks, they were born into a parallel world to the middle class. For them, it was one of life's givens that they would long have been working while others were pursuing higher education. Consequently they are among the 50 million Americans who read at a fourth-grade or fifth-grade level.

They can be thankful, though, that they are not quite among the 42 million American adults who read even more poorly. Nearly one-third of our nation's population is illiterate or barely literate, and cannot read predatory car loans, mortgage documents, or credit-card agreements. The first to be discarded from the work force, they composed the vanguard and the bulk of property foreclosures and personal bankruptcies. That was before the national mortgage rot began eating into the middle class—people who could read well enough, but apparently could not do the maths, or believed that their job tenure as the Empire's paper-shufflers was vouchsafed by God himself. The Krassies and Clay Juniors at least have the excuse of poor literacy.

America's semi-literacy, our general inability to read about the workings of government and the outside world, never gets in the way of our self-esteem. Fed on the delusion that all wisdom resides in the common man, and that our opinions and judgement are all to be equally valued, no matter what frothy dreck issues from our mouths and minds, we never doubt ourselves. This 'every man is a natural fountain of wisdom' myth is a sop, of course, and compensates for the obvious disparities and injustices taking place before our very eyes. No matter how bad things get, the rest of the world is worse off, because, 'By God, I live in the only free nation in a world of dictators and jealous terrorists. I live in an anointed republic where my opinion is just as good as any king's! More so, because I am the common man in a realm where the common man *is* king, dammit!'

Semi-literacy endows its tribe with the absolute surety and conviction of those who don't know what they don't know, rendering them blustering, happy idiots who haven't the slightest damned notion of anything beyond appearances. Delighting in the simple-minded images and slogans that have come to replace language, they buy the T-shirts of Barack Obama dressed as bin Laden, or sporting a Hitler moustache, and believe that the Democratic Party is setting up death panels for the elderly to save on the national cost of healthcare. Most ominously, they are hostages to political manipulation.

In November 2008, during the last days of the presidential elections, I stopped by to visit Clay, Krassie, and the kids. As I walked uphill toward the chicken house, the mountains rolled away in all directions, their leafless trees a smoke-coloured blur against the skyline. Silver-black sleet clouds hovered to the north. November was coming on cold and wet, reminiscent of countless similar late-autumn days I had spent as a child under the same sky. The mood about this place and this season was deeply familiar, and even as a kid such days stirred a strange feeling of poignancy in me, a piercing sense of emptiness and eternity.

My reverie was slammed by a barrage of savage snarls and deep-throated barking. I had forgotten about the lunging, hysterical Doberman kept locked behind a steel-mesh fence during the daytime. Stepping onto the porch of the chicken house, I found the front door wide open before me, despite the cold, and a wood-pellet stove struggled away at full blast. It crossed my mind that Pap would have kicked somebody's arse for wasting heat like that. Visible from the doorway were the three kids on the worn, dirty carpet in a sea of crumbs, eating bright-orange, hyper-sweet cakes out of a box. Clay Junior was off somewhere in his truck scouting for deer signs—hunting season opened the next week. Sprawled on the couch in a grungy pink sweat-suit, Krassie, overweight and fast headed for that permanent post–third child white-trash obesity, was immersed in a Fox News program about the elections, now just a couple of days away.

Somehow, I'd not imagined her having the slightest interest in politics or the elections. As it happened, though, Obama's race had grabbed Krassie's attention. More accurately, America's far right had taken up residence in her vacant political mind. More bluntly, the Republican Party had run its hand up her arse and was now operating her like a puppet, flapping her mouth. After the initial greetings and obligatory Southern small talk, she informed me that, 'If Obama is elected, every white woman will be a slave to some nigger.'

Even I, a man who listens daily to some of the most ridiculous, ignorant sludge that the American mind has to offer, was floored. This was raw-hate stuff here, and Krassie is by no means a hateful person. Dumb as a sack of goat hair, yes; but hateful, absolutely not.

'Where did you learn that?' I asked.

'It's right here on the Internet. I'll show you.'

She sat down at her computer in the kitchen, which was parked beneath a mounted deer head on the wall. We Southerners see no conflict between taxidermy and kitchen décor. Everywhere there were totemic images of deer, leaping from calendar illustrations, gazing from the covers of the dozens of 'hook and bullet' magazines that comprised the family library ... It struck me how much my mountain tribe, meat hunters for two-and-a-half centuries in these hills, are truly people of the deer. It also struck me that as a child I had curled up in that very corner where the computer sat, listening to hunting stories, and/or reading library books. In one of those strange, flitting memory images, I recalled finishing up Jim Bishop's classic, *The Day Lincoln Was Shot*, right there in that corner, right in that spot during one of our Christmas-holiday stays.

The computer was agonisingly slow. While we waited for it to gnaw its way through to a modem connection, Krassie's oldest daughter, age eleven, offered her opinion. 'I like Obama,' she said. 'He's very smart.' There was no objection on Krassie's part. Remember: our people are believers in and defenders of the right to opinion, even the most ill informed— probably because we own the majority of them. Looking at the child, I thought, *Now there's a little niece who's going to feel very trapped in this wasteland, if she doesn't already.* The computer ground on and on. Finally, I hedged my way out of the wait with, 'I'll take your word for it, Krassie.'

Once back at home, I told my wife about Obama's plot to make every white woman a slave to a black man.

'Well, then, half the women I know are really going to enjoy his presidency,' she answered.

Obama's subsequent election as president gave the Krassies of this world even more fuel for their dark speculations. On a later visit, I learned from Krassie that 'The Obamas are practising satanic witchcraft in the White House.' It never lets up. Then I learned that Obama is a Muslim operating out of the White House on a forged US birth certificate. As time went by, the startling updates on Obama and the Democratic Party kept coming. If I had to pick a favourite, I'd probably choose the one about the Democratic Party's 'healthcare plot' to make working heterosexual Americans pay for sex-change operations being demanded by liberals and welfare bums.

Even knowing where Krassie got this stuff, I had to verify it: 'Where did you learn all this?' I asked Krassie.

'On the Townhall website.'

Along with the Fox Network and the rabidly right-wing website Free Republic, Townhall.com helps make up the information trinity for millions of redneck and underclass whites. America's political elites quite well understand that not only is this class disposable, but so are its hand-fed truths. Any expedient lie that works can be used, then flushed and replaced with the next one, *ad infinitum*, even if today's lie contradicts yesterday's lie. Their memories are less than an inch long, and yesterday's lie is completely forgotten.

On the other hand, installing a hot button in their brains is about as easy as it gets. When it comes to the effect of simple repetition on simple minds, you couldn't do better than my native stomping grounds of Virginia and West Virginia, as was demonstrated during packed 'town hall meetings' during President Obama's healthcare reform initiative (this may be a bit of a tangent, but I cannot toss away such a good example of manufacturing opinion among our republic's white underclass of unwashed philosopher kings). In Southwest Virginia's voting district 9, the town hall meetings' sponsoring congressman was Rick Boucher. 'Slick Rick', a 14-termer, is one of those rightist Democrats never examined by our simplistic media, which treat both parties as if they were completely uniform in their make-up. He is pro the Iraq and Afghan wars, he is bought and paid for by the utilities and communications companies, and he is the tenth most powerful person in Congress.

A throng of Krassies—those screaming, red-faced white folks so loved by news cameras—turned out to fill his town hall meeting. Ruddy, overweight working people with neck veins bulging and fists shaking, they made gripping footage for the news hour, even with the sound off. In glaring contrast to them was a lone older black woman, there to tell the senator about her Down syndrome grandchild: 'The child can't get the physical and mental care he needs because our family can't afford any kind of healthcare at all ... We are just too poor,' she concluded, near tears. Her touching plea was interrupted by a sheer burst of redneck compassion. Yessiree! A young white man jumped up and screamed, 'It's a wonder they didn't abort him!' An angry chorus of mob agreement went up.

Between that whole sorry assemblage there was not enough combined brainpower to piss, much less ask: *Who* didn't abort the child? *Who* are we talking about here? And what in the name of heaven does this have to do with fixing the healthcare system? The implied villains were—who else?—those dirty liberal baby-killers. Instantly, abortion rights had become the main theme of the meeting. Goodbye to any further discussion of healthcare reform. All it took was one well-inculcated hot-button word: 'abortion'. My redneck people had responded right on cue.

Few if any of them could be called political types by any stretch. Ordinarily, they would have been home stuffing their pie holes and waiting for that day's winning lottery number on TV. But they had shown up at the behest of local Republican businessmen, the Chamber of Commerce, and fundamentalist pastors, who in turn were orchestrated by healthcare-industry lobbyists and industry public-relations firms. And, by golly, America was gonna hear the genuine, bona fide, straight-from-the-horse's-mouth, unadulterated opinion of the common man! Just as soon as they were all instructed as to that opinion.

Many attendees at town hall meetings and staged 'Tea Party' anti-tax rallies are retired or just plain-bored people to whom the free bus ride and buffet dinner that usually comes with the faux protests look pretty damned good. Not to mention the free tote-bag of goodies: chocolates, coupons, a neat little pen-light key ring. You can dig through this nickel-and-dime loot while the group's organiser gives you the 'orientation' during the bus ride—dividing up the planted questions among the group, giving tips on how to short circuit the opposing side's speaking opportunities, booing on cue, and so on. And sometimes there is that free trip to Washington, DC later to do more of the same, if you show enough talent for the cameras.

Rick Boucher's attendees had little talent, and not even a gnat's arse worth of understanding of the issue. But they knew the Devil's mark, and the Devil's mark is abortion. So they responded for the cameras just as they have been conditioned to do.

I know a slew of these people all over the nation, and I can tell you this: they honestly don't give a tinker's damn about abortion. You'll never hear any of them mention the word, except when their preachers and self-designated spokespersons or news reporters urge them to. The term 'abortion' is tucked away somewhere in their heads in a file holding the vague lexicon of 'Stuff I understand that I should believe in'. There it remains—a stale, unexamined, little brain fart—until the appropriate hot-button word is pressed. And then, right on cue, like serially wired blasting caps, they are detonated at town hall meetings or Tea Party protests, setting off a chain of blasts of 'citizen anger' diatribes.

The sad truth is that the pent-up anger has little to do with feelings about healthcare, but a helluva lot to do with all the shitty breaks, insults, and degradations that come with being an underclass citizen of the Empire. We are conditioned in much the same way as a dog is trained to bite on command. It doesn't matter who gets bitten—the dog gets the satisfaction of biting somebody for a change, and his master looks pleased when he does.

Healthcare reform had 70 per cent support when it began. After a few weeks of orchestrated slap-downs of its proponents at town hall meetings, and staged citizen revolts, public opinion of healthcare reform was in the toilet. Ordinary, quiet people, who never even discuss politics, started to have doubts when they saw folks like themselves on television rising up in what was touted by blonde meat-puppet anchorpersons and jowly, self-important male pundits as 'a nationwide protest by the common man'. Boucher could now go back to Capitol Hill and give evidence that voters in his white underclass district were vehemently against any kind of insurance-industry reform. They prefer the status quo. They like the fuck-job they are getting. They prefer being without health insurance, and going into medical bankruptcy, rather than enjoying the benefits of affordable healthcare.

Once again, my people, the great unwashed and unlettered, had been sicced like dogs onto challengers of the status quo. Every time this kind of thing happens, a cheer goes up from American news consumers dining on the spectacle and hyperbole of it all. 'By God, Helen! The common citizen, the working guy, the little guy, is standing up to Big Gubbyment. Says he ain't gonna take it anymore!'

Ideas like that of 'a white woman slave to some nigger' play to our unlettered and uncultured redneck attraction to the extreme and entertaining. I've heard it said again and again that 'Old people will be killed off to save money when the government has to pay for nursing care,' and I've refrained from pointing out that the vast majority of America's elderly are in facilities that are already being paid for by the government. But the notion of government death panels killing dear Grandma is far more entertaining to our imaginations than guaranteed access to chest-screening tests and blood-pressure medicines. Two generations into this national infantilisation, it's now the only political life that the underclass knows—the ideological spectacle made real. It serves the few against the many, the rich against the poor, in a last big grab at what dwindling wealth remains. Ideology has utterly triumphed. If reaching right down into Krassie's world, way out here on this ridge, isn't utter triumph, I don't know what is.

The reader is free to drop by my home in Winchester, Virginia and get the tour. See for yourselves. By all means come. Dozens of foreign journalists do so each year. It's an inconvenience to me, but it's well worth the effort to watch their jaws drop in stupefaction. So step right up to the arcade of disposable minds and abandoned lives in the Ideological States of America, where we are always psyched and ready to fight for the beliefs we are told we hold. We always show up to fight on the wrong side, and end up killing one another, but we show up for the brawl, by God!

Regardless of appearances, these people have normal IQs. They are born with the same number of brain cells and potential as anyone else. So why is it that when those with the most to lose do manage to rally for the fight, they always show up in the wrong camp? As I am asked in nearly every interview, 'Why do they work so hard to screw themselves?'

It is because the screwees have no language of their own in which to talk to themselves, or to discuss their condition with others of their own class. When they speak at all of these things, they speak in the language of their screwers, a language in which terms such as 'socialism', 'universal healthcare', 'welfare society', 'citizen entitlement', 'social taxes', 'solidarity', 'fair go', and 'common weal' are deemed profanities. Without language and the education to use it in defining concepts, their intellectual life is a constellation of deeply internalised corporate state–media imagery—commercials for the American brand entertainingly presented in a theatre of political and social kitsch.

The people become bored at increasingly higher thresholds, as the media's depiction of life becomes more bizarre. ('Of course it's real, otherwise why would they call it a reality show?') And, like children, they delight in and expect a new and more mesmerising spectacle daily, resulting in what can only be called an induced mass hallucination. Boundaries dissolve between politics and personal fantasies: today they involve white slavery, voodoo, geriatric death panels, and whole political parties getting sex-change operations; tomorrow, it's swarthy terrorist cells in the cul de sacs of cupcake land, and flu vaccines bearing malevolent nano-chips into the public bloodstream.

Entertaining and titillating as it is, life on Planet Tabloid is not as depressing as real America is these days—the America in which your son or daughter is doing a fourth rotation in Iraq because there are no jobs in the home of the brave. It's certainly better than contemplating America falling apart before your very eyes—not to mention the unnerving impression of inhabiting a spent empire locked in its inexorable orbit, and growing darker by the day.

I have rattled on at such length about underclass political consciousness, especially the town hall meetings, because they represent a new development in which the white underclass plays a pivotal role. It feels to me like a build-up to an incitement of violence—if not now, then someday not far off—that will either be purposefully managed or will erupt spontaneously. There is an odour of fascism and nascent brownshirts about. A look around these meetings, for instance, will often reveal a firearm—not as a bulge under a coat or jacket, but worn openly on the hip or in a shoulder-belt holster. This by no means illegal if the wearer has a weapons permit; guns are openly worn in this state and in many of the heartland realms I travel. I grew up accustomed to seeing guns, and seldom found it disconcerting. Until now. There is some new dimension to the presence of handguns at these public events, which are allegedly dedicated to civil public discourse. Until 2009, I never saw a gun worn at a public meeting or civic gathering. People with weapons permits have always considered such behaviour inappropriate and the sign of a boob. But now these guns in public view give me the willies.

Ostensibly, the guns are a display of Second Amendment rights—the right to bear arms. But there is a lack of nonchalance in the way they are worn now, an in-your-face quality to the way they are displayed. Exactly who are the guns supposed to scare? I don't know—liberals, I suppose. What breaks my heart is that the gun-toters are invariably my own people. My family's people. Clayton's people. Krassie's people. What will happen when things get worse for them in this country? And they surely will. Hell, we've got car camps of homeless people now—in some cases, sanctioned and overseen by municipal governments. And by official count—which is always doctored by the regime in power to look better—one in eight Americans now suffer from food insecurity. Undoubtedly we will see a fraudulent, manufactured 'recovery'. For a few years, the powers in charge will manage to waste our remaining resources, human and natural, extending a doomed system long enough to extract those last few trillions, instead of creating something more sustainable. At some point, the country will end up even worse off than now. And my people will be among the worst off. What then? Will they be sicced like dogs, as usual, or will they savage the same people without having to be sicced?

THE NATION IS FLAT BUST, IN HOCK FOR GENERATIONS to come. An America that sees itself as a superpower begs from door to door for gas and ammunition money from Indonesian retirement funds and Chinese bankers. Hundreds of thousands of frightened mid-level managers and urban school teachers-turned-survivalist homesteaders have purchased plots in the countryside, replacing their faith in the market with faith in the growth of the pea vine (and were immediately dubbed 'the new survivalist movement' by the media industry, which launched a TV series and several books in an effort to grow their markets by catering to them).

It didn't even help to be the ultimate insider, the president of the United States. The long run turned out to be an abruptly short jog: the CIA'S top-secret 15-point advisory to incoming president Obama listing American losses of economic stability and global influence by 2025 proved way out—all fifteen points were met during the first year of his presidency. Now, princes and soothsayers inside the Great Walled City issue pronouncements of 'recovery' across the land. And the moon rises over the stones of Catal Huyuk for the 2,810,000th time since the last dweller pondered its light from within those walls.

'If the whole country is goin' to the devil, then let 'er rip!' says Clayton. 'I've got my garden, my guns, and my fishin' gear.' Surely enough, the dwellers of Fort Clayton are safe for the moment. Krassie can sit at her isolated modem connection on this West Virginia ridge, confident that she will never be homeless or hungry on this piece of land, so long as Clayton can hang onto it. In this steadfast place, yet another generation of children run laughing down the creek beds, where at night the eyes of the deer burn like molten green glass, and where you can eat lushly from your own garden in even the toughest of times. This piece of land never abandoned anybody. Elsewhere, a helluva lot of busted working people are 'scratching shit with the chickens', as Maw used to say. I can almost hear Pap from the grave: 'See there, damned ya! I told you them gardening rights was gonna save your arse one day.'

A week after Clayton's birthday party, I found myself driving along Shanghai Road again, with no particular intent, just feeling the hills again, seeing barns and woodsheds that are no longer there. Turning onto a yellow-clay farm road, I parked and walked along a remembered path, also no longer there — one leading to a pond that, like the path, I assumed must also have been long gone.

Pap had built the pond, up in the hills, at the edge of an old grove looking down on the heart of the farm — down on the cantaloupe patch, the house, and the many unpainted outbuildings and surrounding orchards. Fed by springs and run-off rainwater from many acres of even higher terrain, the pond never dried up in even the worst of droughts.

And, by God, it still hadn't! There it was, diminished in size by five decades of silt, and choked by thick green algae, but there it was. The cow pasture next to the pond had gone to pioneer forest, with trees a full seven inches in base diameter, 48 annual rings in thickness. Shelves of ghostly fungi grew step-like on the trees of the older abutting forest, as if to denote the land's fecund and vibrant past amidst its abandoned present. Behind the pond, back there in the darker woods, a scarlet tanager hid, the salamanders slept, the snakes still lay perfectly still in the coolness ...

Rotting fence lines snaked through the dimness, enclosing phantom calf lots, cornfields, and pastures. A corner post wore a helmet of the thinnest lacy membrane of crumbling rust, the remains of an old tin bucket we used to plink at with our rifles from the facing hill — killing imaginary Japs, Germans, and other enemies of democracy foolhardy enough to venture a threat against the firepower of freedom's anointed few. Ours was the vengeance of the just. All that we knew about America said so. The Bible said so. With every crack of the rifle and splink of a bullet passing through that bucket, some enemy of God and this good land died. And with each bullet, our skinny chests grew broader and our righteousness was made stronger. Each bullet was its own streaking, silver prayer — its own offering to the stern God who had blessed us. We dreamed of angels over battlefields yet to come. We dreamed of unimaginable glory.

So potent was the dream that it came to dream the dreamers ... in a realm unto itself, ethereal and beyond any mortal lifetime, beyond the mewling of the newly born and the stillness of the newly dead. And that dream which dreams its dreamers proclaimed itself the American Dream, and caused them to dream of its own divinity among all other nations and peoples — the indisputable source of all rightness and good and progress, a volcanic issuer of wars and food aid, justice untold and technology creasing the starry void with rockets and righteousness. America, oh America, oh silver javelin-thrower who cracked the jewelled movement of the stars with rockets, and who cleaved atoms from their appointed settings ... dream us each day our daily lives, and in thy name thy will be done.

Amen.

The panther is the sign of war. A gun is the mark of a man. Draw Me! Pull me close to your heart and draw me quick! My boys can work, and this here is still good tomater country! Lean on the jake brake and let 'er howl ... watch them stacks turn white hot! Remember this: God don't allow whittlin' Never wear a dead man's shoes, and fer God's sake don't ask me, boy! Just do the next thing that needs doin'!

This has been my story, my own memoir, with a heavy dose of redneck social commentary. It's not the story of all the people, or even most of the people. But I am quite sure it is illustrative of millions of once-rural Americans and their offspring who poured their sweat onto this country's soil and their blood into its wars. It is the story of the many who know they are screwed but don't know how thoroughly, and for damned sure don't understand why or by whom; the many who, no matter how much blood they gave for their country, never 'made good' in their own country, but will never get their country out of their blood.

Call this a memoir for the many.